About This Book

Here, in one book, is all the information that you need in order to create games for the World Wide Web using Java. This book covers everything from design considerations and creating animations to artificial intelligence. All the code listed in the book is also on the accompanying CD-ROM, so you don't have to type in all those lines of code, unless it's something you consider fun.

In addition to game programming, this book provides valuable information to anyone who wants to liven up Web pages with interactive graphics and animations. These types of features are often necessary to make your pages stand out from the rest.

How This Book Is Structured

This book is intended to be read and absorbed over the course of three weeks (and it's a real seven-day week, not a business week). On each day, you read one chapter, which describes a new concept or two related to game programming on the World Wide Web. At the end of the three weeks, you will be ready to design and program your own games using Java.

Conventions

NOTE

A Note box presents interesting pieces of information related to the surrounding discussion.

TIP

A Tip box offers advice or teaches an easier way to do something.

WARNING

A Warning box advises you about potential problems and helps you steer clear of disaster.

Teach
Yourself
INTERNET
GAME

Teach Yourself

INTERNET GAME PROGRAMMING WITH JAVA

in 21 Days

Michael Morrison

201 West 103rd Street
Indianapolis, Indiana 46290

To my dad, who is the embodiment of the perfect father. You have taught me by example how confidence, integrity, and hard work can take me anywhere I want to go. I love you dad, and I will be happy if I can achieve only half of what you have!

Copyright © 1996 by Sams.net Publishing

Trademarks

President, Sams Publishing Richard K. Swadley
Team Leader Greg Wiegand
Managing Editor Cindy Morrow
Director of Marketing John Pierce
Assistant Marketing Managers Kristina Perry
Rachel Wolfe

Acquisitions Editor
Chris Denny

Development Editor
Jeff Koch

Software Development Specialist
Steve Straiger

Production Editor
Ryan Rader

Copy Editor
Cheri Clark

Indexer
Tom Dinse

Technical Reviewer
Brad Jones

Editorial Coordinator
Bill Whitmer

Technical Edit Coordinator
Lynette Quinn

Resource Coordinator
Deborah Frisby

Formatter
Frank Sinclair

Editorial Assistants
Carol Ackerman, Andi Richter, Rhonda Tinch-Mize

Cover Designer
Tim Amrhein

Book Designer
Gary Adair

Copy Writer
Peter Fuller

Production Team Supervisor
Brad Chinn

Production
Mary Ann Abramson, Stephen Adams, Debra Bolhuis, Georgiana Briggs, Charlotte Clapp, Jason Hand, Daniel Harris, Clint Lahnen, Ryan Oldfather, Casey Price, Dana Rhodes, Laura Robbins, Susan Springer

Overview

Week 3 in Review   **369**

Appendixes

Contents

Acknowledgments

I would like to thank Chris Denny for giving me another opportunity to ramble about game programming. A big thanks also goes to Angelique Brittingham for her initial guidance and for treating me to artichoke lasagna.

I'd like to thank the love of my life, Mahsheed, whose jaw was dismantled during much of the development of this book, but who remained incredibly supportive, as always. I love you, girl!

I would also like to thank my parents, who have always encouraged and supported my nerdly interests—I love and miss you lots.

An enormous thanks goes to Dr. James Bertz for seeing to it that Mahsheed stayed healthy throughout her jaw surgery, for educating me about the finer points of orthognathic surgery, and for just being an all-around good person.

A big thanks goes to Greg Turner for his incredibly gracious help in putting together the network code for the NetConnect4 applet. Also, thanks to Sven Wiebus and Keith Pomakis, who were willing to let me rip apart their Connect4 AI code. And thanks to Jonathan Hardwick for his valuable information on Java optimization.

Finally, thanks to my friends in Nashville who are far away but definitely not forgotten: Keith, Heath, Mehrdad, Paul, Justin, Randy, Mike, Shawn, Travis, and Sarah. I miss you guys!

About the Author

Michael Morrison is a contributing author of *Tricks of the Java Programming Gurus* and *Java Unleashed*, and the co-author of *Windows 95 Game Developer's Guide Using the Game SDK.* He currently lives in Scottsdale, Arizona with his now almost legal partner in life, Mahsheed. When not glued to his computer, Michael enjoys skateboarding, mountain biking, and committing flagrant fouls in basketball. You can contact Michael at mmorrison@thetribe.com, or visit his Web site at http://www.thetribe.com.

Tell Us What You Think!

As a reader, you are the most important critic and commentator of our books. We value your opinion and want to know what we're doing right, what we could do better, what areas you'd like to see us publish in, and any other words of wisdom you're willing to pass our way. You can help us make strong books that meet your needs and give you the computer guidance you require.

Do you have access to CompuServe or the World Wide Web? Then check out our CompuServe forum by typing **GO SAMS** at any prompt. If you prefer the World Wide Web, check out our site at http://www.mcp.com.

NOTE

If you have a technical question about this book, call the technical support line at (800) 571-5840, ext. 3668.

As the team leader of the group that created this book, I welcome your comments. You can fax, e-mail, or write me directly to let me know what you did or didn't like about this book—as well as what we can do to make our books stronger. Here's the information:

Fax: (317) 581-4669

E-mail: programming_mgr@sams.mcp.com

Mail: Greg Wiegand
         Comments Department
         Sams Publishing
         201 W. 103rd Street
         Indianapolis, IN 46290

Introduction

Now that the initial hype surrounding Java is starting to settle down, many developers are sitting around wondering what's next. So we have this really cool technology, but now what? The next logical step for Java programmers is to branch out and start applying their newfound skills to specific areas. One such area that has always intrigued me is games. Having a natural interest in games, I decided to apply my Java skills toward seeing what types of games could be written in Java. You're now holding the results of my experiment!

It turned out that even though Java has its weaknesses (namely in the area of performance), it is actually a very competent game development language. It is so competent, in fact, that after finishing the first sample game for this book, I wanted to distance myself from C++. If you are a C++ programmer interested in writing games in Java, this book is for you. However, a knowledge of C++ is by no means a prerequisite for this book. In fact, it is targeted toward beginning and intermediate Java programmers who are looking for some fun ways to use Java. Even if you aren't a programmer at all, you might find this book useful as a guide to incorporating games and entertainment into your Web site.

Throughout this book, you learn about game programming from a very Web-centric perspective. This is only natural because Java is very Web-centric itself. You learn all about the unique benefits (and drawbacks) of developing Internet games in Java for the Web, accompanied by plenty of source code that you can reuse on your own projects. More specifically, you learn about the following major issues related to Internet game programming with Java:

- ☐ Object-oriented game programming
- ☐ Graphics techniques
- ☐ Sprite animation
- ☐ Handling user input
- ☐ Using sound
- ☐ Game debugging
- ☐ Artificial intelligence
- ☐ Multiplayer network game programming
- ☐ Optimizing game code

These topics are covered throughout 21 lessons; hence the title, *Teach Yourself Internet Game Programming with Java in 21 Days*! Over a three-week period, you move from learning the fundamentals of Java game programming to writing three complete games and a variety of other sample applets. The sample games include high-speed animation, sound, and network support for multiple players. By the end of this book, you'll be ready to build your own Internet Java games from scratch. By the way, all you need to build the sample games is the Java Developer's Kit, which is included on the CD-ROM. Good luck and have fun… I sure did!

Week

1

At a Glance

The first week of your journey through Internet game programming with Java covers a lot of territory. You begin by learning the basics about Internet games and how Java impacts them, along with an object-oriented Java programming primer. You then jump into the basics of graphics in games and the support Java provides for working with graphics. You then cover the most crucial topic of the entire book—sprite animation. You use this animation knowledge to finish up the week with an interesting animated simulator—Sim Tarantula.

You cover the following topics this week:

- ☐ Games on the Web
- ☐ Java Game Programming
- ☐ Object-Oriented Programming with Java

- ☐ The Basics of Graphics
- ☐ Java Graphics Techniques
- ☐ Sprite Animation
- ☐ Sim Tarantula: Creepy Crawly Sprites

Day 1

Games on the Web

The Internet and the World Wide Web have energized the already fast-moving world of computing and created previously unthinkable opportunities for communication between computer users. One of the most talked about areas of application for the Web is games. When games are networked on a global scale, they offer a plethora of entertainment possibilities for users. Gaming on the Web will truly change the way we all view entertainment, primarily because it blurs cultural boundaries much like the Internet itself does.

Throughout the next 21 days, you learn how to develop games for the Web using Java. You begin with the basics and move on to learning advanced topics such as networking and artificial intelligence. By the end of the book, you'll have all the information and knowledge necessary to develop your own Java games. And it all begins today!

Today's lesson focuses on the current state of the Internet as a whole, the Web in particular, and how they both impact gaming. Although the point of this book is to develop Internet games using Java, understanding the current scenario surrounding games on the Internet is a major first step in seeing the relevance of writing games in Java. Therefore, with that in mind, buckle up and prepare yourself for a journey through gaming on the Web!

The following topics are covered in today's lesson:

- [ ] The state of the Net
- [ ] What the Web has to offer
- [ ] Internet games
- [ ] Java-based Web games

The State of the Net

With all of the media attention that is focused on the Internet and the World Wide Web, figuring out exactly what they are all about is sometimes difficult. Are they just a neat new way to market products or will they truly offer us a new medium of communication that will someday surpass even televisions and telephones? The answer is, who knows? Unfortunately, the ultimate use for the Internet is still unknown. This is because it is still in such a state of flux that it's pretty much impossible to accurately predict where it will end up. However, you can look at the evidence of what is there now and gain some insight into what the Internet might become, at least in terms of games.

The Web as most people know it consists of a tangled mess of hypertext documents containing text, images, and sound. For the most part, it has consisted of static information; you can search and browse and generate some things on the fly, but Web content is pretty much fixed, at least from a user's perspective. A wide range of add-ons and extensions have begun to appear that promise interactivity and new types of media. These extensions offer everything from movie clips and CD-quality audio to a hot meal embedded right there in a Web page. OK, maybe I'm exaggerating a little, but you get the idea.

No extension to the Web has generated more excitement than Java, which offers complete interactivity within the traditional Web environment. With Java, you have the ability to create full-featured, interactive applications and embed them in the middle of a Web page. It is probably not a shock to you to hear that Java is the technology touted as bringing the Web, and in turn the Internet, to the masses. Therefore, although the Web is already receiving much attention on its own accord, the Internet landscape is rapidly changing to accommodate the opportunities and benefits of Java.

What the Web Has to Offer

The concept of looking at the Web, and the Internet as a whole, as a medium for games is relatively new. It has been technically possible to link games and transfer data over an Internet connection for a while now, but that's only one facet of gaming on the Internet. The next generation of Internet games will more than likely move away from the Internet as simply a communication medium. More likely, the next generation of games will be integrated into the rapidly expanding Web environment.

The marriage of games and the Web is a natural one; like the Web, games are very content-driven, meaning that they are very much dependent on the graphics, sound, and other content that makes them interesting. It makes sense to use the Web to not only browse information, but also to act on that information. It might sound strange to look at games as information systems, but that's really all they are (as is all software). When you view a game in terms of simply being an information system, it's easier to see what the Web has to offer gaming.

The Web is a relatively stable, content-driven, globally distributed environment. The fact that it is stable isn't quite as defining because most operating systems are already fairly stable. Knowing this, it's safe to say that few people would look to the Web as a gaming environment based on its stability alone. Therefore, you have to look to the other two items to see what's important about the Web in regard to games. The fact that the Web is content-driven is important because games are content-driven themselves, and therefore fit naturally into the Web environment. However, this is more of a convenience than a compelling reason to move games to the Web.

The real appeal of moving games to the Web is the fact that the Web is globally distributed. As a result, the Web has a massive global user base that is growing by leaps and bounds even as you read this. What better appeal for a gaming environment than a lot of people anxious to see what the Web can do for them? Even though it's exciting to think of people around the world playing games on the Web, I think the real dynamic in this situation is the idea of these people playing games together.

Even with the prevalence of telephones, interactive communication of a global nature is still very limited. With interactive Web games, you're going far beyond sharing a recipe with someone on the other side of the world; you're exploring dungeons with them or dunking over them in a game of basketball. To me, this whole prospect is just too cool! So, if you haven't gotten the point, I think the Web offers the ultimate gaming environment because of the opportunities it affords for people from all places to interact, have fun, and most important, learn about each other.

NOTE

You might not immediately think of games as a cultural vehicle for learning about other people, but consider the fact that most traditional (noncomputer) children's games have been passed on for countless generations. Just like stories and legends, the games people play say a lot about their culture. Sharing games with people all around the world is indeed an ideal way to learn about other people and teach them about you.

Web-Based versus Non-Web Based Games

When it comes to the Internet, there are really two different kinds of games: Web games and non-Web games. Both types of games can run networked over the Internet, but only Web games have any dependency on the Web. Non-Web games are games that run networked across the Internet but have no connection to Web pages. Furthermore, non-Web games are typically available only for a single platform or a limited number of platforms. It is important for you to understand the distinction between Web games and non-Web games. Figure 1.1 shows an example of a networked non-Web game.

As you can see in Figure 1.1, the game players are connected in a network game directly with the Internet. There is no mention of the Web because the Web has nothing to do with non-Web games. Players in a non-Web game are only responsible for establishing an Internet connection and running the independent game program appropriately.

Figure 1.1.

A networked Internet game.

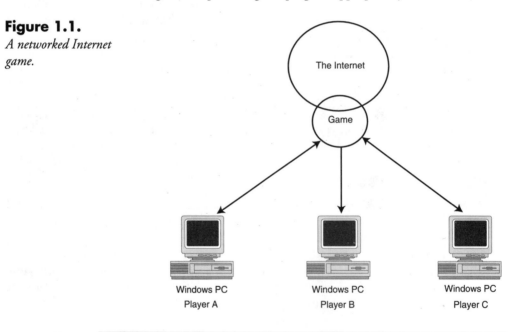

The Internet

Game

Windows PC   Windows PC   Windows PC
Player A   Player B   Player C

> You are probably already familiar with some of the more popular non-Web games such as DOOM and CivNet. These games provide a means to play with other players networked over the Internet, but they have no association with the Web.
>
> **NOTE**

Web games, on the other hand, are platform-independent games that are either launched from or run within the confines of a Web page, and might or might not have networking features. Because the Web itself is built on the Internet, it goes without saying that Web games that are networked use the Internet for networking. Therefore, Web games can be considered platform-independent Internet games that run from or within the confines of a Web page. In this way, Web games are really just a specific type of Internet game. Figure 1.2 shows the relationship between Web games and how they run on the Internet.

Figure 1.2 shows a total of six players involved in four different Web games. Three of the games are non-networked Web games, meaning that the players can't interact with other players over the Internet; the fourth game is a networked Web game involving three different players. These three players are able to play the game together and interact with each other via their Web connection in real time.

Figure 1.2.

Web games running both singly and networked over the Internet.

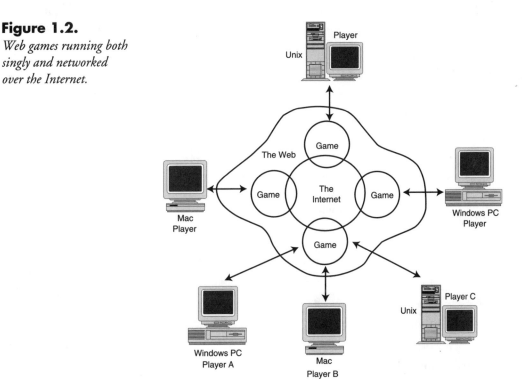

You might be wondering what the significance of a game running inside a Web page is. Integrating games into the Web environment is yet another step toward unifying media on the Internet. The ultimate technical goal of the Web, at least in my humble opinion, is to merge all the disparate media types present on computers into a functionally single presence. In doing so, Web users can seamlessly peruse different media types in conjunction with one another, resulting in a more complete and fulfilling experience.

Games can be considered their own media type, because of their unique system requirements. In actuality, games are a merger of other media types such as graphics, sound, and animation. Integrating games into Web pages further blurs the line between static and interactive content. The real world is highly interactive, and the more interactive the Web becomes, the more natural it will feel to human users. Likewise, game playing will eventually become a standard usage of the Web.

Non-Java Based Games

There are already a variety of gaming environments on the Internet carving out the future of gaming. Some of these environments are Web-based, whereas others have little dependence on the Web. They are all dependent on client software running on a particular platform. Nevertheless, they are worth checking out because they are a solid sign of the changing climate surrounding the commercial game community and how it addresses the Internet. First, let's take a look at the Internet game services that don't rely on Java technology.

NOTE Most of the non-Java based Internet game services don't actually develop their own games. They typically allow you to play existing commercial games having Internet support. The role of the service is mainly to provide a standard means to connect with other players and correlate playing the games.

The following are some of the more popular Internet game services that aren't based on Java:

- ☐ Mpath
- ☐ Cyber Warrior Network
- ☐ ImagiNation Network
- ☐ Total Entertainment Network
- ☐ Outland
- ☐ Sim-Net

Mpath

Mpath Interactive has announced plans for a summer, 1996 release of a Web-based game service called Mplayer, which promises to "bring the excitement of real-time multiplayer gaming to the Internet's World Wide Web for the first time." Mplayer is PC-based and plans to offer games from well-known game publishers aimed at adult gamers. Mpath also plans to have contests, tournaments, and special events all oriented toward gaming and leisure interests.

The Mplayer service will be speech-enabled so that players will be able to share verbal dialog as they play. In addition, the service will provide a general chat area for post-game conversation and strategic planning. The Mpath Web site is located at http://www.mpath.com, and is shown in Figure 1.3.

Figure 1.3.

The Mpath Web site.

Cyber Warrior Network

The Cyber Warrior Network is an Internet game service currently focusing on a single game, Rubies of Eventide. Rubies of Eventide is a PC-based multiplayer 3-D fantasy adventure game that has been developed exclusively for Internet play via the Cyber Warrior Network. For more information about the Cyber Warrior Network and Rubies of Eventide, check out its Web site at http://www.cyberwar.com (see Figure 1.4).

Figure 1.4.
The Cyber Warrior Network Web site.

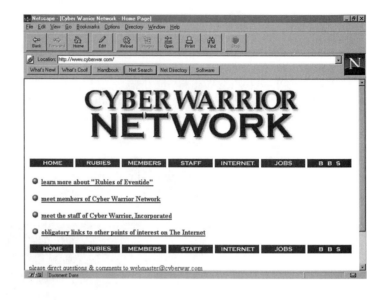

ImagiNation Network

Another PC-based gaming service, the ImagiNation Network, sports more than 40 multiplayer games and hundreds of chat rooms, bulletin boards, and tournaments. The ImagiNation Network even has an e-mail list and newsletter to keep its members informed. To find out more, go to its Web site at `http://www.inngames.com` (see Figure 1.5).

Figure 1.5.
The ImagiNation Network Web site.

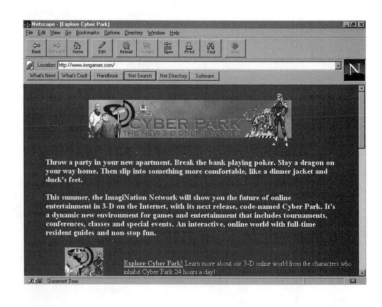

Total Entertainment Network

The Total Entertainment Network (TEN) is one of the more promising Internet game services, because of its connection with established commercial game publishers. Several major companies in the game industry have signed on with TEN, some of them exclusively. The list currently includes Apogee/3D Realms, Maxis, MicroProse, SimTex, Spectrum Holobyte, and SSI. For more information on the Total Entertainment Network, look at its Web site, which is located at `http://www.ten.net` (see Figure 1.6).

Figure 1.6.

The Total Entertainment Network Web site.

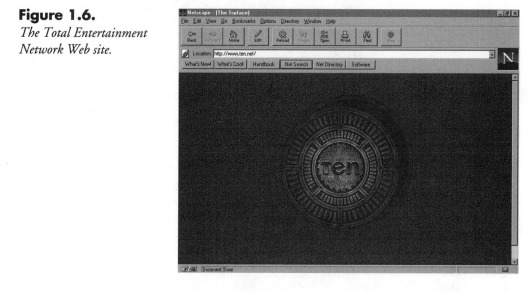

Outland

Outland is a Macintosh-based Internet gaming service offering multiplayer games such as Chess, Go, Backstab, Reversi, and the popular space strategy game, Spaceward Ho! Outland also includes chat rooms and the capability to play multiple games at once. For the latest scoop on Outland, visit its Web site at `http://www.outland.com` (see Figure 1.7).

Figure 1.7.

The Outland Web site.

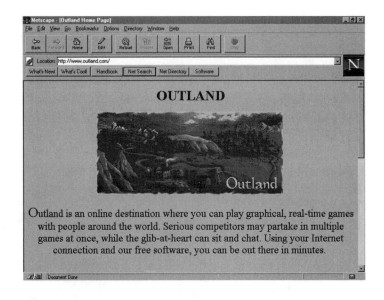

Sim-Net

Sim-Net is the only Internet gaming service mentioned here that supports both PCs and Macintoshes. Sim-Net includes a chat feature as well as organized tournaments. For more information about Sim-Net, check out its Web site at `http://www.simnet1.com` (see Figure 1.8).

Figure 1.8.

The Sim-Net Web site.

Java-Based Web Games

Along with the Internet game services that don't rely on the Java technology, there are already a few online games and services based on Java. These games are good examples of the excitement Java has already generated in an amazingly short amount of time. They are also interesting in how they each handle the details of integrating games into the Web page environment.

The following are some of these Java-based Web games and services:

☐ Avalon

☐ Internet MahJong Server

☐ iChess

☐ Unearthed

Avalon

Avalon is a multiplayer role-playing game that includes both human-controlled characters and imaginary computer-controlled creatures. Although the core gaming environment itself is not based on Java, there is a Java client that interacts with the central game server. Avalon is presented as an entire world that evolves as new players join and contribute their actions. The Avalon Web site, which is shown in Figure 1.9, is located at `http://www.avalon-rpg.com`.

Figure 1.9.

The Avalon Web site.

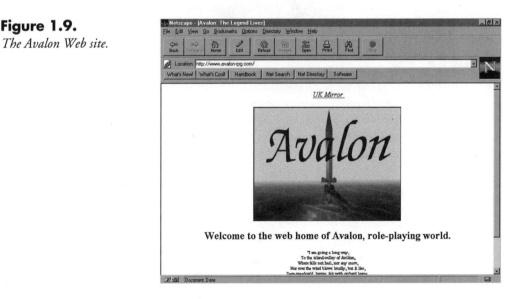

Internet MahJong Server

The Internet MahJong Server (IMS) is an entirely Java-based game server that provides virtual gambling rooms for the popular Chinese tile game MahJong. The fact that it is entirely built on Java means that players using a variety of different types of computer systems can seamlessly play games together. IMS is located at `http://www.real-time.com/MJ/mj.html` and is shown in Figure 1.10.

Figure 1.10.

The MahJong Server Web site.

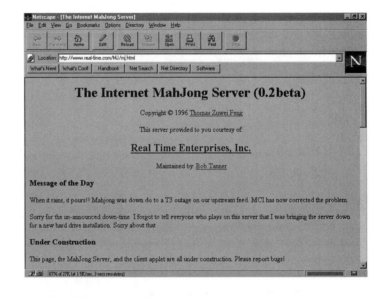

iChess

iChess is a multiplayer chess game written entirely in Java. It includes a chat window and a lot of freedom with regard to how a game is carried out. For example, you can play live with another player or you can connect and make a move when the other player is not connected. In the latter case, the game progresses while players make moves at their own leisure. To try out a game of iChess, check it out at `http://www.ichess.com` (see Figure 1.11).

Figure 1.11.

The iChess Web site.

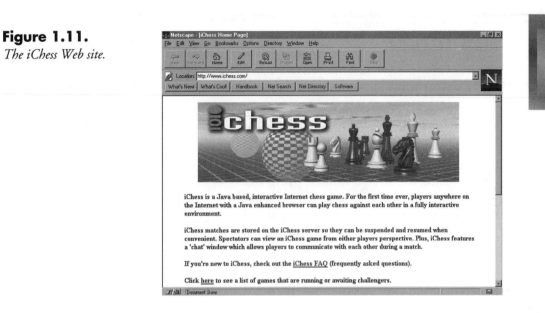

Unearthed

Unearthed is a multiplayer fantasy world that enables different players to interact together in real time. It is written entirely in Java and demonstrates the usage of a high level of graphical content in Java. Although it is still in its early development stages, Unearthed is worth checking out. It is located at `http://www.mit.edu/people/twm/unearthed` and is shown in Figure 1.12.

Figure 1.12.

The Unearthed Web site.

Summary

Today you learned about the current climate surrounding the Internet and the World Wide Web and how it impacts gaming. You found out some of the aspects of the Web that are appealing to game players, which are in turn causing a rush for game developers to move their games to the Web. This discussion gave you some insight into why the Web is so important to the future of games.

The second half of today's lesson focused on some of the more popular Web sites that support online gaming. Some of them are strictly Internet-based and require platform-specific client applications, whereas others consist of full-blown Java games. These Web sites give you a good place to start when you are assessing the state of games on the Web. Tomorrow you move on to learning more specifics about how Java impacts Web games.

Q&A

Q Are interactive commercial Web games poised to replace traditional games as we know them?

A Maybe someday, but not in the immediate future. You can expect to see more games supporting the Internet as a networking medium for multiple players, but games based solely on the Web are still a ways off. This is mainly due to the fact that programming languages supporting Web-based games, such as Java, are still in their infancy. You learn a lot more about this in tomorrow's lesson.

Q Are there any other obstacles slowing the evolution of the Web as a medium for gaming?

A Yes, the other big obstacle facing Web games is the bandwidth limitation imposed by modem connections. Because most Web users connect to the Web over a relatively slow modem connection, there are very real limitations on how much game data can be sent during a game.

Q Because Web games are online, and therefore readily available without any extra software, how do game companies make money from them?

A The current trend is toward charging a monthly membership fee for belonging to an online game service. This membership typically entitles you to a certain number of hours and the option to play a variety of different games. It's not yet clear whether this arrangement will work as Web games get more established. I'm not sure how many game players like the idea of paying a monthly bill for a gaming service, even if it ends up averaging to be around the same cost of buying games outright.

Workshop

The Workshop section provides questions and exercises to help solidify the material you learned today. Try to answer the questions and go over the exercises before moving on to tomorrow's lesson. You'll find the answers to the questions in Appendix A, "Quiz Answers."

Quiz

1. What technology is poised to bring interactive gaming to the Web?
2. What is potentially the most intriguing aspect of writing games for the Web?

Exercises

1. Try out a few of the Internet and Web-based games listed in today's lesson.
2. Think of some of some of your favorite games and how they might scale to the Web environment. Does the Web stand a chance of enhancing their playability?

Day 2

Java Game Programming

On Day 1, you learned what the Web has to offer in terms of games. Most of the games you learned about were not developed in Java because Java is a new technology and programmers haven't had time to gain enough proficiency to turn out interesting games. For the aspiring Java game developer like yourself, this is very good news; the game market is wide open! This level playing field in Java game development should give you the energy to get busy thinking about your own game designs as you go through today's lesson and the rest of the book.

Today's lesson follows up on Day 1's general discussion of Web games to focus on programming Web games in Java. Today you learn about the specific features of Java that make it a very good language for game development. This lesson lays the groundwork for much of the material that you cover throughout the rest of the book. You finish up today's lesson with a brief look at conceptual game design.

The following topics are covered in today's lesson:

- ☐ Java and Web games
- ☐ Java features for games
- ☐ Game design

Java and Web Games

With all the hype surrounding Java and what it will do for the Internet, it should come as no surprise that games are being hyped as one of the most interesting applications of Java. Indeed, that's probably why you bought this book to begin with! Even though Java includes many useful features for games, it still isn't quite the ideal gaming language for the Internet.

NOTE

> Just because Java isn't an ideal Internet gaming language doesn't mean that it doesn't deliver on many accounts. In reality, there probably will never be an ideal gaming language, because games have such unique programming challenges and languages tend to be designed for general use.

Although it's not the ideal language, Java does have much to offer for mixing games with the Web equation. Java as a technology is poised to bring interactivity to the Web in a general sense. Java games are only one aspect of this "interactive revolution." Java provides a level of platform independence, security, and network support that is still unattainable in any other language. All these issues are of utmost importance in any technology that is to bring interactive games to the Web.

NEW TERM   *Platform independence* refers to the capability of a single executable program to run on a variety of different computer systems.

This discussion might make a little more sense in the context of an example, so let's look at one. Consider an educational Web page attempting to discuss desert animals and how they interact with one another. Before Java, without using complex platform-dependent programming languages, the Web presentation would have been limited to text and inlined graphics. Now imagine a Java game inserted right into the Web pages, which allows students to play the role of a desert animal contending with other desert predators. This level of interactivity combined with the accessibility of the Web can't be matched by any other media. Web games written in Java will truly change the way you perceive the Web as a whole. By the way, this example isn't just something I made up for the purposes of this discussion; you will actually develop a game on Day 10 that is very similar to this example.

2

Java Features for Games

You've seen some of the aspects of Java that are beneficial in making Web games a reality. It's now time to look at the specifics of the functionality that Java provides for developing games for the Web. The primary areas of importance for game programming are the following:

- [ ] Graphics and animation
- [ ] User input
- [ ] Sound
- [ ] Networking
- [ ] Media management

As you learn about each of these different areas of game programming, I want to help put them into perspective by explaining how they would impact the development of a Java Space Invaders game. This will help you to see how each of these areas impacts a real game, and it might also help you get ideas about designing a real game.

Graphics and Animation

What good is a game without graphics? In most cases, not much! Fortunately, Java delivers the goods when it comes to graphics. The standard Java API includes wide support for all kinds of neat graphics features such as images, color models, and 2D graphics primitives. Although Java as a whole is still largely limited by its relatively slow performance, the support is in place for very powerful graphics. As future releases of Java address the speed concerns, game programmers will be able to more fully exploit the graphics capabilities Java provides. You get the whole scoop on graphics later this week on Day 5, "Java Graphics Techniques."

What about animation? Most games would be pretty boring without it! Although the standard Java API doesn't provide any specific animation support, it is riddled with features that make implementing animation very easy. One of the most important aspects of Java is its multithreaded design, which provides a powerful framework for establishing the all-important timing necessary for animations. You learn all about implementing animation in Java later this week on Day 6, "Sprite Animation."

In the context of a real game, the graphics and animation form the majority of the look of the game. In a Space Invaders game, for example, the graphics and animation account for the aliens, the player's ship, any barriers that the player can hide behind, the missiles being fired back and forth, and any explosions that take place when a missile collides with something. Furthermore, the display of the title screen and score would also fall under the area of graphics programming.

User Input

User input is a very critical area of game development because it dictates how a game "feels" to the game player. User input is also important because it establishes the primary interface between the player and the game. Java provides support for the two major input devices in use on most computer systems these days—the keyboard and mouse. When programming in Java, you monitor these input devices by responding to user input events generated when the user manipulates one of the devices.

Although it would certainly be nice if Java supported other input devices such as joysticks and flight yokes, the reality is that these devices aren't available on a wide variety of platforms. Hopefully a future version of Java will provide some degree of support for these gaming devices, because they are typically used in addition to the keyboard and mouse.

Even without the support for game-specific input devices, the support for the keyboard and mouse is enough to provide an effective user interface to most games. If you're skeptical, you can judge for yourself next week on Day 9, "Handling User Input with Java."

Using the Space Invaders example again, the user input requirements of the game consist of the inputs necessary to control the player's ship and fire missiles. For a game like this in which the ship simply moves from side to side, the best approach is probably to just use the left and right arrow keys to handle the ship's movement. You could also detect side to side mouse movement and use it to control the ship. You would designate another key, such as the spacebar, as the fire button. Likewise, a mouse click could also serve as the fire button for the mouse interface.

Sound

Rounding out the "big three" areas of game development is sound. Sound is currently the weakest area of Java's support for gaming. Release 1.0 of Java supports playing sound waves only in the ULAW format, which is popular on Sun workstations. Although the current Java sound support provides built-in sound mixing and the capability to play looped sounds, it is pretty limited because all sounds must be in the ULAW format (which is a low-quality sound format). Furthermore, there is no support for manipulating sounds at a lower level, which is often useful in games. A future release of Java will no doubt remedy many of the current limitations in regard to sound.

NOTE

Sun is already busy at work on a future add-on to Java that will provide lots of neat sound features such as MIDI (Musical Instrument Digital Interface) music and support for other sound formats.

Even with its limitations, the current Java sound support is enough to add simple sound effects and music to Java games. Actually, the fact that Java provides a built-in sound mixer in the first release is a big deal. Contrast this situation with that of Windows 3.1, which didn't have any sound mixing support until very late in the product cycle.

NOTE

It might seem strange that I'm comparing Java to an operating system (or shell, at least) in Windows 3.1. This brings up an interesting point regarding what Java really is. Java is not just a language; it is also a runtime system that acts very much like an operating system at times.

2

You learn all about sound programming in Java, as well as the ULAW sound format, next week on Day 12, "Playing Sound with Java."

Going back to the Space Invaders example, the sound programming aspect of the game consists of writing code to handle all the sound effects in the game, as well as the background music. You might wonder how to add music considering the fact that Java doesn't yet support the popular MIDI music standard. The truth is that the original Space Invaders arcade game was developed well before the MIDI standard, so someone improvised back then! Similarly, you have to improvise music in Java by playing looped wave sounds repeatedly. Admittedly, this isn't the ideal approach, but it's the only approach you have—for now.

Networking

Now that the concept of a "computer in every home" is inching closer to reality, game developers can no longer ignore the potential of multiplayer network games. The desire of game players to connect and play games with other real people is just too strong to ignore. This is evident in the recent surge of commercial games that support network play. CivNet comes to mind as an example of a popular single player game (Civilization) that has been revamped for network play.

Networking is the one area where Java really shines because it is such an integral part of the Java runtime system. Unlike other popular game programming languages such as C and C++, Java was designed from the ground up to support networking over the Internet. For this reason, the networking support in Java is much easier to use and a lot more secure than add-on networking libraries for C/C++.

Network programming has long been a very complex and highly specialized area of software development. Prior to Java, most programmers had to focus all their efforts on network programming alone just to develop enough skills to do anything useful. Java has changed all that and made network programming a realistic pursuit for the rest of us.

Combine Java's extensive network support with its platform independence and you have a gaming platform that crosses all boundaries for availability to users. With a networked Java game, you could be sitting in front of a Windows 95 machine playing a game of Poker with players in other parts of the world using completely different machines, such as Sun workstations or Macintoshes. That's about as good as it gets when it comes to distributed game play! You learn all about network programming in Java on Day 18, "Networking with Java."

Using the Space Invaders example again, there isn't a very clear way to add network support because the original game was basically a single player game. However, nothing is stopping you from adding a mode in which two players join forces and battle the aliens. Using this approach, you have to define a means of sending data back and forth between the players so that each player's game is up to date with the other player's actions. This technique is known as synchronization and is a key topic on Day 17, "The Basics of Multiplayer Gaming."

Media Management

The last issue in regard to Java's support for games is *media management*. Media management refers to the tracking of media objects (graphics, sounds, and so on) as they are being transferred across the Internet. If you didn't guess, the whole issue of media management is unique to Web games because traditional games reside on a single machine and get all their data from a CD-ROM or hard drive.

To understand why media management is an issue, think about where the data comes from when a game is playing. In a traditional game, the data comes straight from the hard drive or CD-ROM. When you consider distributed Java games, it becomes difficult to nail down exactly where the game's content is coming from. Of course, a Java game executes locally on the end user's machine, but it is initially transferred from whatever Web server it is installed on. Java games could certainly still be shipped on a CD-ROM like traditional games, but doing so would bypass the whole point of incorporating Java games into online Web content. For this reason, most Java games transfer their data (media objects) over an Internet connection.

Because transferring data over the Internet takes a finite amount of time (often too finite!), it becomes necessary for Java games to keep up with the time at which certain data is available for use. In other words, you don't have the luxury of speedy hard drive access, so you have to take into account the amount of time it takes to transfer data over an Internet connection. For example, it would be a bad thing to display a game screen when you have the graphics for only half of the objects being displayed. Java provides a feature for keeping up with which media objects have been transferred, and therefore which ones are available for use. Unfortunately, the current release of Java only supports the tracking of images, and not sounds. You learn the details about tracking images later this week on Day 5, "Java Graphics Techniques." Media tracking support for sounds and other types of media has been promised in a future release of Java.

Returning to the trusted Space Invaders example, it's not too difficult to determine what media objects the game is composed of. Basically, each graphic element in the game is stored as an image, which has to be transferred for the game to run correctly. In addition to the images, you also have to deal with the individual sound effects and the looped music sound. These elements are equally important media content that have to be transferred along with the images.

Game Design

Now that you understand some of the reasons that Java is cool for writing games, let's take a conceptual look at game design. The rest of today's lesson focuses on the flow of thought necessary to come up with a game plan. This thought should take place before you begin to write any Java code. I know you're probably itching to get into the technical side of things, but please be patient. You'll get a good dose of Java code in due time!

Do you have some ideas of games you would like to write? If so, you probably already realize that coming up with a good game idea is often the easy part. Taking a game concept and making it reality is where most of us fall short. That's okay; you just have to take it a step at a time and think through the development process.

The first step in taking a game from concept to reality is to get a solid idea of what you want the game to be. This doesn't need to be an itemized list of every scene and every little creature and interaction. It simply needs to state some minimal ground rules about what your goal is for the final game.

Here are the key items you should address when beginning the game development process:

- ☐ Basic idea
- ☐ Storyline
- ☐ Play modes

Basic Idea

The first thing you should do is determine the basic idea behind your game. Is it a shoot-em-up, a maze game, a role-playing adventure game, or some mixed combination? Or do you have an idea of a game that doesn't really fit in an existing category? Is the object to rescue good guys, kill bad guys, or just explore a strange environment? What time frame is your game set in, or does it even have a time frame? Write all this stuff down. Whatever comes to mind, write it down, because brainstorms come and go and you don't want to forget anything. Forcing yourself to formalize your ideas causes you to think more about the game and clears up a lot of things.

If you are having trouble coming up with a basic game idea, think about the influences of a lot of the popular computer games. Many games are based on movies, some on historical events, and others on sports. Ultimately, computer games are models of the world around us, whether fantasy or real, so look no farther when dreaming up your game. Movies in particular can provide a lot of good creative settings and storylines for games.

NOTE

Currently, there are even a few cases in which a game idea has served as the basis for a movie, which is pretty surprising. The really strange thing is that some of the movies are based on games with a very limited plot. For example, the immensely popular Mortal Kombat game, which is basically a straight-up fighting game with no plot, was made into a movie.

Regardless of your inspiration, just remember that your game has to be fun. Actually, that's why I think computer games are so alluring to programmers. The overriding design goal is always to maximize fun! Who wouldn't want to spend all day trying to figure out the best way to have fun? If your game isn't fun to play, the most dazzling graphics and sound won't be able to save it. The point I'm trying to make is that you must make fun the priority when designing your game. After you have a basic idea of what your game will be and you've decided that you're going to make it fun at all costs, you can develop a storyline.

Storyline

Even if your game is a simple action game, developing a storyline helps you to establish the landscape and think up creatures to populate your game world. Putting your game in the context of a story also brings the game player closer to your world. For games in which the story is a more integral part, it is often useful to develop a storyboard along with the storyline. A *storyboard* tells the story scene by scene by using rough sketches of each scene.

A storyboard basically enables you to create a visual layout of the entire game, based on the story. Having a storyboard to reference helps ensure that you don't lose sight of the story when you get into heavy development.

Play Modes

The final thing to consider when laying out your initial game design is what play modes you will support. Will it be single player, two player, networked, or some combination? This might sound like a fairly simple decision, but it can have huge repercussions on the game logic later. Even though Java provides a lot of support for networking, network games typically incur a significantly more complex design.

On the other hand, many single-player games will require some degree of artificial intelligence to make the computer opponent challenging to play against. Artificial intelligence can easily get complicated and difficult to implement, so you need to weigh your resources heavily into your game design when deciding on play modes. Speaking of artificial intelligence, you learn all about it on Day 15, "Teaching Games to Think."

Summary

Today you learned what Java has to offer games on the Web. Some of the requirements of Web games were discussed, along with how Java addresses many of the problems inherent in moving games to the Web. You learned about the primary features of Java that directly impact game development, along with their benefits and limitations. In short, you learned today that Java, although not perfect (yet), is positioned to be an extremely viable development tool for games on the Web.

You finished up today's lesson with a discussion of general game design ideas. Although not etched in stone, these ideas and suggestions serve as good guidelines when you start working out your masterpiece. This discussion also serves as a good ending to today's lesson, because you will continue with more theory on Day 3. Tomorrow's lesson focuses on object-oriented programming in Java, a topic you won't want to miss!

Q&A

Q Does Java provide support for 3D graphics?

A No, not yet. The standard Java 1.0 API has no support for 3D graphics, but a future release of Java could well fix this. Also, there are some third-party Java graphics libraries in the works that might make viable alternatives to writing your own 3D graphics code.

Q How do you play music in Java?

A Currently, the only way to play music is to loop a sampled sound clip stored in the ULAW sound format. There is talk of MIDI extensions for Java, but nothing real has surfaced yet. Keep your eyes open, though!

Q Are there any limitations to how Java games can be networked?

A Not really. As long as you stay within the network security bounds imposed by Java, which you are forced to do anyway, the options available for network games are wide open. You can theoretically have as many players as you want, interacting however you choose to allow them.

Workshop

The Workshop section provides questions and exercises to help solidify the material you learned today. Try to answer the questions and at least go over the exercises before moving on to tomorrow's lesson. You'll find the answers to the questions in Appendix A, "Quiz Answers."

Quiz

1. What user input devices does Java currently support?
2. What are some limitations of the sound support in Java 1.0?
3. What is a media object?
4. What is a storyboard used for?

Exercises

1. Get on the Web and check out some Java games. Hint: A good place to start is the Gamelan Web site, which is located at `http://www.gamelan.com`. Gamelan has an entire section devoted to Java games.
2. Perform the preliminary design for a game of your own, addressing each of the issues mentioned at the end of today's lesson.
3. Check out Javasoft's Web site at `http://www.javasoft.com` for the latest news on Java; who knows, by the time you read this there could be new enhancements to Java such as more advanced sound support.

Day 3

Object-Oriented Programming with Java

Object-oriented programming (OOP) is a programming paradigm that is fundamentally different from traditional procedural programming styles. It is centered around the concept of objects—programming constructs that have both properties and the procedures for manipulating those properties. This approach models the real world much more closely than conventional programming methods and is ideal for the simulation-type problems commonly encountered in games.

You're probably already aware that Java is an object-oriented language, but you might not fully understand what that means. To successfully use Java to write Internet games, you need to embrace object-oriented programming techniques and design philosophies. The goal of today's lesson is to present the conceptual aspects of object-oriented programming as they relate to Java. By the end of today's lesson, you will fully understand what OOP means to Java and maybe even have some new buzz words to share with your friends! More important, you will gain some insight into why the OOP paradigm built into Java is a perfect match for game programming.

The following topics are covered in today's lesson:

- ☐ What is OOP?
- ☐ OOP and games
- ☐ Java and other OOP languages

What Is OOP?

If you've been anywhere near the computer section of a bookstore or picked up a programming magazine in the last five years, you've certainly seen the hype surrounding object-oriented programming. It's the most popular programming technology to come about in a long time, and it all revolves around the concept of an object. The advent of Java has only served to elevate the hype surrounding OOP. You might wonder what the big deal is with objects and object-oriented technology? Is it something you should be concerned with, and if so, why? Is it really that crucial when working with Java? If you sift through the hype surrounding the whole object-oriented issue, you'll find a very powerful technology that provides a lot of benefits to software design.

But the question still remains: What is OOP? OOP is an approach to programming that attempts to bridge the gap between problems in the real world and solutions in the computer programming world. Prior to OOP, a conceptual stumbling block always existed for programmers when trying to adapt the real world into the constraints imposed by a traditional programming language. In the real world, people tend to think in terms of "things," but in the pre-OOP programming world people have been taught to think in terms of blocks of code (procedures) and how they act on data. These two modes of thinking are very different from each other and pose a significant problem when it comes to designing complex systems that model the real world. Games happen to be very good examples of complex systems that often model the real world.

OOP presents an approach to programming that allows programmers to think in terms of objects, or things, much like people think of things in the real world. Using OOP techniques, a programmer can focus on the objects that naturally make up a system, rather than trying to rationalize the system into procedures and data. The OOP approach is a very natural and logical application of the way humans already think.

The benefits of OOP go beyond easing the pain of resolving real world problems in the computer domain. Another key issue in OOP is code reuse, when you specifically design objects and programs with the goal of reusing as much of the code as possible, whenever possible. Fortunately, it works out that the fundamental approaches to OOP design naturally encourage code reuse, meaning that it doesn't take much of an extra effort to reuse code after you employ standard OOP tactics.

The OOP design approach revolves around the following major concepts:

- ☐ Objects
- ☐ Classes
- ☐ Encapsulation
- ☐ Messages
- ☐ Inheritance

Objects

NEW TERM *Objects* are bundles of data and the code, or procedures, that act on that data.

The procedures in an object are also known as *methods*. The merger of data and methods provides a means of more accurately representing real-world objects. Modeling a real-world problem through traditional programming constructs, without objects, requires a significant logical leap. Objects, on the other hand, enable programmers to solve real-world problems in the software domain much more easily and logically.

As evident by the name, objects are at the heart of object-oriented technology. To understand how software objects are beneficial, think about the common characteristics of all real-world objects. Lions, cars, and calculators all share two common characteristics: state and behavior.

NEW TERM The *state* of an object is the condition that the object is in, as defined by its attributes.

NEW TERM The *behavior* of an object is the collection of actions that the object can take.

For example, the state of a lion might include color, weight, and whether the lion is tired or hungry. Lions also have certain behaviors such as roaring, sleeping, and hunting. The state of a car includes the current speed, the type of transmission, whether it is two- or four-wheel-drive, whether the lights are on, and the current gear, among other things. The behaviors for a car include turning, braking, and accelerating.

Just like real-world objects, software objects possess two common characteristics: state and behavior. To relate this back to programming terms, the *state* of an object is determined by its data and the *behavior* of an object is defined by its methods. By making this connection between real-world objects and software objects, you begin to see how objects help bridge the gap between the real world and the world of software living inside your computer.

3

Because software objects are modeled after real-world objects, you can more easily represent real-world objects in object-oriented programs. You could use the lion object to represent a real lion in an interactive software zoo. Similarly, car objects would be very useful in a racing game. However, you don't always have to think of software objects as modeling physical real-world objects; software objects can be just as useful for modeling abstract concepts. For example, the standard Java API provides a thread object that represents a stream of execution in a multithreaded program.

Figure 3.1 shows a visualization of a Java software object, including the primary components and how they relate.

Figure 3.1.

A software object.

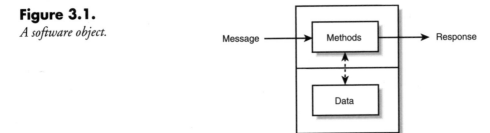

The software object in Figure 3.1 clearly shows the two primary components of an object: data and methods. The figure also shows some type of communication, or access, between the data and the methods. Additionally, it shows how messages are sent through the methods, which result in responses from the object. You'll learn more about messages later today in the "Messages" section.

The data and methods within an object express everything that the object knows (state), along with what all it can do (behavior). A software object modeling a real-world car would have variables (data) that indicate the car's current state: it's traveling at 75 mph, it is in 4th gear, and the lights are on. The software car object would also have methods that enable it to brake, accelerate, steer, change gears, and turn the lights on and off. Figure 3.2 shows what a Java car object might look like.

In both Figures 3.1 and 3.2 you probably noticed the line separating the methods from the data within the object. This line is a little misleading, because methods have full access to the data within an object. The line is there to illustrate the difference between the visibility of the methods and the data to the outside. In this sense, an object's visibility refers to what parts of the object another object has access to. Because object data defaults to being invisible, or inaccessible to other objects, all interaction between objects must be handled via methods. This hiding of data within an object is called *encapsulation*.

Figure 3.2.
A car object.

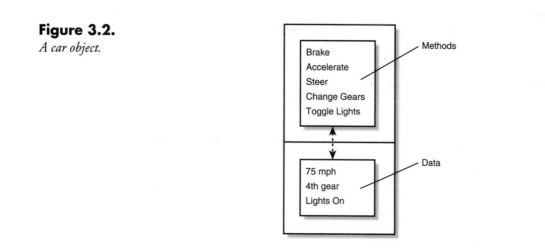

Classes

Throughout this discussion of object-oriented programming, you've only dealt with the concept of an object already existing in a system. You might be wondering how objects get into a system in the first place. This question brings you to the most fundamental structure in object-oriented programming: the class.

NEW TERM   A *class* is a template or prototype that defines a type of object.

A class is to an object what a blueprint is to a house. Many houses can be built from a single blueprint; the blueprint outlines the makeup of the houses. Classes work exactly the same way, except that they outline the makeup of objects.

In the real world, there are often many objects of the same kind. Using the house analogy, there are many different houses around the world, but as houses they all share common characteristics. In object-oriented terms, you would say that your house is a specific instance of the class of objects known as houses.

NEW TERM   An *instance* of a class is an object that has been created in memory using the class as a template. Instances are also sometimes referred to as *instantiated objects*.

All houses have states and behaviors in common that define them as houses. When a builder starts building a new development of houses, he or she typically will build them all from a set of blueprints. It wouldn't be as efficient to create a new blueprint for every single house, especially when there are so many similarities shared between each one. The same thing applies in object-oriented software development; why rewrite a lot of code when you can reuse code that solves similar problems?

In object-oriented programming, as in construction, it's also common to have many objects of the same kind that share similar characteristics. And like the blueprints for similar houses, you can create blueprints for objects that share certain characteristics. What it boils down to is that classes are software blueprints for objects.

As an example, the class for the car object discussed earlier would contain several variables representing the state of the car, along with implementations for the methods that enable the driver to control the car. The state variables of the car remain hidden underneath the interface. Each instance, or instantiated object, of the car class gets a fresh set of state variables. This brings you to another important point: When an instance of an object is created from a class, the variables declared by that class are allocated in memory. The variables are then modified via the object's methods. Instances of the same class share method implementations but have their own *object data*. Classes can also contain class data.

NEW TERM *Object data*, or *instance data*, is the information that models an object's state. Each object in memory has its own set of instance data, which determines what state the object is in.

NEW TERM *Class data* is data that is maintained on a class-wide basis, independent of any objects that have been created.

There is only one instance of class data in memory no matter how many objects are created from the class. Class data is typically used to store common information that needs to be shared among all instances of a class. A common example of class data is a count of how many instantiated objects exist of a particular class. When a new object is created, the count is incremented, and when an existing object is destroyed, the count is decremented.

Objects provide the benefits of modularity and information hiding, whereas classes provide the benefit of reusability. Just as the builder reuses the blueprint for a house, the software developer reuses the class for an object. Software programmers can use a class over and over again to create many objects. Each of these objects gets its own data but shares a single method implementation.

Encapsulation

NEW TERM *Encapsulation* is the process of packaging an object's data together with its methods.

A powerful benefit of encapsulation is the hiding of implementation details from other objects. This means that the internal portion of an object has more limited visibility than the external portion.

The external portion of an object is often referred to as the object's interface, because it acts as the object's interface to the rest of the program. Because other objects must communicate with the object only through its interface, the internal portion of the object is protected from outside tampering. And because an outside program has no access to the internal implementation of an object, the internal implementation can change at any time without affecting other parts of the program.

Encapsulation provides two primary benefits to programmers:

☐ Implementation hiding

☐ Modularity

NEW TERM *Implementation hiding* refers to the protection of the internal implementation of an object.

An object is composed of a public interface and a private section that can be a combination of internal data and methods. The internal data and methods are the sections of the object that can't be accessed from outside the object. The primary benefit is that these sections can change without affecting programs that use the object.

NEW TERM *Modularity* means that an object can be maintained independently of other objects.

Because the source code for the internal sections of an object is maintained separately from the interface, you are free to make modifications and feel confident that your object won't cause problems. This makes it easier to distribute objects throughout a system, which is a crucial point when it comes to Java and the Internet.

Messages

An object acting alone is rarely very useful; most objects require other objects to really do anything. For example, the car object is pretty useless by itself with no other interaction. Add a driver object, however, and things get more interesting! Knowing this, it's pretty clear that objects need some type of communication mechanism in order to interact with each other.

Software objects interact and communicate with each other via *messages*. When the driver object wants the car object to accelerate, it sends a message to the car object. If you want to think of messages more literally, think of two people as objects. If one person wants the other person to come closer, they send the other person a message. More accurately, one might say to the other person "come here, please." This is a message in a very literal sense. Software messages are a little different in form, but not in theory; they tell an object what to do. In Java, the act of sending an object a message is actually carried out by calling a method of the object. In other words, methods are the mechanism through which messages are sent to objects in the Java environment.

Many times, the receiving object needs more information along with a message so that it knows exactly what to do. When the driver tells the car to accelerate, the car must know by how much. This information is passed along with the message as message *parameters*.

From this discussion, you can see that messages consist of three things.

1. The object to receive the message (car)
2. The name of the action to perform (accelerate)
3. Any parameters the method requires (15 mph)

These three components are sufficient information to fully describe a message for an object. Any interaction with an object is handled by passing a message. This means that objects anywhere in a system can communicate with other objects solely through messages.

Just so you don't get confused, understand that "message passing" is another way of saying "method calling." When an object sends another object a message, it is really just calling a method of that object. The message parameters are actually the parameters to a method. In object-oriented programming, messages and methods are synonymous.

Because everything that an object can do is expressed through its methods (interface), message passing supports all possible interactions between objects. In fact, interfaces enable objects to send messages to and receive messages from each other even if they reside in different locations on a network. Objects in this scenario are referred to as *distributed objects*. Java is specifically designed to support distributed objects.

Inheritance

What happens if you want an object that is very similar to one you already have, but with a few extra characteristics? You just derive a new class based on the class of the similar object.

NEW TERM   *Inheritance* is the process of creating a new class with the characteristics of an existing class, along with additional characteristics unique to the new class.

Inheritance provides a powerful and natural mechanism for organizing and structuring programs.

So far, the discussion of classes has been limited to the data and methods that make up a class. Based on this understanding, you build all classes from scratch by defining all of the data and all of the associated methods. Inheritance provides a means to create classes based on other classes. When a class is based on another class, it inherits all of the properties of that class, including the data and methods for the class. The class doing the inheriting is referred to as the *subclass* (child class) and the class providing the information to inherit is referred to as the *superclass* (parent class).

NOTE

Child classes are sometimes referred to as *descendants*, and parent classes are sometimes referred to as *ancestors*. The family tree analogy works quite well for describing inheritance.

Using the car example, gas-powered cars and cars powered by electricity can be child classes inherited from the car class. Both new car classes share common "car" characteristics, but they also have a few characteristics of their own. The gas car would have a fuel tank and a gas cap, and the electric car might have a battery and a plug for recharging. Each subclass inherits state information (in the form of variable declarations) from the superclass. Figure 3.3 shows the car parent class with the gas and electric car child classes.

Figure 3.3.

Inherited car objects.

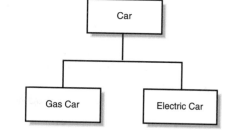

3

The real power of inheritance is the ability to inherit properties and add new ones; subclasses can have variables and methods in addition to the ones they inherit from the superclass. Remember, the electric car has an additional battery and a recharging plug. Subclasses also have the capability to override inherited methods and provide different implementations for them. For example, the gas car would probably be able to go much faster than the electric car. The accelerate method for the gas car could reflect this difference.

Class inheritance is designed to allow as much flexibility as possible. You can create inheritance trees as deep as necessary to carry out your design. An inheritance tree, or class hierarchy, looks much like a family tree; it shows the relationships between classes. Unlike a family tree, the classes in an inheritance tree get more specific as you move down the tree. The car classes in Figure 3.3 are a good example of an inheritance tree.

By using inheritance, you've learned how subclasses can allow specialized data and methods in addition to the common ones provided by the superclass. This enables programmers to reuse the code in the superclass many times, thus saving extra coding effort and therefore eliminating potential bugs.

One final point to make in regard to inheritance: It is possible and sometimes useful to create superclasses that act purely as templates for more usable subclasses. In this situation, the superclass serves as nothing more than an abstraction for the common class functionality shared by the subclasses. For this reason, these types of superclasses are referred to as *abstract classes*. An abstract class cannot be instantiated, meaning that no objects can be created from an abstract class. An abstract class cannot be instantiated because parts of it have been specifically left unimplemented. More specifically, these parts are made up of methods that have yet to be implemented, which are referred to as abstract methods.

Using the car example once more, the accelerate method really can't be defined until the car's acceleration capabilities are known. Of course, how a car accelerates is determined by the type of engine it has. Because the engine type is unknown in the car superclass, the accelerate method could be defined but left unimplemented, which would make both the accelerate method and the car superclass abstract. Then the gas and electric car child classes would implement the accelerate method to reflect the acceleration capabilities of their respective engines or motors.

NOTE

The discussion of inheritance naturally leads to the concept of *polymorphism*, which is the notion of an object having different forms. Using polymorphism, it is possible to have objects with similar interfaces but different responses to method calls. In this way, an object is able to maintain its original interface within a program while taking on a different form.

OOP and Games

So far, I've talked a lot about the general programming advantages of using objects to simplify complex programming tasks, but I haven't talked too much about how they specifically apply to games. To understand how you can benefit from OOP design methods as a game programmer, you must first take a closer look at what a game really is.

Think of a game as a type of abstract simulation. If you think about most of the games you've seen or played, it's almost impossible to come up with one that isn't simulating something. All the adventure games and sports games, and even the far-out space games, are modeling some type of objects present in the real world (maybe not *our* world, but *some* world nevertheless). Knowing that games are models of worlds, you can make the connection that most of the things (landscapes, creatures, and so on) in games correspond to things in these worlds. And as soon as you can organize a game into a collection of "things," you can apply OOP techniques to the design. This is possible because things can be translated easily into objects in an OOP environment.

Look at an OOP design of a simple adventure game as an example. In this hypothetical adventure game, the player controls a character around a fantasy world and fights creatures, collects treasure, and so on. You can model all the different aspects of the game as objects by creating a hierarchy of classes. After you design the classes, you create them and let them interact with each other just as objects do in real life.

The world itself probably would be the first class you design. The world class would contain information such as its map and images that represent a graphical visualization of the map. The world class also would contain information such as the current time and weather. All other classes in the game would derive from a positional class containing coordinate information specifying where in the world the objects are located. These coordinates would specify the location of objects on the world map.

The main character class would maintain information such as life points and any items picked up during the game, such as weapons, lanterns, keys, and so on. The character class would have methods for moving in different directions based on the player's input. The items carried by the character also would be objects. The lantern class would contain information such as how much fuel is left and whether the lantern is on or off. The lantern would have methods for turning it on and off, which would cause it to use up fuel.

There would be a general creature class from which all creatures would be derived. This creature class would contain information such as life points and how much damage the creature inflicts when fighting. It would have methods for moving in different directions. Unlike the character class, however, the creature's move methods would be based on some type of intelligence programmed into the creature class. The mean creatures might always go after the main character if they are on the same screen together, for example, but passive creatures might just ignore the main character. Derived creature classes would add extra attributes, such as the capability to swim or fly. Figure 3.4 shows the class hierarchy for this hypothetical game.

I've obviously left out a lot of detail in the descriptions of these hypothetical objects. This is intentional because I want to highlight the benefit of the object approach, not the details of fully implementing a real example. Although you already might see the benefits of the object design so far, the real gains come when you put all the objects together in the context of the complete game.

After you have designed all the object classes, you just create objects from them and let them go. You already will have established methods that enable the objects to interact with each other, so in a sense the game world is autonomous. The intelligence of any object in the game is hidden in the object implementation, so no external manipulation is required of them. All you really must do is provide a main game loop that updates everything. Each object would have some method for updating its status. For creatures, this update would entail determining the direction in which to move and whether they should attack. For the main character object, an update would involve performing an action based on the user input. The key point to understand here is that the objects are independent entities that know how to maintain themselves.

Figure 3.4.

Class hierarchy for a hypothetical adventure game.

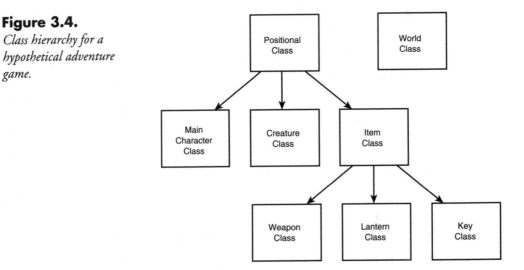

Of course, this game also could be designed using a procedural approach, but then there would be no concept of an object linked with its actions. You would have to model the objects as data structures and then have a bunch of functions that act on those structures. No function would be more associated with a particular data structure than any other. And more importantly, the data structures would know nothing about the functions. You also would lose all the benefits of deriving similar objects from a common parent object. This means that you would have duplicate code for all these types of objects that would have to be maintained independently.

> **NOTE**
>
> Procedural programming is the precursor to object-oriented programming. In procedural programming, the focus to solving programmatic problems is on using blocks of code called procedures that independently act on data. This is in direct contrast to object-oriented programming, in which procedures and data are combined in a single unit: the object.

A more dramatic benefit of using OOP becomes apparent when you develop new games in the future. By following an OOP design in the first game, you will be able to reuse many of the objects for new games. This is not just a side effect of using OOP techniques, it is a fundamental goal of OOP design. Although you can certainly cut and paste code in a procedural approach, this hardly compares to reusing and deriving from entire objects. As an example, the creature class developed in the hypothetical adventure game could be used as a base class for any kind of creature object, even those in other games.

Although this example is brief, it should illustrate the advantages of using an OOP design for games. If nothing else, I wanted to at least get you thinking about how OOP design techniques can make games easier to develop, which ultimately makes your job more fun!

The good news about all this OOP stuff is that Java is designed from the ground up as an OOP language. As a matter of fact, you don't even have the option of writing procedural code in Java. Nevertheless, it still takes effort to maintain a consistent OOP approach when you are writing Java games, which is why I've spent so much time today discussing OOP theory.

Java and Other OOP Languages

You've learned that OOP has obvious advantages over procedural approaches, especially when it comes to games. OOP was conceived from the ground up with the intention of simulating the real world. However, in the world of game programming, the faster language has traditionally always won. This is evident by the amount of assembly language still being written in the commercial game-development community. No one can argue the fact that carefully written assembly language is faster than C, and that even more carefully written C is sometimes faster than C++. And unfortunately, Java ranks a distant last behind all these languages in terms of efficiency and speed.

However, the advantages of using Java to write games stretch far beyond the speed benefits provided by these faster languages. This doesn't mean that Java is poised to sweep the game community as the game development language of choice; far from it! It means that Java provides an unprecedented array of features that scale well to game development. The goal for Java game programmers is to write games in the present within the speed limitations of Java, while planning games for the future that will run well when faster versions of Java are released.

NOTE

In fact, two separate speed issues are involved in Java game programming. The first is the issue of the speed of the Java language and runtime environment, which will no doubt improve as better compilers and more efficient versions of the runtime environment are released. The second issue is that of Internet connection speed, which is limited by the speed of the modem or physical line used to connect to the Internet. Both of these issues are important, but they impact Java games in different ways: The first speed limitation affects how fast a game runs, while the second limitation affects how fast a game loads.

Due to languages such as Smalltalk, which treats everything as an object (an impediment for simple problems), and their built-in memory-allocation handling (a sometimes very slow process), OOP languages have developed a reputation for being slow and inefficient. C++ remedied this situation in many ways but brought with it the pitfalls and complexities of C, which are largely undesirable in a distributed environment such as the Internet. Java includes many of the nicer features of C++, but incorporates them in a more simple and robust language.

For more information about exactly how Java improves C++, see Appendix C, "Differences Between Java and C/C++."

The current drawback to using Java for developing games is the speed of Java programs, which is significantly slower than C++ programs because Java programs execute in an interpreted fashion. The just-in-time compilation enhancements promised in future versions of Java should help remedy this problem. You learn about some optimization techniques to help speed up Java code near the end of this book on Day 20, "Optimizing Java Code for Games."

Currently, Java programs are interpreted, meaning that they go through a conversion process as they are being run. Although this interpreted approach is beneficial because it allows Java programs to run on different types of computers, it greatly affects the speed of the programs. A promising solution to this problem is just-in-time compilation, which is a technique in which a Java program is compiled into an executable native to a particular type of computer before being run.

Today, Java is still not ready for prime time when it comes to competing as a game programmer's language. It just isn't possible yet in the current release of Java to handle the high-speed graphics demanded by commercial games. To alleviate this problem, you have the option of integrating native C code to Java programs. This might or might not be a workable solution, based on the particular needs of a game.

Regardless of whether Java can compete as a high-speed gaming language, it is certainly capable of meeting the needs of many other types of games that are less susceptible to speed restrictions. The games you develop throughout this book are examples of the types of games that can be developed in the current release of Java.

Summary

Today you learned about object-oriented programming and how it relates to Java. You saw that the concept of an object is at the heart of the OOP paradigm and serves as the conceptual basis for all Java code design. You also found out exactly what an object is, along with some of the powerful benefits of following an object-centric design approach.

You learned in today's lesson how OOP design principles can be applied to games. Games are a very natural application of OOP strategies, because they typically resemble simulations. You then learned that OOP game programming in Java is not without its drawbacks. Execution speed is often the killer in game programming, and Java game programming is no exception. However, future enhancements to Java should lessen the performance gap between Java and other popular OOP languages such as C++.

Now that the conceptual groundwork for Java game programming has been laid, you are ready to move on to more specific game programming issues. To be exact, you now are ready to learn about the basics of using graphics in games, which are covered in tomorrow's lesson.

Q&A

Q What is an object-oriented language?

A A language that supports the concept of an object, which is the merger of data and methods into a logically single element. Furthermore, object-oriented languages typically support features such as encapsulation, inheritance, and polymorphism, which combine to encourage code reuse.

Q What is the difference between a class and an object?

A A class is a blueprint, or template, that defines the data and methods necessary to model a "thing." An object is an instance of a class that exists in the computer's memory and can be interacted with much like a "thing" in the real world. You can create as many objects from a single class as memory will allow.

Q What's the difference between a message and a method?

A Nothing, really. "Sending a message" is another way of saying "calling a method" and is often used in more general OOP discussions.

Workshop

The Workshop section provides questions and exercises to help solidify the material you learned today. Try to answer the questions and at least study the exercises before moving on to tomorrow's lesson. You'll find the answers to the questions in Appendix A, "Quiz Answers."

Quiz

1. What is an object?
2. What is encapsulation?
3. Why is implementation hiding important?
4. What is the major problem with Java in regard to game programming?

Exercises

1. Develop a class hierarchy for a game idea of your own, similar to the one created for the hypothetical adventure game.
2. Play some computer games, paying particular attention to how they can each be broken down into groups of objects.
3. If you are a C or C++ programmer new to Java, read Appendix C, "Differences Between Java and C/C++."

Week 1

Day 4

The Basics of Graphics

The graphical appearance of a game is the first impression a user has of the game. And even though game play is the ultimate measure of how engaging a game is, weak graphics can often kill a potentially cool game. For this reason, it's important for you to take the time to carefully create graphics and animation for your games that are sure to catch someone's attention. You'll learn more about the technical details of using graphics in Java tomorrow. Today, the focus is on how to create game graphics and animation.

If you aren't fortunate enough to have a staff of artists at your disposal, then you are like the rest of us and have to work graphical magic with the limited resources at hand. Even if you decide to get help from an artist on your game graphics, you still need to have a solid understanding of the role of the graphics in your game. Either way, any insight that a game developer has into the process of creating game graphics can only serve to ease the development and improve the visual appeal of the game. Today's lesson gives you a good dose of this insight.

The following topics are covered in today's lesson:

- ☐ Graphics in games
- ☐ The GIF image format
- ☐ Graphics utilities
- ☐ Creating and editing graphics
- ☐ Finding graphics

Graphics in Games

Before you begin any actual graphics creation, it's important to decide exactly what you need in terms of game graphics. You already should have the game pretty well defined before progressing to this stage. The next step is to take what you know about the game and assess the graphical content required to make it a reality. This consists of making decisions regarding the game's graphical elements and itemizing the graphics needed.

Game Window Size

The first major decision to make regarding a game's graphics is the size of the game window.

NEW TERM The *game window* is the rectangular surface on the screen where the game applet is displayed.

Because Java games typically run within the confines of a Web page, you have pretty wide control over the size of the game window. The only potential limitation on the game window is performance.

You might wonder how performance could be related to the size of the game window. In games with animation, the game window is usually constantly redrawn with animation frames. The amount of time it takes to redraw the game window is based on the window's size; the larger the game window, the longer it takes to redraw, because there is more to draw. Therefore, in games that use extensive animation, you need to weigh the game window size against the performance of the game. I've found that a game window size in the range of 200 to 300 pixels in both width and height yields decent performance results on a wide variety of systems.

Keep in mind that games that don't use animation aren't necessarily restricted to the game-window size limitation. However, it is still generally a good idea to keep the game window size within reason, because the game will be embedded inside a Web page.

Target Audience

The target audience for your game can impact the graphics requirements a great deal. Games for children typically use graphics with bright colors to help keep their interest. Games aimed at very young children often use highly contrasting bright colors and larger graphic images. Very young children have much more difficulty with mouse precision and timing, so you need to address these issues in your game design. Most children are drawn toward animals and cartoon-type characters. These types of graphics make a good addition to almost any children's game.

If you're developing a game aimed at teenagers or an older crowd, the graphics pretty much depend on the game itself. Many teens and young adults are attracted to games with realistic violence and a lot of gory graphics. Both inside and outside the commercial game community, there has been much debate about violence in video games, and the decision to include bloody graphics in your game is ultimately your own to make. I personally don't see gory graphics as being any different than special effects in movies; they have their place in some games and certainly can add to the excitement.

Movies are a good example of how the target audience dictates the graphic detail. Children gravitate toward cartoons; the characters are easily recognizable and contrast well with the background. Within cartoons, there are varying levels of graphic detail typically associated with the target age group for the cartoon. Older kids usually are more interested in cartoons that more closely approach realism. Similarly, most adults prefer movies with human actors instead of cartoons.

NOTE

It is sometimes possible to aim primarily for a particular target audience while also including elements that appeal to other audiences. This approach is sometimes referred to as *shotgun marketing*, because the appeal of a game spreads across a wide group of people. Shotgun marketing is regularly employed in movies with great success. As examples, consider the immensely popular Disney animated movies, which clearly target children but always include plenty of humor that adults can appreciate.

Setting and Mood

Perhaps even more important than the target audience of your game is the setting and mood of the game. Where is your game taking place, both in time and in location? If it's a futuristic space game, your graphics might include metallic colors contrasting with dark space backgrounds. A gothic vampire game probably would have dark, gloomy graphics based mostly at night. By using dark colors, you can more effectively portray the gloomy mood of the game, with creatures emerging from the moonlit shadows.

NOTE

> Keep in mind that the setting of the game can also be enhanced with graphics in the surrounding Web page containing the embedded game applet.

In these two game examples, I've alluded a great deal to the colors used for the graphics. This is important because colors can really dictate the mood of a game more effectively than specific graphical images. The best way to understand the impact of the colors on the mood of a game is to think about the dimmer switch on a light. Have you ever dimmed the lights in a room and noticed the immediate change in mood reflected by the dimming? Whether the mood is interpreted as gloomy or romantic, it is altered nevertheless. This lighting technique is used frequently in movies and certainly can be used in games as well.

You can easily apply the dimmer idea to your game graphics by altering the brightness of the graphics in a graphics editor. Most graphics editors provide image filtering features that enable you to specifically alter the brightness of an image. You learn some popular shareware graphics editors a little later today in the "Graphics Utilities" section.

Graphics Style

The style you choose for your game graphics is the final requirement you need to address before moving on to creating them. You more than likely already have an idea of the style, so this decision probably won't take too much time. *Graphics style* basically means the look of the images, such as cartoon style, lifelike, rendered, and so on. Lifelike graphics, such as scanned photographs or digitized video, usually contain a very broad range of colors. On the other hand, cartoon-type graphics usually consist of black edges with solid color fills.

After you select a graphics style, you should try to keep all the graphics consistent throughout the game. It probably wouldn't be a good idea to have a scanned background with cartoon characters moving around in front of it. On the other hand, maybe your game has some Roger Rabbit–type theme to back up this mix of graphics. It's totally up to you; just remember that a more consistent style used for graphics results in a more absorbing and realistic game.

The graphics style of the game is related closely to how the graphics are created. It will be hard to commit to a cartoon style for the graphics if you don't have access to an artist and have no artistic abilities yourself, for example. So, while you're thinking about the style you want for the game, weigh into your decision the resources you have for carrying out the graphics development.

The GIF Image Format

Graphic images in Java are usually represented using the GIF image format. The GIF (Graphics Interchange Format) image format is a platform-independent format created by CompuServe in 1987 to help facilitate image compatibility across a wide range of computer systems. At the time of the GIF format creation, most other image formats were designed around a specific computer platform, and therefore were difficult to transport to other platforms. This isn't much of a problem today, but the GIF format has lived on and thrived nevertheless.

The most current version of the GIF image format is version 89a, which provides a lot of neat features beyond the primary purpose of encapsulating a bitmapped image. The GIF89a format supports up to 256 colors with a transparency color, data compression, and interlacing.

New Term *Transparency colors* are colors in an image that are unused, meaning that they aren't drawn when the rest of the colors in the image are drawn. The significance of transparency colors is that they allow the background behind an image to show through.

New Term *Data compression* is a technique involving the conversion of data into a smaller, more efficient format so that it takes up less space in memory or on a hard drive or takes less time to transfer over a modem connection.

New Term *Interlaced images* are images that can be displayed in incremental stages as they are being loaded. You've no doubt witnessed this effect in Web pages when images go from blurry to clear as they are being loaded.

More advanced features of the GIF89a format include hidden text comments, multiple animation frame sub-images, and animation frame rate, among others.

New Term *Hidden text comments* are comments you can insert into an image that aren't displayed. These comments are sometimes useful for making notes about an image.

Java doesn't currently support all these features, namely animation, but it supports enough of them to still make GIFs a very viable format for image representation in Java games.

NOTE

The animation support in the GIF89a format consists of the capability to specify a sequence of images (frames) that are displayed in succession to give the illusion of movement. You can specify a frame rate, which determines how fast the frames are displayed or animated.

4

I mentioned that the GIF89a format supports up to 256 colors, which means that there can be less than 256 colors in an image. GIF images can contain anywhere from 2 to 256 colors; the number of colors impacts the size of the image greatly.

 NEW TERM A *color palette* is a group of colors available to an image. All 256-color GIF images have an associated color palette defining the colors that the image can contain.

You can reduce the colors used in a GIF image by using a graphics utility that supports the GIF format. You find out about some of the popular shareware graphics utilities that support the GIF89a format in the next section.

> **NOTE**
>
> When working with GIF images, you have the ability to specify which colors make up the 256 color palette. Tweaking the color palette to fit the particular color needs of an image is referred to as *palette optimization*. Using palette optimization, you can usually get pretty good results with 256 colors.

If you want more detailed information about the GIF image format, check out the All About GIF89a image format Web site at `http://members.aol.com/royalef/gifabout.htm`. This site also contains a link to the original CompuServe GIF image format specification, for inquiring minds that have to know! Figure 4.1 shows what the All About GIF89a image format Web site looks like.

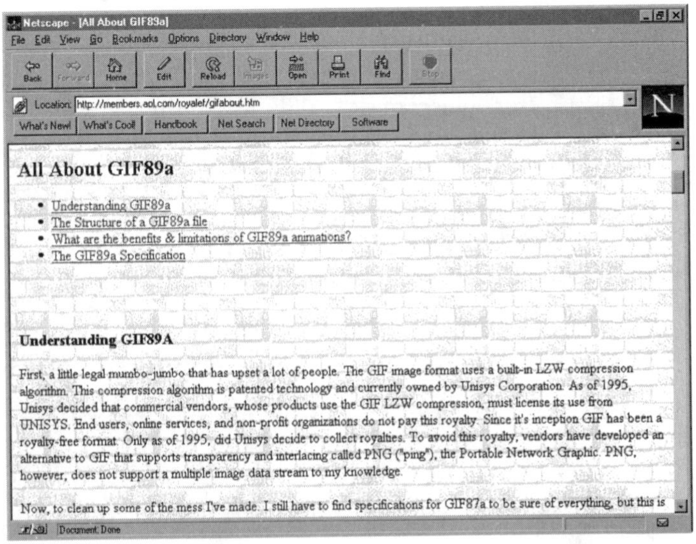

Figure 4.1.

The All About GIF89a image format Web site.

4

Creating and Editing Graphics

You've learned how to assess the graphical requirements for games and the different types of game graphics, but you still haven't really covered the specifics of how to create graphics. Unfortunately, there is no simple explanation of how to create graphics. As in all art forms, there is much about the subject that must be grafted out of experience. However, I want to cover the basic techniques of creating graphics for games, and then you can chart your own course. Before getting into these techniques, however, let's take a quick look at some of the shareware graphics utilities that are available on the Web.

Graphics Utilities

Whether you create your own graphics or hire an artist, you will need a graphics utility at some point in the graphics development process. Even if you don't need to change the content of the graphics, you often will need to resize or change the transparency color of the images. A nice graphics editor is the most important tool for developing and maintaining game graphics. Although you might end up wanting to invest in a professional graphics editor with a wider range of features, such as Adobe Photoshop, you can't go wrong by starting out with a good shareware editor.

The rest of this section focuses on some popular shareware graphics editors you can use to create and edit GIF images for Java games. They all support the GIF89a graphics format and provide varying degrees of image processing features.

Image Alchemy

Image Alchemy, by Handmade Software, is a very extensive graphics editor and conversion utility with versions available on a wide range of platforms. Image Alchemy reads and writes over 70 different image formats. Although it is geared more toward image conversion than editing, its strong conversion features and incredibly wide support for multiple platforms make it a very useful graphics utility to have.

Handmade Software has versions of Image Alchemy for almost every major computer platform. It even has an online version that enables you to convert images over the Web via a connection to its Image Alchemy server. Very cool!

You can get information about Image Alchemy and download the latest version from the Image Alchemy Web site, which is located at `http://www.handmadesw.com/hsi/alchemy.html`. Figure 4.2 shows the Image Alchemy Web site.

Figure 4.2.

The Image Alchemy Web site.

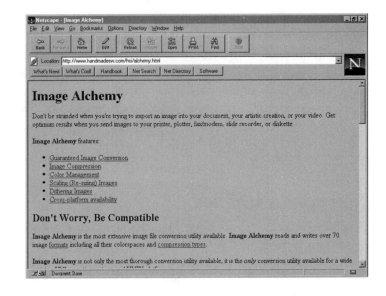

Paint Shop Pro

Paint Shop Pro, by JASC Software, is a graphics editor for Windows 95 with a full suite of editing, conversion, and image processing tools. Paint Shop Pro contains a wide variety of paint tools, as well as image filters and conversion features for most of the popular image formats. Paint Shop Pro is arguably the best shareware graphics editor for Windows 95.

You can get information about Paint Shop Pro and download the latest version from the Paint Shop Pro Web site, which is located at `http://www.jasc.com/psp.html`. Figure 4.3 shows the Paint Shop Pro Web site.

Graphics Workshop

Graphics Workshop, by Alchemy Mindworks, is another graphics editor for Windows 95 that is comparable to Paintshop Pro. Graphics Workshop is geared more toward image conversion rather than editing. However, you might find some useful features in it that complement Paintshop Pro, so definitely take a look at them both.

You can get information about Graphics Workshop and download the latest version from the Graphics Workshop Web site, which is located at `http://www.mindworkshop.com/alchemy/gww.html`. Figure 4.4 shows the Graphics Workshop Web site.

Figure 4.3.
The Paint Shop Pro Web site.

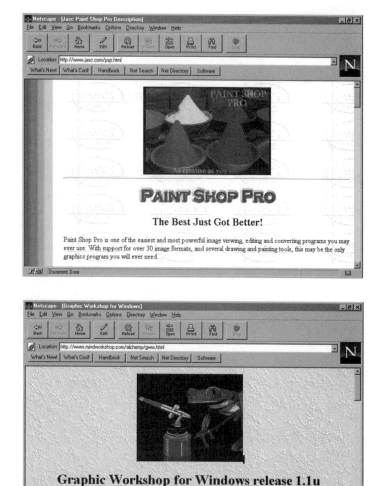

Figure 4.4.
The Graphics Workshop Web site.

Imaging Machine

Imaging Machine, by E. I. du Pont de Nemours and Company, puts an interesting twist on the concept of image manipulation. The entire graphics utility is online and consists of a variety of image processing tools that are accessible from the Imaging Machine Web site. The goal of Imaging Machine is to free users from the unwanted hassles of downloading, installing, and configuring complex imaging software. There is also a stand-alone non-network version called ImageMagick that runs on most UNIX systems. The ANSI C++ source code is available for ImageMagick, so you can rebuild it for your platform if you desire.

You can find information about Imaging Machine and try it out for yourself at the Imaging Machine Web site, which is located at `http://www.vrl.com/Imaging`. Figure 4.5 shows the Imaging Machine Web site.

Figure 4.5.

The Imaging Machine Web site.

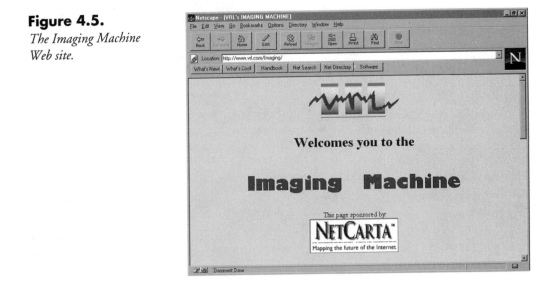

Line-Art Graphics

Getting back to graphics creation, the first method of creating graphics is called *line-art* graphics. I call this method line art because it encompasses practically all hand-drawn graphics, whether drawn and scanned from paper or drawn in a software paint program. Either way, you have total control over the colors used and the resulting image. Cartoon-type graphics fall in this category.

You usually draw line-art graphics by hand on paper and scan them with a digitizing scanner, or you use a graphics editor to draw and modify the image. The freehand technique is useful if you have some traditional art experience. The graphics editor approach usually is better if you don't have any art experience, because you can "cheat" to a certain extent by using software image processing tools. An in-between solution is to draw rough outlines of what you want on paper, scan them as digitized images, and color and clean them up in a graphics editor. This is a really nice way to create graphics because you get to draw freehand and still benefit from software tools, while ultimately maintaining complete control over the image.

3-D Rendered Graphics

You don't have to look far these days to see how popular 3-D rendered graphics have become in the game world. There is a reason for this; rendering provides the capability to create incredibly complex and realistic 3-D graphics that sometimes aren't even possible with freehand drawing, especially when it comes to animation. Before I get into that, you should quickly learn how modeling and rendering works.

Using 3-D modeling software such as Caligari's trueSpace or AutoDesk's 3D Studio, you create mathematical wireframe 3-D objects. Of course, the majority of the math is hidden, so all you really have to worry about is learning how to model 3-D objects using the software tools. These modeling programs provide all kinds of methods for creating and manipulating the wireframe objects into just about any shape you can imagine. After you come up with a shape with which you're happy, you specify the surface of the object along with any sources of light. You even can place cameras to get different views of the object. After specifying all these attributes, you tell the application to render the image of the object.

NEW TERM   *Rendering* is the process of composing a graphical image of a purely mathematical object.

Rendering can yield incredible results for game graphics, and I highly suggest looking into it. However, it usually takes a fair amount of practice to get good at creating and working with wireframe objects to a point where you can create complex models. On the other hand, it might come easy to you. Either way, rendering can be a lot of fun and can yield results far beyond the artistic grasp of most game programmers.

Generally speaking, rendered objects have a certain graphical style that is hard to shake. Remember that rendering is a computer process, so it's hard to make rendered objects show emotion like you can with hand-drawn images. Keep in mind that a delicate balance of tools usually generates the most effective results. You might find that rendering is great for producing backgrounds, whereas hand-drawn images are better for individual characters. If you do decide on a mixture of graphics-creation techniques, be sure to blend their respective styles with each other as best you can.

One final note about rendering: I mentioned that rendering can make creating animations much easier. Most modeling/rendering software packages come with tools that enable you to place and move a camera. You usually have the option of moving individual objects, as well as the camera, over time to generate animations. You can generate amazing animations with very little work using these types of tools.

4

Scanned Photography and Video-Captured Graphics

Another interesting way to create graphics for games is by using scanned photography and video-captured graphics. *Scanned photography* basically consists of scanned photographic images captured with a digitizing scanner. These can be useful, but because of the two-phase photographic development/image scan process, they aren't used too much in games. On the other hand, *video-captured graphics*, which rely on a very similar concept, have been used a great deal; these graphics were used in DOOM. Using video-captured graphics involves setting up a video camera and grabbing frames of video of an object as bitmapped images. Video-captured graphics differ from video sequences in that video-captured graphics are used to generate snapshots of different views of an object, and not a real-time animation.

This technique is useful primarily because it enables you to create real-world models of the objects in your game and then convert them to images automatically. The primary problem with video capturing is that the resulting images have a broad range of colors that usually have to be dithered down to the 256-color GIF format. However, sometimes an optimized palette can help yield better results.

 Dithering is a process in which the colors in an image are reduced to a lesser amount of colors. This is carried out by using different patterns of the lesser colors to represent the colors lost. Many graphics editors provide dithering features.

The only other problem with video capturing is that it usually involves having to build a small video studio with lighting and a backdrop, not to mention buying the video camera and video hardware that supports NTSC (National Television Standards Committee) video input. You also have to be able to somehow construct physical models of the game objects. However, if you are willing to go the extra step and do these things, the results certainly are worth the trouble.

 NTSC video is the type of video signal used by many televisions, VCRs, and video cameras. To be able to retrieve images in this format, you need to have graphics hardware that supports NTSC input.

Background Graphics and Textures

 Background graphics are any graphics that appear behind the main objects in the game, such as walls, forests, clouds, and so on.

Many background graphics, such as walls, benefit from textured bitmap images.

 A *texture* is an image that models a piece of a graphical surface that can be tiled without notice.

Textures are very useful primarily because they take up relatively little space; this is because they are tiled repeatedly to create a larger image at runtime. I highly recommend using textures whenever possible. You've no doubt already seen many textures at work as backgrounds in Web pages.

There are libraries of royalty-free textures that often serve as a good resource. Of course, you are free to draw your own textures, but be warned that drawing a textured image so that it can be tiled correctly with the edges blending smoothly is pretty tricky. Although textures are nice for creating tiled backgrounds, you can also draw the background graphics as complete images; just remember that the size of the images will usually increase. You can find much texture artwork at The Clip Art Connection Web site, which you learn about a little later today in the "Finding Graphics" section.

Animated Graphics

Although you don't learn about the details of animation until later this week, it's okay now to look at the graphical requirements of animated graphics. Because animation typically involves a series of images, most animated graphics will be in the form of a series of animation frame images.

The animation frames for an object in a game sometimes are referred to as *phases* of the object. The phases depict the movements that the object goes through independent of positional motion. The phase animations usually mean different things for different objects. A fire object might have four frames of animation that depict the movement of the flames, for example. On the other hand, a tank's phases in a battle game might consist of the rotations of the tank. Figure 4.6 shows these two types of animation frames.

It also is possible for objects to change phase in more than one way. In this case, you will have a two-dimensional array of animation frames rather than a horizontal strip. An example would be a crawling soldier with different animations reflecting the crawling motion. You might have eight rotations for the soldier along with two different frames to show the leg and arm crawling movement. Figure 4.7 shows how these animations might look.

Practically speaking, you would need more frames of animation than these examples show, especially when it comes to rotation. Four frames is hardly enough to depict smooth rotation of an object. I recommend a minimum of eight frames when you are showing an object rotating, unless the object is very small, in which case four frames might work.

I mentioned earlier that the GIF89a image format supports animation by enabling you to include multiple frame images in a single GIF image. Unfortunately, the current release of Java doesn't support animated GIF images, so you'll have to implement Java animations using multiple separate GIF images. You learn much more about this later this week on Day 6, "Sprite Animation."

4

Figure 4.6.
Animation frames for a fire and a tank.

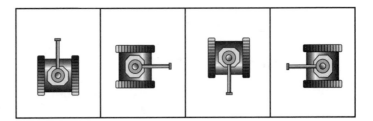

Figure 4.7.
Animation frames for a crawling soldier.

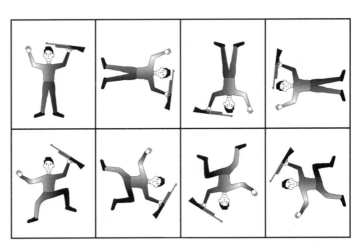

Finding Graphics

If you've decided that creating game graphics isn't for you, you have a few options. The first is to try to find royalty-free art. This isn't always a very viable option, because games typically require very unique graphics. However, you might be able to find interesting clip art that will work for your game graphics. The last thing I want to do is to discourage you from trying a possibly useful outlet for obtaining graphics.

A good starting point for finding existing clip-art graphics is The Clip Art Connection Web site, which is located at `http://www.acy.digex.net/~infomart/clipart/index.html`. The Clip Art Connection contains links to many different clip-art sites, as well as sites to artists and commercial stock art collections. This site is definitely worth checking out! Figure 4.8 shows what The Clip Art Connection Web site looks like.

Figure 4.8.

The Clip Art Connection Web site.

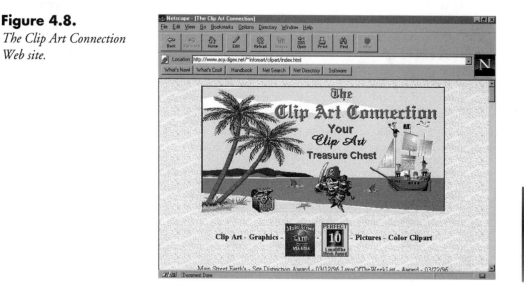

Another option, and the one I suggest when you don't have the ability to create your own graphics, is to hire an artist to draw or render the graphics for you. You might be surprised by how inexpensive it can be; some people might even be willing to draw the graphics for free just to be involved in a Java game (just don't forget to give them full credit, a free copy of the end product, and probably a nice thank-you card or e-mail).

The best place to look for artists is on the Internet or online services such as CompuServe. Finding artists through one of these channels has an additional benefit; the artists are probably already comfortable with computers and software drawing tools. This will ease the communication gap between you and them. Additionally, they probably will already have a scanner and can handle any image conversions. Some of the art-related forums on CompuServe are the Artist Forum (ARTIST), Computer Art Forum (COMART), and the Computer Animation Forum (COMANI). On the Internet, you can either search for artists using one of the popular search engines, such as Yahoo!, or you can start with the artist list provided at The Clip Art Connection Web site.

Before you contact an artist, be sure to have a very solid idea of what you want. It's a good idea to write down all your thoughts on the game and what it should look like, including sketches or written descriptions of the graphics. The better the communication between you and the artist, the more likely he or she will deliver graphics to your liking. You might want to ask for some samples of the artist's work to check out the style and see whether it matches what you have in mind. The last step is to work up a formal agreement with the artist, outlining exactly what is expected on both ends of the deal, along with a due date that is agreeable to both parties.

Summary

Today's lesson covered the basics of creating graphics for games. Along with establishing what is required of game graphics, you learned about some specific techniques for creating them. Unfortunately, I don't have the space (or the qualifications!) to try to teach you art, which is exactly what game graphics are. If you are weak in the art area, you might want to hire an artist to draw or render the graphics for your game.

The main goal today was to give you enough background information about game graphics to give you a better idea of what you will need to create graphics for your own games. As fun as creating graphics can be, the real joy is seeing them in action. Tomorrow's lesson gets into the specifics of using graphics in Java.

Q&A

Q Does Java support any image formats other than GIF?

A Yes. Java also supports the JPEG image format, which is geared more toward photographic images.

Q If the GIF format supports only 256 colors, what do I do about images using more than 256 colors?

A The reality is that you can have a maximum of 256 colors in GIF images, and therefore a maximum of 256 colors in your game graphics. However, you can side-step this limitation a little by using a graphics utility to dither images that have more colors down to 256-color GIF images.

Q I have no artistic abilities, I haven't found any interesting graphics on the Web, and I don't know if I can afford hiring an artist. Is there anything I can do?

A Yes! In this case, your best bet is to buy a color scanner and start looking for interesting artwork everywhere you go. The best source is to look in bookstores for stock art books. I have a little confession to make: Much of the artwork used for games in this book was scanned from stock art books and then resized, colored, and cleaned up using a graphics editor. I'm not incredibly artistic, just resourceful!

Q **I have a game idea that has graphics consisting of lines, rectangles, and other simple graphics primitives. Do I still need to create images?**

A Absolutely not. If your game needs only graphics primitives, you can easily use the Java AWT graphics features to generate the graphics at runtime. This is cool because it completely eliminates the delays associated with transferring images over the Internet.

Workshop

The Workshop section provides questions and exercises to help you get a better feel for the material you learned today. Try to answer the questions and at least peruse the exercises before moving on to tomorrow's lesson. You'll find the answers to the questions in Appendix A, "Quiz Answers."

Quiz

1. Who created the GIF image format and why?
2. What is interlacing?
3. What is dithering?
4. What is a phased graphical object?
5. What things should you consider when hiring an artist?

Exercises

1. Play a few commercial games and pay special attention to the style of the graphics used in different scenes.
2. Find a cool graphics editor and learn how to use its basic features.
3. Get on the Web and check out some of the clip-art graphics archives. See anything that might be useful in a game?
4. Connect to the Imaging Machine Web site and try it out on some of the clip-art graphics you found.

4

Day 5

Java Graphics Techniques

Graphics are at the heart of most games. Knowing this, you need to understand a certain degree of Java graphics fundamentals before you get into full-blown game graphics. Today's lesson focuses on some of the basic Java graphics techniques that will be important as you move on to programming game graphics. You aren't going to get into too many gritty details today, because this lesson is meant to only lay the groundwork of using Java graphics. Don't worry, you'll build some serious Java graphics skills throughout the rest of the book.

You begin today's lesson by learning about the Java graphics coordinate system and the class used as the basis for most of the Java graphics operations. You then move on to images and how they are used in the context of a Java applet. The lesson finishes with an in-depth discussion of how to track the loading of images over a Web connection, which is a very important topic in regard to game graphics.

The following topics are covered in today's lesson:

- ☐ The graphics coordinate system
- ☐ The basics of color
- ☐ The graphics class
- ☐ Tracking images

The Graphics Coordinate System

All graphical computing systems use some sort of coordinate system to specify the nature of points in the system. Coordinate systems typically spell out the origin (0,0) of a graphical system, as well as the axes and directions of increasing value for each of the axes. The traditional mathematical coordinate system familiar to most of us is shown in Figure 5.1.

Figure 5.1.

The traditional coordinate system.

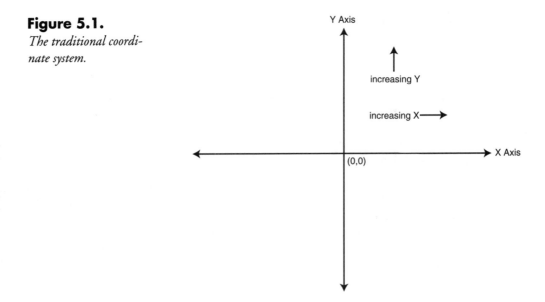

The graphical system in Java uses a coordinate system of its own to specify how and where drawing operations take place. Because all drawing in Java takes place within the confines of an applet window, the Java coordinate system is realized by the applet window. The coordinate system in Java has an origin that is located in the upper-left corner of the window; positive X values increase to the right and positive Y values increase down. All values in the Java coordinate system are positive integers. Figure 5.2 shows how this coordinate system looks.

Figure 5.2.
The Java graphics coordinate system.

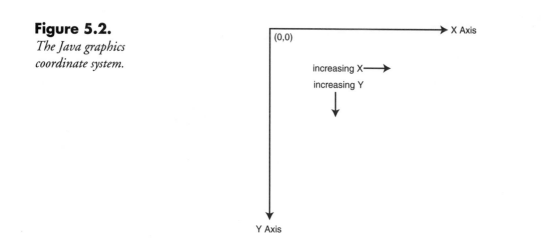

The Basics of Color

A topic that impacts almost every area of Java graphics is color. Therefore, it's important to understand the underlying nature of color and how it is modeled in Java and in computer systems in general. Most computer systems take a similar approach to representing color. The main function of color in a computer system is to accurately reflect the physical nature of color within the confines of a graphical system. This physical nature isn't hard to figure out; anyone who has experienced the joy of Play-Doh can tell you that colors react in different ways when they are combined with each other. Like Play-Doh, a computer color system needs to be able to mix colors with accurate, predictable results.

Color computer monitors provide possibly the most useful insight into how software systems implement color. A color monitor has three electron guns: red, green, and blue. The output from these three guns converges on each pixel of the screen, exciting phosphors to produce the appropriate color (see Figure 5.3). The combined intensities of each gun determine the resulting pixel color. This convergence of different colors from the monitor guns is very similar to the convergence of different colored Play-Doh.

NOTE

Technically speaking, the result of combining colors on a monitor is different than that of combining similarly colored Play-Doh. The reason for this is that color combinations on a monitor are additive, meaning that mixed colors are emitted by the monitor; Play-Doh color combinations are subtractive, meaning that mixed colors are absorbed. The additive or subtractive nature of a color combination is dependent on the physical properties of the particular medium involved.

5

Figure 5.3.

Electron guns in a color monitor converging to create a unique color.

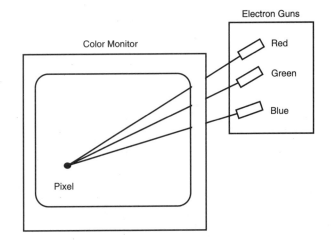

The Java color system is very similar to the physical system used by color monitors; it forms unique colors by using varying intensities of the colors red, green, and blue. Therefore, Java colors are represented by the combination of the numeric intensities of the primary colors (red, green, and blue). This color system is known as RGB (Red Green Blue) and is standard across most graphical computer systems.

> Although RGB is the most popular computer color system in use, there are others. Another popular color system is HSB, which stands for Hue Saturation Brightness. In this system, colors are defined by varying degrees of hue, saturation, and brightness. The HSB color system is also supported by Java.

Table 5.1 shows the numeric values for the red, green, and blue components of some basic colors. Notice that the intensities of each color component range from 0 to 255 in value.

Table 5.1. RGB component values for some basic colors.

Color	Red	Green	Blue
White	255	255	255
Black	0	0	0
Light Gray	192	192	192
Dark Gray	128	128	128
Red	255	0	0

Color	Red	Green	Blue
Green	0	255	0
Blue	0	0	255
Yellow	255	255	0
Purple	255	0	255

Java provides a class, Color, for modeling colors. The Color class represents an RGB color and provides methods for extracting and manipulating the primary color components. Color also includes constant members representing many popular colors. You typically use the Color class to specify the color when you are using many of Java's graphical functions, about which you learn next.

The Graphics **Class**

Most of Java's graphics functions are accessible through a single class, Graphics, found in the Java AWT (Advanced Windowing Toolkit) package. The Graphics class models a graphics context.

NEW TERM A *graphics context* is an abstract representation of a graphical surface that can be drawn upon.

An abstract drawing surface (graphics context) is basically a way to allow you to draw in a generic manner, without worrying about where the drawing is physically taking place. Graphics contexts are necessary so that the same graphics routines can be used regardless of whether you are drawing to the screen, to memory, or to a printer. The Graphics class provides you with a graphics context to which you perform all graphics funtions. As you learn about the functionality provided by the Graphics class, keep in mind that its output is largely independent of the ultimate destination thanks to graphics contexts.

Graphical output code in a Java applet is usually implemented in the applet's paint method. A Graphics object is passed into the paint method, which is then used to perform graphical output to the applet window (output surface). Because the Graphics object is provided by paint, you never explicitly create a Graphics object.

NOTE

Actually, you couldn't explicitly create a Graphics object even if you wanted to because it is an abstract class. If you recall from Day 3, an abstract class is a class containing unimplemented methods, meaning that objects can't be directly created from the class.

Even though graphics operations often take place within the context of an applet window, the output of the Graphics object is really tied to a component.

> **NEW TERM** A *component* is a generic graphical window that forms the basis for all other graphical elements in the Java system. Java components are modeled at the highest level by the Component class, which is defined in the AWT package.

An applet window is just a specific type of component. Thinking of graphics in terms of the Component class rather than an applet window shows you that graphics can be output to any object that is derived from Component. As a matter of fact, every Component object contains a corresponding Graphics object that is used to render graphics on its surface.

Java graphics contexts (Graphics objects) have a few attributes that determine how different graphical operations are carried out. The most important of these attributes is the color attribute, which determines the color used in graphics operations such as drawing lines. You set this attribute using the setColor method defined in the Graphics class. setColor takes a Color object as its only parameter. Similar to setColor is setBackground, which is a method in the Component class that determines the color of the component's background. Graphics objects also have a font attribute that determines the size and appearance of text. This attribute is set using the setFont method, which takes a Font object as its only parameter. You learn more about drawing text and using the Font object, which is covered a little later today in the "Drawing Text" section.

Most of the graphics operations provided by the Graphics class fall into one of the following categories:

- ☐ Drawing graphics primitives
- ☐ Drawing text
- ☐ Drawing images

Drawing Graphics Primitives

Graphics primitives consist of lines, rectangles, circles, polygons, ovals, and arcs. You can create pretty impressive graphics by using these primitives in conjunction with each other; the Graphics class provides methods for drawing these primitives. Certain methods also act on primitives that form closed regions. You can use these methods to erase the area defined by a primitive or fill it with a particular color.

> **NEW TERM** *Closed regions* are graphical elements with a clearly distinctive inside and outside. For example, circles and rectangles are closed regions, whereas lines and points are not.

I'm not going to go through an exhaustive explanation of how to draw each type of primitive, because they don't usually impact game graphics that much. Most games rely more on images, which you learn about later today in the "Drawing Images" section. Nevertheless, look at a few of the primitives just so you can see how they work.

Lines

Lines are the simplest of the graphics primitives and are therefore the easiest to draw. The drawLine method handles drawing lines, and is defined as follows:

```
void drawLine(int x1, int y1, int x2, int y2)
```

The first two parameters, x1 and y1, specify the starting point for the line, and the x2 and y2 parameters specify the ending point. To draw a line in an applet, call drawLine in the applet's paint method, as in the following:

```
public void paint(Graphics g) {
  g.drawLine(5, 10, 15, 55);
}
```

The results of this code are shown in Figure 5.4.

Figure 5.4.

A line drawn using the drawLine *method.*

Most graphical programming environments provide a means to draw lines (and other graphics primitives) in various widths. Java doesn't currently provide a facility to vary the width of lines, which is a pretty big limitation. A future release of Java will probably alleviate this problem.

NOTE

Rectangles

Rectangles are also very easy to draw. The drawRect method enables you to draw rectangles by specifying the upper-left corner and the width and height of the rectangle. The drawRect method is defined in Graphics as follows:

```
void drawRect(int x, int y, int width, int height)
```

The x and y parameters specify the location of the upper-left corner of the rectangle, whereas the width and height parameters specify their namesakes. To draw a rectangle using drawRect, just call it from the paint method like this:

```
public void paint(Graphics g) {
  g.drawRect(5, 10, 15, 55);
}
```

The results of this code are shown in Figure 5.5.

Figure 5.5.

A rectangle drawn using the drawRect *method.*

You can also use a drawRoundRect method, which allows you to draw rectangles with rounded corners.

Other Primitives

The other graphics primitives (circles, polygons, ovals, and arcs) are drawn in a very similar fashion to lines and rectangles. Because you won't actually be using graphics primitives much throughout this book, there's no need to go into any more detail with them. If you're curious, feel free to check out the documentation that comes with the Java Developer's Kit. I'm not trying to lessen the importance of graphics primitives, because they are very useful in many situations. It's just that the game graphics throughout this book are more dependent on images, with a little text sprinkled in.

Drawing Text

Because Java applets are entirely graphical in nature, you must use the Graphics object even when you want to draw text. Fortunately, drawing text is very easy and yields very nice results. You will typically create a font for the text and select it as the font to be used by the graphics context before actually drawing any text. As you learned earlier, the setFont method selects a font into the current graphics context. This method is defined as follows:

```
void setFont(Font font)
```

The Font object models a textual font, and includes the name, point size, and style of the font. The Font object supports three different font styles, which are implemented as the following constant members: BOLD, ITALIC, and PLAIN. These styles are really just constant numbers, and can be added together to yield a combined effect. The constructor for the Font object is defined as follows:

```
public Font(String name, int style, int size)
```

As you can see, the constructor takes as parameters the name, style, and point size of the font. You might be wondering exactly how the font names work; you simply provide the string name of the font you want to use. The names of the most common fonts supported by Java are Times Roman, Courier, and Helvetica. Therefore, to create a bold, italic, Helvetica, 22-point font, you would use the following code:

```
Font f = new Font("Helvetica", Font.BOLD + Font.ITALIC, 22);
```

TIP

Some systems support other fonts beyond the three common fonts mentioned here (Times Roman, Courier, and Helvetica). Even though you are free to use other fonts, keep in mind that these three common fonts are the only ones guaranteed to be supported across all systems. In other words, it's much safer to stick with these fonts.

After you've created a font, you will often want to create a FontMetric object to find out the details of the font's size. The FontMetric class models very specific placement information about a font, such as the ascent, descent, leading, and total height of the font. Figure 5.6 shows what each of these font metric attributes represent.

Figure 5.6.

The different font metric attributes.

> Really cool text! — baseline / } ascent } height / descent

You can use the font metrics to precisely control the location of text you are drawing. After you have the metrics under control, you just need to select the original Font object into the Graphics object using the setFont method, as in the following:

```
g.setFont(f);
```

Now you're ready to draw some text using the font you've created, sized up, and selected. The drawString method, defined in the Graphics class, is exactly what you need. drawString is defined as follows:

```
void drawString(String str, int x, int y)
```

drawString takes a String object as its first parameter, which determines the text that is drawn. The last two parameters specify the location in which the string is drawn; x specifies the left edge of the text and y specifies the baseline of the text. The baseline of the text is the bottom of the text, not including the descent. Refer to Figure 5.6 if you are having trouble visualizing this.

The DrawText sample applet demonstrates drawing a string centered in the applet window. Figure 5.7 shows the DrawText applet in action.

Figure 5.7.

The DrawText sample applet.

It's just a mere shadow of itself.

The source code for the DrawText sample applet is shown in Listing 5.1.

Listing 5.1. The DrawText sample applet.

```
// DrawText Class
// DrawText.java

// Imports
import java.applet.*;
import java.awt.*;

public class DrawText extends Applet {
  public void paint(Graphics g) {
    Font        font = new Font("Helvetica", Font.BOLD +
      Font.ITALIC, 22);
    FontMetrics fm = g.getFontMetrics(font);
    String      str = new
      String("It's just a mere shadow of itself.");
```

```
        g.setFont(font);
        g.drawString(str, (size().width - fm.stringWidth(str)) / 2,
          ((size().height - fm.getHeight()) / 2) + fm.getAscent());
    }
}
```

DrawText uses the font-related methods you just learned to draw a string centered in the applet window. You might be wondering about the calls to the size method when the location to draw the string is being calculated. The size method is a member of Component and returns a Dimension object specifying the width and height of the applet window.

That sums up the basics of drawing text using the Graphics object. Now it's time to move on to the most important aspect of Java graphics in regard to games: images.

Drawing Images

NEW TERM *Images* are rectangular graphical objects composed of colored pixels.

Each pixel in an image describes the color at that particular location of the image. Pixels can have unique colors that are usually described using the RGB color system. Java provides support for working with 32-bit images, which means that each pixel in an image is described using 32 bits. The red, green, and blue components of a pixel's color are stored in these 32 bits, along with an alpha component.

NEW TERM The *alpha component* of a pixel refers to the transparency or opaqueness of the pixel.

Before getting into the details of how to draw an image, you first need to learn how to load images. The getImage method, defined in the Applet class, is used to load an image from a URL. getImage comes in two versions, which are defined as follows:

```
Image getImage(URL url)
Image getImage(URL url, String name)
```

These two versions essentially perform the same function; the only difference is that the first version expects a fully qualified URL, including the name of the image, and the second version enables you to specify a separate URL and image name.

You probably noticed that both versions of getImage return an object of type Image. The Image class represents a graphical image, such as a GIF or JPEG file image, and provides a few methods for finding out the width and height of the image. Image also includes a method for retrieving a graphics context for the image, which enables you to draw directly onto an image.

The Graphics class provides a handful of methods for drawing images, which follow:

```
boolean drawImage(Image img, int x, int y, ImageObserver observer)
boolean drawImage(Image img, int x, int y, int width, int height,
  ImageObserver observer)
```

5

```
boolean drawImage(Image img, int x, int y, Color bgcolor, ImageObserver
  observer)
boolean drawImage(Image img, int x, int y, int width, int height, Color
  bgcolor, ImageObserver observer)
```

All these methods are variants on the same theme: they all draw an image at a certain location as defined by the parameters x and y. The last parameter in each method is an object of type ImageObserver, which is used internally by drawImage to get information about the image.

The first version of drawImage draws the image at the specified x and y location—x and y represent the upper-left corner of the image. The second version draws the image inside the rectangle formed by x, y, width, and height. If this rectangle is different than the image rectangle, the image will be scaled to fit. The third version of drawImage draws the image with transparent areas filled in with the background color specified in the bgcolor parameter. The last version of drawImage combines the capabilities in the first three, enabling you to draw an image within a given rectangle and with a background color.

> Don't worry if you haven't heard of transparency before; you learn all about it in Day 6, "Sprite Animation." For now, just think of it as areas in an image that aren't drawn, resulting in the background showing through.
>
> **Note**

The process of drawing an image involves calling the getImage method to load the image, followed by a call to drawImage, which actually draws the image on a graphics context. The DrawImage sample applet shows how easy it is to draw an image (see Figure 5.8).

Figure 5.8.

The DrawImage sample applet.

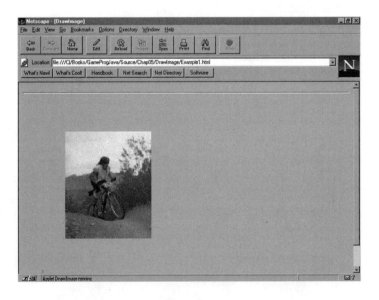

The source code for the DrawImage sample applet is shown in Listing 5.2.

Listing 5.2. The DrawImage sample applet.

```
// DrawImage Class
// DrawImage.java

// Imports
import java.applet.*;
import java.awt.*;

public class DrawImage extends Applet {
  public void paint(Graphics g) {
    Image img = getImage(getCodeBase(), "Res/Ride.gif");

    g.drawImage(img, (size().width - img.getWidth(this)) / 2,
      (size().height - img.getHeight(this)) / 2, this);
  }
}
```

The DrawImage sample applet loads an image in the paint method using getImage. The getCodeBase method is used to specify the applet directory where applet resources are usually located, while the image name itself is simply given as a string. The image is actually stored in the *Res* subdirectory beneath the applet directory, as evident by the image name ("Res/Ride.gif") passed into getImage. The image is then drawn centered in the applet window using the drawImage method. It's as simple as that!

Tracking Images

Even though images are a very neat way of displaying high-quality graphics within a Java applet, they aren't without their drawbacks. The biggest problem with using images is the fact that they must be transmitted over the Web as needed, which brings up the issue of transmitting multimedia content over a limited bandwidth. This means that the speed at which images are transferred over a Web connection will often cause a noticeable delay in a Java applet reliant on them, such as games.

There is a standard technique for dealing with transmission delay as it affects static images. You've no doubt seen this technique at work in your Web browser when you've viewed images in Web pages. The technique is known as *interlacing*, and it makes images appear blurry until they have been completely transferred. To use interlacing, images must be stored in an interlaced format (usually GIF version 89a), which means that the image data is arranged in a way so that the image can be displayed before it is completely transmitted. Interlacing is a good approach to dealing with transmission delays for static images because it enables you to see the image as it is being transferred. Without interlacing, you have to wait until the entire image has been transferred before seeing it at all.

Before you get too excited about interlacing, keep in mind that it is useful only for static images. You're probably wondering why this is the case. It has to do with the fact that animations (dynamic images) rely on rapidly displaying a sequence of images over time, all of which must be readily available to successfully create the effect of movement.

> Don't worry if this animation stuff is new to you; you learn all the juicy details on Day 6.

NOTE

An animation sequence wouldn't look right using interlacing, because some of the images would be transferred before others. A good solution would be to just wait until all the images have been transferred before displaying the animation. That's fine, but how do you know when the images have all been transferred? Enter the Java media tracker.

The Java media tracker is an object that tracks when media objects, such as images, have been successfully transferred. Using the media tracker, you can keep track of any number of media objects and query to see when they have finished being transmitted. For example, suppose you have an animation with four images. Using the media tracker, you would register each of these images and then wait until they have all been transferred before displaying the animation. The media tracker keeps up with the load status of each image. When the media tracker reports that all the images have been successfully loaded, you are guaranteed that your animation has all the necessary images to display correctly.

The `MediaTracker` Class

The Java `MediaTracker` class is part of the AWT package and contains a variety of members and methods for tracking media objects. Unfortunately, the `MediaTracker` class that ships with release 1.0 of the Java development kit supports only image tracking. Future versions of Java are expected to add support for other types of media objects such as sound and music.

The `MediaTracker` class provides member flags for representing various states associated with tracked media objects. These flags are returned by many of the member functions of `MediaTracker` and are as follows:

☐ `LOADING`: Indicates that a media object is currently in the process of being loaded.

☐ `ABORTED`: Indicates that the loading of a media object has been aborted.

☐ `ERRORED`: Indicates that some type of error occurred while loading a media object.

☐ `COMPLETE`: Indicates that a media object has been successfully loaded.

The `MediaTracker` class provides a variety of methods for helping to track media objects:

5

```
MediaTracker(Component comp)

void addImage(Image image, int id)

synchronized void addImage(Image image, int id, int w, int h)

boolean checkID(int id)

synchronized boolean checkID(int id, boolean load)

boolean checkAll()

synchronized boolean checkAll(boolean load)

void waitForID(int id)

synchronized boolean waitForID(int id, long ms)

void waitForAll()

synchronized boolean waitForAll(long ms)

int statusID(int id, boolean load)

int statusAll(boolean load)

synchronized boolean isErrorID(int id)

synchronized boolean isErrorAny()

synchronized Object[] getErrorsID(int id)

synchronized Object[] getErrorsAny()
```

The constructor for MediaTracker takes a single parameter of type Component. This parameter specifies the Component object on which tracked images will eventually be drawn. This parameter reflects the current limitation of being able to track only images with the MediaTracker class and not sounds or other types of media.

The addImage methods add an image to the list of images currently being tracked. Both methods take as their first parameter an Image object and as their second parameter an identifier that uniquely identifies the image. If you want to track a group of images together, you can use the same identifier for each image. The second addImage method has additional parameters for specifying the width and height of a tracked image. This version of addImage is used for tracking images that you are going to scale; you pass the width and height that you want to use for the scaled the image.

After you have added images to the MediaTracker object, you are ready to check their status. You use the checkID methods to check whether images matching the passed identifier have finished loading. Both versions of checkID return false if the images have not finished loading, and true otherwise. Both methods return true even if the loading has been aborted or if an error has occurred. You must call the appropriate error checking methods to see whether an error has occurred. (You learn the error checking methods a little later in this section.) The only difference between the two checkID methods is how each loads an image. The first version of checkID does not load an image if that image has not already begun loading. The second version enables you to specify that the image should be loaded even if it hasn't already begun loading, which is carried out by passing true in the load parameter.

The checkAll methods are very similar to the checkID methods, except that they apply to all images, not just those matching a certain identifier. Similar to the checkID methods, the checkAll methods come in two versions. The first version checks to see whether the images have finished loading, but doesn't load any images that haven't already begun loading. The second version also checks the status of loading images but enables you to indicate that images are to be loaded if they haven't started already.

You use the waitForID methods to begin loading images with a certain identifier. This identifier should match the identifier used when the images were added to the media tracker with the addImage method. Both versions of waitForID are synchronous, meaning that they do not return until all the specified images have finished loading or an error occurs. The second version of waitForID enables you to specify a timeout period, in which case the load will end and waitForID will return true. You specify the timeout period in milliseconds by using the ms parameter.

The waitForAll methods are very similar to the waitForID methods, except they operate on all images. Like the waitForID methods, there are versions of waitForAll both with and without timeout support.

You use the statusID method to determine the status of images matching the identifier passed in the id parameter. statusID returns the bitwise OR of the status flags related to the images. The possible flags are LOADING, ABORTED, ERRORED, and COMPLETE. To check for a particular status flag, you mask the flag out of the return value of statusID, like this:

```
if (tracker.statusID(0, true) & MediaTracker.ERRORED) {
  // there was an error!
}
```

The second parameter to statusID, load, should be familiar to you by now because of its use in the other media tracker methods. It specifies whether you want the images to begin loading if they haven't begun already. This functionality is very similar to that provided by the second version of the checkID and waitForID methods.

The statusAll method is very similar to the statusId method; the only difference is that statusAll returns the status of all the images being tracked rather than those matching a specific identifier.

Finally, you arrive at the error-checking methods mentioned earlier in this section. The isErrorID and isErrorAny methods check the error status of images being tracked. The only difference between the two is that isErrorID checks on images with a certain identifier, whereas isErrorAny checks on all images. Both of these methods basically check the status of each image for the ERRORED flag. Note that both methods will return true if any of the images have errors; it's up to you to determine which specific images had errors.

If you use isErrorID or isErrorAny and find out that there are load errors, you need to find out which images have errors. You do this by using the getErrorsID and getErrorsAny methods. These two methods both return an array of Objects containing the media objects that have load errors. In the current implementation of the MediaTracker class, this array is always filled with Image objects. If there are no errors, these methods return null. Similar to the isErrorID and isErrorAny methods, getErrorsID and getErrorsAny differ only by the images that they check; getErrorsID returns errored images matching the passed identifier, and getErrorsAny returns all errored images.

That wraps up the description of the MediaTracker class. Now that you understand what the class is all about, you're probably ready to see it in action. Read on!

Using the Media Tracker

With the media tracker, you know exactly when certain images have been transferred and are ready to use. This enables you to display alternative output based on whether or not images have finished transferring. The Tarantulas sample applet, which is located on the accompanying CD-ROM, demonstrates how to use the media tracker to track the loading of multiple images and display them only when they have all finished transferring. Figure 5.9 shows the Tarantulas applet while the images are still being loaded.

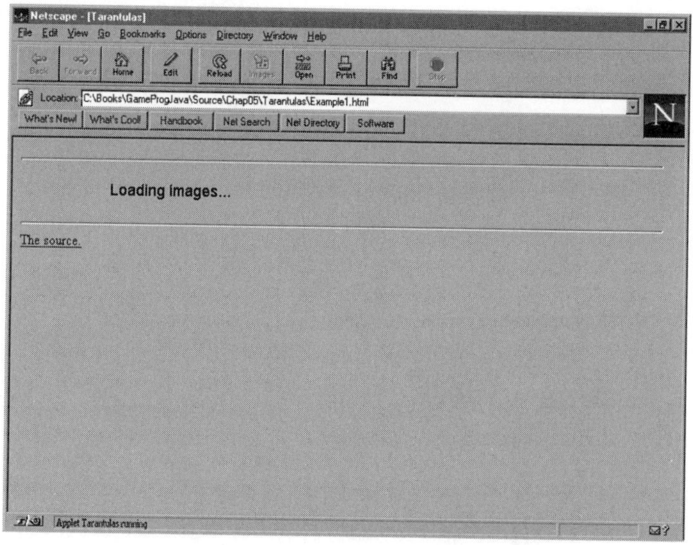

Figure 5.9.

The Tarantulas applet with images partially loaded.

5

As you can see, none of the images are displayed until they have all been successfully transferred. While they are loading, a text message is displayed informing the user that the images are still in the process of loading. This is a pretty simple enhancement to the applet, but one that makes the applet look much more professional. By displaying a simple message while media objects are loading, you solve the problem of drawing partially transferred images, and more important, the problem of displaying animations with missing images. The source code for Tarantulas is shown in Listing 5.3.

Listing 5.3. The Tarantulas sample applet.

```java
import java.applet.*;
import java.awt.*;

public class Tarantulas extends Applet implements Runnable {
  Image         img[] = new Image[8];
  Thread        thread;
  MediaTracker  tracker;

  public void init() {
    tracker = new MediaTracker(this);
    for (int i = 0; i < 8; i++) {
      img[i] = getImage(getDocumentBase(), "Res/Tarant" + i + ".gif");
      tracker.addImage(img[i], 0);
    }
  }

  public void start() {
    thread = new Thread(this);
    thread.start();
  }

  public void stop() {
    thread.stop();
    thread = null;
  }

  public void run() {
    try {
      tracker.waitForID(0);
    }
    catch (InterruptedException e) {
      return;
    }
    repaint();
  }

  public void paint(Graphics g) {
    if ((tracker.statusID(0, true) & MediaTracker.ERRORED) != 0) {
      g.setColor(Color.red);
      g.fillRect(0, 0, size().width, size().height);
      return;
    }
    if ((tracker.statusID(0, true) & MediaTracker.COMPLETE) != 0) {
```

```
      for (int i = 0; i < 8; i++)
        g.drawImage(img[i], i * img[i].getWidth(this), 0, this);
    }
    else {
      Font         font = new Font("Helvetica", Font.PLAIN, 18);
      FontMetrics fm = g.getFontMetrics(font);
      String       str = new String("Loading images...");
      g.setFont(font);
      g.drawString(str, (size().width - fm.stringWidth(str)) / 2,
        ((size().height - fm.getHeight()) / 2) + fm.getAscent());
    }
  }
}
```

Begin examining the Tarantulas sample applet by looking at the member variables. The thread member is a Thread object that is used by the media tracker to wait for the images to load. The tracker member is the MediaTracker object used to track the images.

In the init method, the MediaTracker object is created by passing this as the only parameter to its constructor. Because the init method is a member of the applet class, Tarantulas, this refers to the applet object. If you recall from the discussion of the MediaTracker class earlier in this chapter, the sole constructor parameter is of type Component and represents the component on which the tracked images will be drawn. All Applet objects are derived from Component, so passing the Applet object (this) correctly initializes the media tracker.

Also notice that the images are added to the media tracker in the init method. You do this by calling the addImage method of MediaTracker and passing the Image object and an identifier. Notice that 0 is passed as the identifier for all the images. This means that you are tracking them as a group using 0 to uniquely identify them.

The start and stop methods are used to manage the creation and destruction of the Thread member object. These are pretty standard implementations for adding basic multithreading support to an applet. You'll see these methods several times throughout the book because most of the sample applets use threads extensively.

The tracking actually starts taking place with the run method. The waitForID method of MediaTracker is called within a try-catch clause. It must be placed in this exception-handling clause because an InterruptedException will be thrown if another thread interrupts this thread. Recall that waitForID is synchronous, meaning that it won't return until all the images with the specified identifier have been loaded. This means that the call to repaint will not occur until the images have all been loaded.

To understand why this works, you need to look at the last method in Tarantulas, paint. The paint method begins by checking to see whether an error has occurred in loading the images. It does this by calling statusID and checking the result against the ERRORED flag. If an error has occurred, paint fills the applet window with the color red to indicate an error. Figure 5.10 shows what Tarantulas looks like when an error occurs.

Figure 5.10.

The Tarantulas applet with an error loading the images.

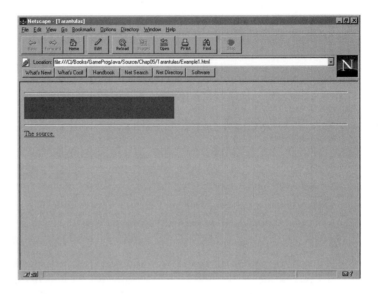

The next check performed by paint is to see whether the images have finished loading. It does this by calling statusID and comparing the result with the COMPLETE flag. If the images have finished loading, the image array is iterated through and each image is drawn on the applet window. If the images have not finished loading, the text message Loading images... is displayed. Figure 5.11 shows the Tarantulas applet with all the images successfully loaded.

Figure 5.11.

The Tarantulas applet with all the images loaded.

That's all there is to tracking images. Too bad all of Java game programming isn't this easy—actually, it almost is!

Summary

Today you were bombarded with a lot of information about the graphics support in Java. Most of it was centered around the Graphics object, which is fortunately pretty straightforward to use. You began by learning about color and what it means in the context of Java. You then moved on to drawing graphics primitives, text, and images. The lesson concluded with a detailed look at how images are tracked and managed using the Java media tracker.

Today marked your first major foray into real Java coding for games. Even though no game-specific code was developed, you learned a great deal about the Java graphics system, which is used extensively in games. If you're still hungry for more, don't worry, because tomorrow's lesson picks up where you left off and dives into animation. If you think you learned a lot today, you better brace yourself for tomorrow!

Q&A

Q **If the Color class already contains predefined colors, why does it still have a constructor that accepts the three primary colors?**

A Because there might be times when you want to use a color that isn't defined in the Color class, in which case you would create a Color object using the desired levels of red, green, and blue.

Q **Why are graphics primitives not as important as images in regard to game graphics?**

A Because most games take advantage of the high level of realism afforded by images, and therefore rely heavily on images rather than primitive graphics types. However, there are exceptions to this rule; for example, vector games are made up entirely of lines, and some 3-D games are made up entirely of polygons.

Q **When exactly is the paint method called, and why?**

A The paint method is called any time a portion of a component, such as the applet window, needs to be updated. For example, if a dialog pops up on top of the applet and then disappears, the applet needs to be updated, so paint is called. You can force a call to paint by calling the repaint method; you did this very thing in the Tarantulas applet to update the status of the loading images.

5

Workshop

The Workshop section provides questions and exercises to help you get a better feel for the material you learned today. Try to answer the questions and at least study the exercises before moving on to tomorrow's lesson. You'll find the answers to the questions in Appendix A, "Quiz Answers."

Quiz

1. What are the four components of a 32-bit Java color?

2. What is a graphics context?

3. What class provides information about fonts and enables you to fine-tune the placement of text?

4. What is the purpose of the media tracker?

Exercises

1. Study the Java Developer's Kit documentation and try out some of the other graphics primitives not demonstrated in today's lesson.

2. Modify the DrawText applet to draw a different string and make sure the centering code works correctly.

3. Modify the Tarantulas applet to run without the media tracker and notice the change in behavior.

Day 6

Sprite Animation

The heart of graphics in almost all games is animation. Without animation, there would be no movement, and without movement, we'd all be stuck playing board games and card games. Today's lesson presents the fundamental concepts surrounding animation in games and, more specifically, sprite animation. As you'll soon learn, practically every game with animation employs some type of animation engine, typically involving sprites.

After learning the basics of animation and how it applies to games, you dig into building a set of sprite animation classes that are powerful and extensive enough to handle all of your Java game animation needs. As a matter of fact, you'll reuse the sprite classes in every game throughout the rest of the book. These sprite classes handle all the details of managing multiple animated sprite objects with support for transparency, Z-order, collision detection, and custom actions. You don't understand some of those last features? Well, don't worry; you will soon enough. Read on!

What Is Animation?

Before getting into animation as it relates to Java and games, it's important to understand the basics of what animation is and how it works. Let's begin by asking this fundamental question: What is animation? Put simply, animation is the illusion of movement. Am I saying that every animation you've ever seen is really just an illusion? That's exactly right! And probably the most surprising animated illusion is one that captured attentions long before computers—the television. When you watch television, you see lots of things moving around. But what you perceive as movement is really just a trick being played on your eyes.

NEW TERM *Animation* is the illusion of movement.

In the case of television, the illusion of movement is created by displaying a rapid succession of images with slight changes in content. The human eye perceives these changes as movement because of its low visual acuity, which means that your eyes are fairly easy to trick into believing the illusion of animation. More specifically, the human eye can be tricked into perceiving animated movement with as low as 12 frames of movement per second. It should come as no surprise that this animation speed is the minimum target speed for most computer games. Animation speed is measured in frames per second (fps).

NEW TERM *Frames per second* (fps) is the number of animation frames, or image changes, presented every second.

Although 12 fps is technically enough to fool your eyes into seeing animation, animations at speeds this low often end up looking somewhat jerky. Therefore, most professional animations use a higher frame rate. Television, for example, uses 30 fps. When you go to the movies, you see motion pictures at about 24 fps. It's pretty apparent that these frame rates are more than enough to captivate your attention and successfully create the illusion of movement.

Unlike television and motion pictures, computer games are much more limited when it comes to frame rate. Higher frame rates in games correspond to much higher processor overhead, so game developers are left to balance the frame rate against the system speed and resources. That is why some games provide different resolution and graphics quality options. By using a lower resolution and more simple graphics, a game can increase its frame rate and generate smoother animations. Of course, the trade-off is a lower resolution and more simple graphics.

When programming animation in Java, you typically have the ability to manipulate the frame rate a reasonable amount. The most obvious limitation on frame rate is the speed at which the computer can generate and display the animation frames. Actually, the same limitation must be dealt with by game developers, regardless of the programming language or platform. However, it is a little more crucial in Java because Java applets are currently much slower than native applications. Hopefully, the advent of just-in-time Java compilers will speed up Java applets and therefore give Java games a boost.

When determining the frame rate for a Java game, you usually have some give and take in establishing a low enough frame rate to yield a smooth animation, while not bogging down the processor and slowing the system down. But don't worry too much about this right now. For now, just keep in mind that when programming animation for Java games, you are acting as a magician creating the illusion of movement.

Types of Animation

Although the focus of today's lesson is ultimately on sprite animation, it is important to understand the primary types of animation used in Java programming. Actually, a lot of different types of animation exist, all of which are useful in different instances. However, for the purposes of implementing animation in Java, I've broken animation down into two basic types: frame-based animation and cast-based animation.

Frame-Based Animation

The most simple animation technique is frame-based animation, which finds a lot of usage in nongaming animations. Frame-based animation involves simulating movement by displaying a sequence of pregenerated, static frame images. A movie is a perfect example of frame-based animation: Each frame of the film is a frame of animation, and when the frames are shown in rapid succession, they create the illusion of movement.

NEW TERM *Frame-based animation* simulates movement by displaying a sequence of pregenerated, static frame images.

Frame-based animation has no concept of a graphical object distinguishable from the background; everything appearing in a frame is part of that frame as a whole. The result is that each frame image contains all the information necessary for that frame in a static form. This is an important point because it distinguishes frame-based animation from cast-based animation, which you learn about next.

Cast-Based Animation

A more powerful animation technique employed by many games is cast-based animation, which is also known as *sprite animation*. Cast-based animation involves graphical objects that move independently of a background. At this point, you might be a little confused by the usage of the term *graphical object* when referring to parts of an animation. In this case, a graphical object is something that logically can be thought of as a separate entity from the background of an animation image. For example, in the animation of a space shoot-em-up game, the aliens are separate graphical objects that are logically independent of the starfield background.

NEW TERM *Cast-based animation* simulates movement using graphical objects that move independently of a background.

Each graphical object in a cast-based animation is referred to as a *sprite*, and can have a position that varies over time. In other words, sprites have a velocity associated with them that determines how their position changes over time. Almost every video game uses sprites to some degree. For example, every object in the classic Asteroids game is a sprite that moves independently of the background.

NEW TERM A *sprite* is a graphical object that can move independently of a background or other objects.

You might be wondering where the term *cast-based animation* comes from. It comes from the fact that sprites can be thought of as cast members moving around on a stage. This analogy of relating computer animation to theatrical performance is very useful. By thinking of sprites as cast members and the background as a stage, you can take the next logical step and think of an animation as a theatrical performance. In fact, this isn't far from the mark, because the goal of theatrical performances is to entertain the audience by telling a story through the interaction of the cast members. Likewise, cast-based animations use the interaction of sprites to entertain the user, while often telling a story.

Even though the fundamental principle behind sprite animation is the positional movement of a graphical object, there is no reason you can't incorporate frame-based animation into a sprite. Incorporating frame-based animation into a sprite enables you to change the image of the sprite as well as alter its position. This hybrid type of animation is actually what you will implement later in today's lesson in the Java sprite classes.

I mentioned in the frame-based animation discussion that television is a good example of frame-based animation. But can you think of something on television that is created in a manner similar to cast-based animation (other than animated movies and cartoons)? Have you ever wondered how weatherpeople magically appear in front of a computer-generated map showing the weather? The news station uses a technique known as *blue-screening*, which enables them to overlay the weatherperson on top of the weather map in real time. It works like this: The person stands in front of a blue backdrop, which serves as a transparent background. The image of the weatherperson is overlaid onto the weather map; the trick is that the blue background is filtered out when the image is overlaid so that it is effectively transparent. In this way, the weatherperson is acting exactly like a sprite!

Transparency

The weatherperson example brings up a very important point regarding sprites: *transparency*. Because bitmapped images are rectangular by nature, a problem arises when sprite images aren't rectangular in shape. In sprites that aren't rectangular in shape, which is the majority of sprites, the pixels surrounding the sprite image are unused. In a graphics system without transparency, these unused pixels are drawn just like any others. The end result is sprites that have visible rectangular borders around them, which completely destroys the effectiveness of having sprites overlaid on a background image.

What's the solution? Well, one solution is to make all of your sprites rectangular. Because this solution isn't very practical, a more realistic solution is transparency, which allows you to define a certain color in an image as unused, or transparent. When pixels of this color are encountered by drawing routines, they are simply skipped, leaving the original background intact. Transparent colors in images act exactly like the weatherperson's blue screen in the example earlier.

NEW TERM *Transparency colors* are colors in an image that are unused, meaning that they aren't drawn when the rest of the colors in the image are drawn.

You're probably thinking that implementing transparency involves a lot of low-level bit twiddling and image pixel manipulation. In some programming environments, you would be correct in this assumption, but not in Java. Fortunately, transparency is already supported in Java by way of the GIF 89a image format. In the GIF 89a image format, you simply specify a color of the GIF image that serves as the transparent color. When the image is drawn, pixels matching the transparent color are skipped and left undrawn, leaving the background pixels unchanged.

Z-Order

In many instances, you will want some sprites to appear on top of others. For example, in a war game you might have planes flying over a battlefield dropping bombs on everything in sight. If a plane sprite happens to fly over a tank sprite, you obviously want the plane to appear above the tank and, therefore, hide the tank as it passes over. You handle this problem by assigning each sprite a screen depth, which is also referred to as *Z-order*.

NEW TERM *Z-order* is the relative depth of sprites on the screen.

6

The depth of sprites is called *Z-order* because it works sort of like another dimension—like a Z axis. You can think of sprites moving around on the screen in the XY axis. Similarly, the Z axis can be thought of as another axis projected into the screen that determines how the sprites overlap each other. To put it another way, Z-order determines a sprite's depth within the screen. By making use of a Z axis, you might think that Z-ordered sprites are 3D. The truth is that Z-ordered sprites can't be considered 3D because the Z axis is a hypothetical axis that is only used to determine how sprite objects hide each other.

Just to make sure that you get a clear picture of how Z-order works, let's go back for a moment to the good old days of traditional animation. Traditional animators, such as those at Disney, used celluloid sheets to draw animated objects. They drew on celluloid sheets because the sheets could be overlaid on a background image and moved independently. This was known as *cel animation* and should sound vaguely familiar. (Cel animation is an early version of sprite animation.) Each cel sheet corresponds to a unique Z-order value, determined by where in the pile of sheets the sheet is located. If a sprite near the top of the pile happens to be in the same location on the cel sheet as any lower sprites, it conceals them. The location of each sprite in the stack of cel sheets is its Z-order, which determines its visibility precedence. The same thing applies to sprites in cast-based animations, except that the Z-order is determined by the order in which the sprites are drawn, rather than the cel sheet location. This concept of a pile of cel sheets representing all the sprites in a sprite system will be useful later today when you develop the sprite classes.

Collision Detection

No discussion of animation as it applies to games would be complete without covering collision detection. *Collision detection* is simply the method of determining whether sprites have collided with each other. Although collision detection doesn't directly play a role in creating the illusion of movement, it is tightly linked to sprite animation and extremely crucial in games.

NEW TERM   *Collision detection* is the process of determining whether sprites have collided with each other.

Collision detection is used to determine when sprites physically interact with each other. In an Asteroids game, for example, if the ship sprite collides with an asteroid sprite, the ship is destroyed. Collision detection is the mechanism employed to find out whether the ship collided with the asteroid. This might not sound like a big deal; just compare their positions and see whether they overlap, right? Correct, but consider how many comparisons must take place when lots of sprites are moving around; each sprite must be compared to every other sprite in the system. It's not hard to see how the overhead of effective collision detection can become difficult to manage.

Not surprisingly, there are many approaches to handling collision detection. The most simple approach is to compare the bounding rectangles of each sprite with the bounding rectangles of all the other sprites. This method is very efficient, but if you have objects that are not rectangular, a certain degree of error occurs when the objects brush by each other. This is because the corners might overlap and indicate a collision when really only the transparent areas are overlapping. The more irregular the shape of the sprites, the more error typically occurs. Figure 6.1 shows how simple rectangle collision works.

Figure 6.1.

*Collision detection using
simple rectangle collision.*

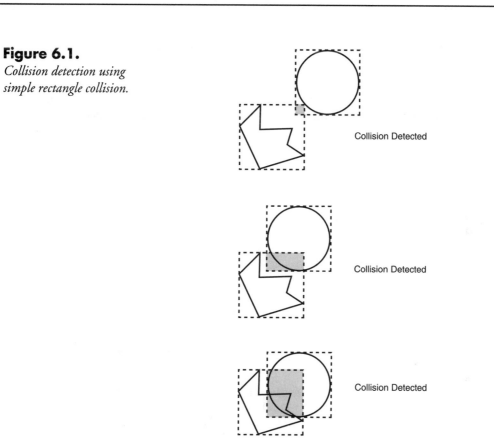

Collision Detected

Collision Detected

Collision Detected

In Figure 6.1, the areas determining the collision detection are shaded. You can see how simple rectangle collision detection isn't very accurate, unless you're dealing with sprites that are rectangular in shape. An improvement on this technique is to shrink the collision rectangles a little, which reduces the corner error. This method improves things a little, but it has the potential of causing error in the reverse direction by allowing sprites to overlap in some cases without signaling a collision. Figure 6.2 shows how shrinking the collision rectangles can improve the error on simple rectangle collision detection. Shrunken rectangle collision is just as efficient as simple rectangle collision because all you are doing is comparing rectangles for intersection.

The most accurate collision detection technique is to detect collision based on the sprite image data, which involves actually checking to see whether transparent parts of the sprite or the sprite images themselves are overlapping. In this case, you get a collision only if the actual sprite images are overlapping. This is the ideal technique for detecting collisions because it is exact and allows objects of any shape to move by each other without error. Figure 6.3 shows collision detection using the sprite image data.

6

Figure 6.2.

Collision detection using shrunken rectangle collision.

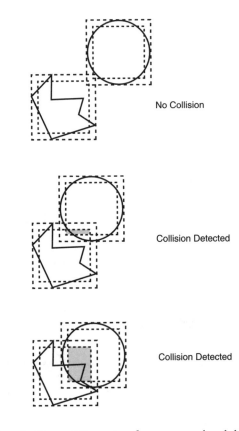

Unfortunately, the technique shown in Figure 6.3 requires far more overhead than rectangle collision detection and is often a major bottleneck in performance. Furthermore, implementing image data for collision detection can get very messy. Considering these facts, it's safe to say that you won't be worrying about image data collision detection in this book. It might be an avenue worth considering in the future if the just-in-time Java compilers can squeeze enough additional performance out of Java, and if you are willing to dig into the programming complexities involved in pulling it off.

Figure 6.3.

Collision detection using sprite image data.

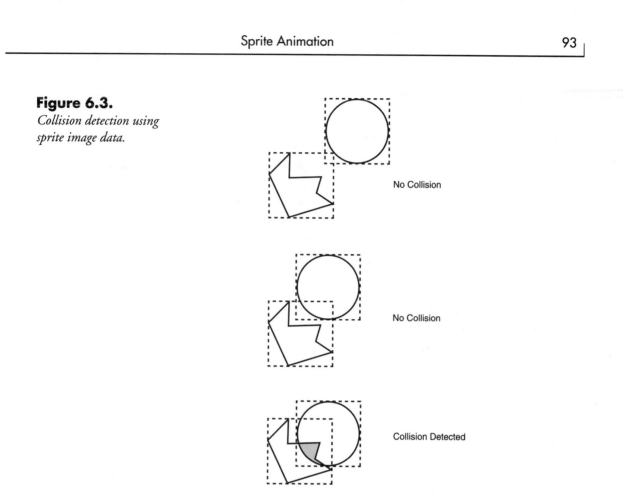

No Collision

No Collision

Collision Detected

Implementing Sprite Animation

As you learned earlier in today's lesson, sprite animation involves the movement of individual graphic objects called sprites. Unlike simple frame animation, sprite animation involves considerably more overhead. More specifically, it is necessary to develop not only a sprite class, but also a sprite management class for keeping up with all the sprites in the system. This is necessary because sprites need to be able to interact with each other through a common mechanism. Furthermore, it is useful to extract the background behind the sprites into a class of its own.

In this section, you learn how to implement sprite animation in Java by creating a suite of sprite classes. The primary sprite classes are Sprite and SpriteVector. However, there are also a few support classes that you will learn about as you get into the details of these two primary classes. The Sprite class models a single sprite and contains all the information and methods necessary to get a single sprite up and running. However, the real power of sprite animation is harnessed by combining the Sprite class with the SpriteVector class, which is a container class that manages multiple sprites and their interaction with each other.

6

The Sprite Class

Although sprites can be implemented simply as moveable graphical objects, you saw earlier that the sprite class developed here will also contain support for frame animation. A frame-animated sprite is basically a sprite with multiple frame images that can be displayed in succession. The Sprite class you are about to see supports frame animation in the form of an array of frame images and some methods for setting the current frame image. Using this approach, you end up with a Sprite class that supports both fundamental types of animation and is much more suitable for Java games.

Before jumping into the details of how the Sprite class is implemented, take a moment to think about the different pieces of information that a sprite must keep up with. When you understand the components of a sprite at a conceptual level, it will be much easier to understand the Java code. So, exactly what information should a Sprite class maintain? The following list contains the key information that the Sprite class needs to include:

- ☐ Array of frame images
- ☐ Current frame
- ☐ XY position
- ☐ Velocity
- ☐ Z-order
- ☐ Boundary

The first component, an array of frame images, is necessary to carry out the frame animations. Even though this sounds like you are forcing a sprite to have multiple animation frames, a sprite can also use a single image. In this way, the frame animation aspects of the sprite are optional. The current frame keeps up with the current frame of animation. In a typical frame-animated sprite, the current frame is incremented to the next frame when the sprite is updated.

The XY position stores the position of the sprite. You can move the sprite simply by altering this position. Alternatively, you can set the velocity and let the sprite alter its position internally.

The Z-order represents the depth of the sprite in relation to other sprites. Ultimately, the Z-order of a sprite determines its drawing order (more on that a little later).

Finally, the boundary of a sprite refers to the bounded region in which the sprite can move. All sprites are bound by some region—usually the size of the applet window. The sprite boundary is important because it determines the limits of a sprite's movement.

Now that you understand the core information required by the Sprite class, it's time to get into the specific Java implementation. Keep in mind that the Sprite class contains all the features necessary to implement sprites in the sample games throughout the rest of the book. Let's begin with the Sprite class's member variables, which follow:

```
public static final int SA_KILL = 0,
                        SA_RESTOREPOS = 1,
                        SA_ADDSPRITE = 2;
public static final int BA_STOP = 0,
                        BA_WRAP = 1,
                        BA_BOUNCE = 2,
                        BA_DIE = 3;
protected Component     component;
protected Image[]       image;
protected int           frame,
                        frameInc,
                        frameDelay,
                        frameTrigger;
protected Rectangle     position,
                        collision;
protected int           zOrder;
protected Point         velocity;
protected Rectangle     bounds;
protected int           boundsAction;
protected boolean       hidden = false;
```

The member variables include the important sprite information mentioned earlier, along with some other useful information. Most notably, you are probably curious about the static final members at the beginning of the listing. These members are constant identifiers that define actions for the sprite. Two different types of actions are supported by Sprite: sprite actions and bounds actions. *Sprite actions* are general actions that a sprite can perform, such as killing itself or adding another sprite. *Bounds actions* are actions that a sprite takes in response to reaching a boundary, such as wrapping to the other side or bouncing. Unlike sprite actions, bounds actions are mutually exclusive, meaning that only one can be set at a time.

After the actions, the Component member variable is the next member variable that you might be curious about. It is necessary because an ImageObserver object is required to retrieve information about an image. But what does Component have to do with ImageObserver? The Component class implements the ImageObserver interface, and the Applet class is derived from Component. So, a Sprite object gets its image information from the Java applet itself, which is used to initialize the Component member variable.

NOTE

> ImageObserver is an interface defined in the java.awt.image package that provides a means for receiving information about an image.

The frameInc member variable is used to provide a means to change the way that the animation frames are updated. For example, in some cases you might want the frames to be displayed in the reverse order. You can easily do this by setting frameInc to -1 (its typical value is 1). The frameDelay and frameTrigger member variables are used to provide a means of varying the speed of the frame animation. You'll see how the speed of animation is controlled when you learn about the incFrame method later today.

Another member variable that you might be curious about is collision, which is a Rectangle object. This member variable is used to support rectangle collision detection, in which a rectangle is used in collision detection tests. You'll see how collision is used later in today's lesson when you learn about the setCollision and testCollision methods.

The last member variable, hidden, is a boolean flag that determines whether or not the sprite is hidden. When you set this variable to true, the sprite is hidden from view. Its default setting is true, meaning that the sprite is visible.

The Sprite class has two constructors. The first constructor creates a Sprite without frame animations, meaning that it uses a single image to represent the sprite. The code for this constructor is as follows:

```
public Sprite(Component comp, Image img, Point pos, Point vel, int z,
    int ba) {
    component = comp;
    image = new Image[1];
    image[0] = img;
    setPosition(new Rectangle(pos.x, pos.y, img.getWidth(comp),
        img.getHeight(comp)));
    setVelocity(vel);
    frame = 0;
    frameInc = 0;
    frameDelay = frameTrigger = 0;
    zOrder = z;
    bounds = new Rectangle(0, 0, comp.size().width, comp.size().height);
    boundsAction = ba;
}
```

This constructor takes an image, position, velocity, Z-order, and boundary action as parameters. The second constructor takes an array of images and some additional information about the frame animations. The code for the second constructor is as follows:

```
public Sprite(Component comp, Image[] img, int f, int fi, int fd,
    Point pos, Point vel, int z, int ba) {
    component = comp;
    image = img;
    setPosition(new Rectangle(pos.x, pos.y, img[f].getWidth(comp),
        img[f].getHeight(comp)));
    setVelocity(vel);
    frame = f;
    frameInc = fi;
    frameDelay = frameTrigger = fd;
    zOrder = z;
    bounds = new Rectangle(0, 0, comp.size().width, comp.size().height);
    boundsAction = ba;
}
```

The additional information required of this constructor includes the current frame, frame increment, and frame delay.

The Sprite class contains a number of access methods, which are simply interfaces to get and set certain member variables. These methods consist of one or two lines of code and are pretty self-explanatory. Check out the code for the getVelocity and setVelocity access methods to see what I mean about the access methods being self-explanatory:

```
public Point getVelocity() {
  return velocity;
}

public void setVelocity(Point vel)
{
  velocity = vel;
}
```

More access methods exist for getting and setting other member variables in Sprite, but they are just as straightforward as getVelocity and setVelocity. Rather than spending time on those, let's move on to some more interesting methods!

The incFrame method is the first Sprite method with any real substance:

```
protected void incFrame() {
  if ((frameDelay > 0) && (--frameTrigger <= 0)) {
    // Reset the frame trigger
    frameTrigger = frameDelay;

    // Increment the frame
    frame += frameInc;
    if (frame >= image.length)
      frame = 0;
    else if (frame < 0)
      frame = image.length - 1;
  }
}
```

incFrame is used to increment the current animation frame. It first checks the frameDelay and frameTrigger member variables to see whether the frame should actually be incremented. This check is what allows you to vary the frame animation speed for a sprite, which is done by changing the value of frameDelay. Larger values for frameDelay result in a slower animation speed. The current frame is incremented by adding frameInc to frame. frame is then checked to make sure that its value is within the bounds of the image array, because it is used later to index into the array when the frame image is drawn.

The setPosition methods set the position of the sprite. The following is their source code:

```
void setPosition(Rectangle pos) {
  position = pos;
  setCollision();
}
```

6

```
public void setPosition(Point pos) {
  position.move(pos.x, pos.y);
  setCollision();
}
```

Even though the sprite position is stored as a rectangle, the setPosition methods allow you to specify the sprite position as either a rectangle or a point. In the latter version, the position rectangle is simply moved to the specified point. After the position rectangle is moved, the collision rectangle is set with a call to setCollision. setCollision is the method that sets the collision rectangle for the sprite. The source code for setCollision is as follows:

```
protected void setCollision() {
  collision = position;
}
```

Notice that setCollision sets the collision rectangle equal to the position rectangle, which results in simple rectangle collision detection. Because there is no way to know what sprites will be shaped like, you leave it up to derived sprite classes to implement versions of setCollision with specific shrunken rectangle calculations. Therefore, to implement shrunken rectangle collision, you just calculate a smaller collision rectangle in setCollision.

This isPointInside method is used to test whether a point lies inside the sprite. The source code for isPointInside is as follows:

```
boolean isPointInside(Point pt) {
  return position.inside(pt.x, pt.y);
}
```

This method is very handy for determining whether the user has clicked on a certain sprite. A good example of this is a board game in which the user drags pieces around with the mouse. You could implement the pieces as sprites and use the isPointInside method to see whether the mouse has clicked on one of the pieces.

The method that does most of the work in Sprite is the update method, which is shown in Listing 6.1.

Listing 6.1. The Sprite class's update method.

```
public BitSet update() {
  BitSet action = new BitSet();

  // Increment the frame
  incFrame();

  // Update the position
  Point pos = new Point(position.x, position.y);
  pos.translate(velocity.x, velocity.y);

  // Check the bounds
  // Wrap?
```

```
    if (boundsAction == Sprite.BA_WRAP) {
      if ((pos.x + position.width) < bounds.x)
        pos.x = bounds.x + bounds.width;
      else if (pos.x > (bounds.x + bounds.width))
        pos.x = bounds.x - position.width;
      if ((pos.y + position.height) < bounds.y)
        pos.y = bounds.y + bounds.height;
      else if (pos.y > (bounds.y + bounds.height))
        pos.y = bounds.y - position.height;
    }
    // Bounce?
    else if (boundsAction == Sprite.BA_BOUNCE) {
      boolean bounce = false;
      Point   vel = new Point(velocity.x, velocity.y);
      if (pos.x < bounds.x) {
        bounce = true;
        pos.x = bounds.x;
        vel.x = -vel.x;
      }
      else if ((pos.x + position.width) >
        (bounds.x + bounds.width)) {
        bounce = true;
        pos.x = bounds.x + bounds.width - position.width;
        vel.x = -vel.x;
      }
      if (pos.y < bounds.y) {
        bounce = true;
        pos.y = bounds.y;
        vel.y = -vel.y;
      }
      else if ((pos.y + position.height) >
        (bounds.y + bounds.height)) {
        bounce = true;
        pos.y = bounds.y + bounds.height - position.height;
        vel.y = -vel.y;
      }
      if (bounce)
        setVelocity(vel);
    }
    // Die?
    else if (boundsAction == Sprite.BA_DIE) {
      if ((pos.x + position.width) < bounds.x ||
        pos.x > bounds.width ||
        (pos.y + position.height) < bounds.y ||
        pos.y > bounds.height) {
        action.set(Sprite.SA_KILL);
        return action;
      }
    }
    // Stop (default)
    else {
      if (pos.x  < bounds.x ||
        pos.x > (bounds.x + bounds.width - position.width)) {
        pos.x = Math.max(bounds.x, Math.min(pos.x,
          bounds.x + bounds.width - position.width));
        setVelocity(new Point(0, 0));
```

continues

Listing 6.1. continued

```
      }
      if (pos.y  < bounds.y ||
        pos.y > (bounds.y + bounds.height - position.height)) {
        pos.y = Math.max(bounds.y, Math.min(pos.y,
          bounds.y + bounds.height - position.height));
        setVelocity(new Point(0, 0));
      }
    }
    setPosition(pos);

    return action;
}
```

The `update` method handles the task of updating the animation frame and position of the sprite. `update` begins by creating an empty set of action flags, which are stored in a `BitSet` object. The animation frame is then updated with a call to `incFrame`. The position of the sprite is updated by translating the position rectangle based on the velocity. You can think of the position rectangle as sliding a distance determined by the velocity.

> **NOTE**
>
> The `BitSet` class is included in the standard Java package `java.util` and provides a means of maintaining a set of boolean flags or bit fields.

The rest of the code in `update` is devoted to handling the various bounds actions. The first bounds action flag, `BA_WRAP`, causes the sprite to wrap around to the other side of the bounds rectangle. This flag is useful in an Asteroids type game, in which the asteroids float off one side of the screen and back from the other. The `BA_BOUNCE` flag causes the sprite to bounce if it encounters a boundary. This flag is useful in a Breakout or Pong type game, in which a ball bounces off the edges of the screen. The `BA_DIE` flag causes the sprite to die if it encounters a boundary. This flag is useful for sprites such as bullets, which you often want destroyed when they travel beyond the edges of the screen. Finally, the default flag, `BA_STOP`, causes the sprite to stop when it encounters a boundary.

Notice that `update` finishes by returning a set of sprite action flags, `action`. Derived sprite classes can return different sprite action values to trigger different actions. Judging by its size, it's not hard to figure out that the `update` method is itself the bulk of the code in the `Sprite` class. This is logical though, because the `update` method is where all the action takes place; `update` handles all the details of updating the animation frame and position of the sprite, along with carrying out different bounds actions.

Another important method in the `Sprite` class is `draw`, whose source code is as follows:

```
public void draw(Graphics g) {
  // Draw the current frame
  if (!hidden)
    g.drawImage(image[frame], position.x, position.y, component);
}
```

After wading through the update method, the draw method looks like a piece of cake! It simply uses the drawImage method to draw the current sprite frame image to the Graphics object that is passed in. Notice that the drawImage method requires the image, XY position, and component (ImageObserver) to carry this out.

The addSprite method is used to add sprites to the sprite list:

```
protected Sprite addSprite(BitSet action) {
  return null;
}
```

The sprite list contains all the sprites and is maintained by the SpriteVector class, which you'll learn about a little later today. The reason for having the addSprite method is that a sprite occasionally needs to create and add another sprite to the sprite list. However, there is a big problem in that an individual sprite doesn't know anything about the sprite list. To get around this problem, you use sprite actions. Sprite actions work like this: A sprite notifies the sprite list that it wants to add a sprite by setting the SA_ADDSPRITE action flag in the set of action flags returned by the update method. The sprite list, in turn, calls the addSprite method for the sprite and adds the new sprite to the list. I know this sounds like a convoluted way to handle sprite creation, but it actually works quite well and fits in with the object-oriented design of the sprite classes. The remaining question, then, is why does this implementation of addSprite return null? The answer is that it is up to derived sprites to provide a specific implementation for addSprite. Knowing this, you could make addSprite abstract, but then you would be forced to derive a new sprite class any time you want to create a sprite.

The last method in Sprite is testCollision, which is used to check for collisions between sprites:

```
protected boolean testCollision(Sprite test) {
  // Check for collision with another sprite
  if (test != this)
    return collision.intersects(test.getCollision());
  return false;
}
```

The sprite to test for collision is passed in the test parameter. The test simply involves checking to see whether the collision rectangles intersect. If so, testCollision returns true. testCollision isn't all that useful within the context of a single sprite, but it is very handy when you put together the SpriteVector class, which you are going to do next.

6

The `SpriteVector` Class

At this point, you have a `Sprite` class with some pretty impressive features, but you don't really have any way to manage it. Of course, you could go ahead and create an applet with some `Sprite` objects, but how would they be able to interact with each other? The answer to this question is the `SpriteVector` class, which handles all the details of maintaining a list of sprites and the handling of interactions between them.

The `SpriteVector` class is derived from the `Vector` class, which is a standard class provided in the `java.util` package. The `Vector` class models a growable array of objects. In this case, the `SpriteVector` class is used as a container for a growable array of `Sprite` objects.

The `SpriteVector` class has only one member variable, `background`, which is a `Background` object:

```
protected Background background;
```

This `Background` object represents the background upon which the sprites appear. It is initialized in the constructor for `SpriteVector`, like this:

```
public SpriteVector(Background back) {
  super(50, 10);
  background = back;
}
```

The constructor for `SpriteVector` simply takes a `Background` object as its only parameter. You'll learn about the `Background` class a little later today. Notice that the constructor for `SpriteVector` calls the `Vector` parent class constructor and sets the default storage capacity (`50`) and amount to increment the storage capacity (`10`) if the vector needs to grow.

`SpriteVector` contains the following two access methods for getting and setting the `background` member variable:

```
public Background getBackground() {
  return background;
}

public void setBackground(Background back) {
  background = back;
}
```

These methods are useful in games in which the background changes based on the level of the game. To change the background, you simply call `setBackground` and pass in the new `Background` object.

The `getEmptyPosition` method is used by the `SpriteVector` class to help position new sprites. Listing 6.2 contains the source code for `getEmptyPosition`.

Listing 6.2. The `SpriteVector` class's `getEmptyPosition` method.

```
public Point getEmptyPosition(Dimension sSize) {
  Rectangle pos = new Rectangle(0, 0, sSize.width, sSize.height);
  Random     rand = new Random(System.currentTimeMillis());
  boolean    empty = false;
  int        numTries = 0;

  // Look for an empty position
  while (!empty && numTries++ < 50) {
    // Get a random position
    pos.x = Math.abs(rand.nextInt() %
      background.getSize().width);
    pos.y = Math.abs(rand.nextInt() %
      background.getSize().height);

    // Iterate through sprites, checking if position is empty
    boolean collision = false;
    for (int i = 0; i < size(); i++) {
      Rectangle testPos = ((Sprite)elementAt(i)).getPosition();
      if (pos.intersects(testPos)) {
        collision = true;
        break;
      }
    }
    empty = !collision;
  }
  return new Point(pos.x, pos.y);
}
```

`getEmptyPosition` is a method whose importance might not be readily apparent to you right now; it is used to find an empty physical position in which to place a new sprite in the sprite list. This doesn't mean the position of the sprite in the list; rather, it means its physical position on the screen. This method is very useful when you want to randomly place multiple sprites on the screen. By using `getEmptyPosition`, you eliminate the possibility of placing new sprites on top of existing sprites. For example, in an adventure game you could randomly place scenery objects such as trees using `getEmptyPosition` to make sure none of them overlap each other.

The `isPointInside` method in `SpriteVector` is similar to the version of `isPointInside` in `Sprite`, except it goes through the entire sprite list checking each sprite. Check out the source code for it:

```
Sprite isPointInside(Point pt) {
  // Iterate backward through the sprites, testing each
  for (int i = (size() - 1); i >= 0; i--) {
    Sprite s = (Sprite)elementAt(i);
    if (s.isPointInside(pt))
      return s;
  }
  return null;
}
```

If the point passed in the parameter pt lies in a sprite, isPointInside returns the sprite. Notice that the sprite list is searched in reverse, meaning that the last sprite is checked before the first. The sprites are searched in this order for a very important reason: Z-order. The sprites are stored in the sprite list sorted in ascending Z-order, which specifies their depth on the screen. Therefore, sprites near the beginning of the list are sometimes concealed by sprites near the end of the list. If you want to check for a point lying within a sprite, it only makes sense to check the topmost sprites first—that is, the sprites with larger Z-order values. If this sounds a little confusing, don't worry; you'll learn more about Z-order later today when you get to the add method.

As in Sprite, the update method is the key method in SpriteVector because it handles updating all the sprites. Listing 6.3 contains the source code for update.

Listing 6.3. The SpriteVector class's update method.

```
public void update() {
  // Iterate through sprites, updating each
  Sprite    s, sHit;
  Rectangle lastPos;
  for (int i = 0; i < size(); ) {
    // Update the sprite
    s = (Sprite)elementAt(i);
    lastPos = new Rectangle(s.getPosition().x, s.getPosition().y,
      s.getPosition().width, s.getPosition().height);
    BitSet action = s.update();

    // Check for the SA_ADDSPRITE action
    if (action.get(Sprite.SA_ADDSPRITE)) {
      // Add the sprite
      Sprite sToAdd = s.addSprite(action);
      if (sToAdd != null) {
        int iAdd = add(sToAdd);
        if (iAdd >= 0 && iAdd <= i)
          i++;
      }
    }

    // Check for the SA_RESTOREPOS action
    if (action.get(Sprite.SA_RESTOREPOS))
      s.setPosition(lastPos);

    // Check for the SA_KILL action
    if (action.get(Sprite.SA_KILL)) {
      removeElementAt(i);
      continue;
    }

    // Test for collision
    int iHit = testCollision(s);
    if (iHit >= 0)
```

```
        if (collision(i, iHit))
          s.setPosition(lastPos);
      i++;
    }
}
```

The update method iterates through the sprites, calling Sprite's update method on each one. It then checks for the various sprite action flags returned by the call to update. If the SA_ADDSPRITE flag is set, the addSprite method is called on the sprite and the returned sprite is added to the list. If the SA_RESTOREPOS flag is set, the sprite position is set to the position of the sprite prior to being updated. If the SA_KILL flag is set, the sprite is removed from the sprite list. Finally, testCollision is called to see whether a collision has occurred between sprites. You get the whole scoop on testCollision in this section. If a collision has occurred, the old position of the collided sprite is restored and the collision method is called.

The collision method is used to handle collisions between two sprites:

```
protected boolean collision(int i, int iHit) {
  // Swap velocities (bounce)
  Sprite s = (Sprite)elementAt(i);
  Sprite sHit = (Sprite)elementAt(iHit);
  Point swap = s.getVelocity();
  s.setVelocity(sHit.getVelocity());
  sHit.setVelocity(swap);
  return true;
}
```

The collision method is responsible for handling any actions that result from a collision between sprites. The action in this case is to simply swap the velocities of the collided Sprite objects, which results in a bouncing effect. This method is where you provide specific collision actions in derived sprites. For example, in a space game, you might want alien sprites to explode upon collision with a meteor sprite.

The testCollision method is used to test for collisions between a sprite and the rest of the sprites in the sprite list:

```
protected int testCollision(Sprite test) {
  // Check for collision with other sprites
  Sprite  s;
  for (int i = 0; i < size(); i++)
  {
    s = (Sprite)elementAt(i);
    if (s == test)  // don't check itself
      continue;
    if (test.testCollision(s))
      return i;
  }
  return -1;
}
```

The sprite to be tested is passed in the test parameter. The sprites are then iterated through and the testCollision method in Sprite is called for each. Notice that testCollision isn't called on the test sprite if the iteration refers to the same sprite. To understand the significance of this code, consider the effect of passing testCollision the same sprite on which the method is being called; you would be checking to see whether a sprite was colliding with itself, which would always return true. If a collision is detected, the Sprite object that has been hit is returned from testCollision.

The draw method handles drawing the background, as well as drawing all the sprites:

```
public void draw(Graphics g) {
  // Draw the background
  background.draw(g);

  // Iterate through sprites, drawing each
  for (int i = 0; i < size(); i++)
    ((Sprite)elementAt(i)).draw(g);
}
```

The background is drawn with a simple call to the draw method of the Background object. The sprites are then drawn by iterating through the sprite list and calling the draw method for each.

The add method is probably the trickiest method in the SpriteVector class. Listing 6.4 contains the source code for add.

Listing 6.4. The SpriteVector class's add method.

```
public int add(Sprite s) {
  // Use a binary search to find the right location to insert the
  // new sprite (based on z-order)
  int   l = 0, r = size(), i = 0;
  int   z = s.getZOrder(),
        zTest = z + 1;
  while (r > l) {
    i = (l + r) / 2;
    zTest = ((Sprite)elementAt(i)).getZOrder();
    if (z < zTest)
      r = i;
    else
      l = i + 1;
    if (z == zTest)
      break;
  }
  if (z >= zTest)
    i++;

  insertElementAt(s, i);
  return i;
}
```

The add method handles adding new sprites to the sprite list. The catch is that the sprite list must always be sorted according to Z-order. Why is this? Remember that Z-order is the depth at which sprites appear on the screen. The illusion of depth is established by the order in which the sprites are drawn. This works because sprites drawn later are drawn on top of sprites drawn earlier, and therefore appear to be at a higher depth. Therefore, sorting the sprite list by ascending Z-order and then drawing them in that order is an effective way to provide the illusion of depth. The add method uses a binary search to find the right spot to add new sprites so that the sprite list remains sorted by Z-order.

That wraps up the SpriteVector class! You now have not only a powerful Sprite class, but also a SpriteVector class for managing and providing interactivity between sprites. All that's left is putting these classes to work in a real applet.

The Background Classes

Actually, there is some unfinished business to deal with before you try out the sprite classes. I'm referring to the Background class used in SpriteVector. While you're at it, let's look at a few different background classes that will come in handy later in the book.

Background

If you recall, I mentioned earlier today that the Background class provides the overhead of managing a background for the sprites to appear on top of. The source code for the Background class is shown in Listing 6.5.

Listing 6.5. The Background class.

```
public class Background {
  protected Component component;
  protected Dimension size;

  public Background(Component comp) {
    component = comp;
    size = comp.size();
  }

  public Dimension getSize() {
    return size;
  }

  public void draw(Graphics g) {
    // Fill with component color
    g.setColor(component.getBackground());
    g.fillRect(0, 0, size.width, size.height);
    g.setColor(Color.black);
  }
}
```

6

As you can see, the Background class is pretty simple. It basically provides a clean abstraction of the background for the sprites. The two member variables maintained by Background are used to keep up with the associated component and dimensions for the background. The constructor for Background takes a Component object as its only parameter. This Component object is typically the applet window, and it serves to provide the dimensions of the background and the default background color.

The getSize method is an access method that simply returns the size of the background. The draw method fills the background with the default background color, as defined by the component member variable.

You're probably thinking that this Background object isn't too exciting. Couldn't you just stick this drawing code directly into SpriteVector's draw method? Yes, you could, but then you would miss out on the benefits provided by the more derived background classes, ColorBackground and ImageBackground, which are explained next. The background classes are a good example of how object-oriented design makes Java code much cleaner and easier to extend.

ColorBackground

The ColorBackground class provides a background that can be filled with any color. Listing 6.6 contains the source code for the ColorBackground class.

Listing 6.6. The ColorBackground class.

```
public class ColorBackground extends Background {
  protected Color color;

  public ColorBackground(Component comp, Color c) {
    super(comp);
    color = c;
  }

  public Color getColor() {
    return color;
  }

  public void setColor(Color c) {
    color = c;
  }

  public void draw(Graphics g) {
    // Fill with color
    g.setColor(color);
    g.fillRect(0, 0, size.width, size.height);
    g.setColor(Color.black);
  }
}
```

ColorBackground adds a single member variable, color, which is a Color object. This member variable holds the color used to fill the background. The constructor for ColorBackground takes Component and Color objects as parameters. There are two access methods for getting and setting the color member variable. The draw method for ColorBackground is very similar to the draw method in Background, except that the color member variable is used as the fill color.

ImageBackground

A more interesting Background derived class is ImageBackground, which uses an image as the background. Listing 6.7 contains the source code for the ImageBackground class.

Listing 6.7. The ImageBackground class.

```
public class ImageBackground extends Background {
  protected Image image;

  public ImageBackground(Component comp, Image img) {
    super(comp);
    image = img;
  }

  public Image getImage() {
    return image;
  }

  public void setImage(Image img) {
    image = img;
  }

  public void draw(Graphics g) {
    // Draw background image
    g.drawImage(image, 0, 0, component);
  }
}
```

The ImageBackground class adds a single member variable, image, which is an Image object. This member variable holds the image to be used as the background. Not surprisingly, the constructor for ImageBackground takes Component and Image objects as parameters. There are two access methods for getting and setting the image member variable. The draw method for ImageBackground simply draws the background image using the drawImage method of the passed Graphics object.

6

Sample Applet: Atoms

It's time to take all the hard work that you put into the sprite classes and see what it amounts to. You didn't come this far for nothing. Figure 6.4 shows a screen shot of the Atoms applet, which shows off the sprite classes you've toiled over for so long. The complete source code, images, and executable classes for the Atoms applet are on the accompanying CD-ROM.

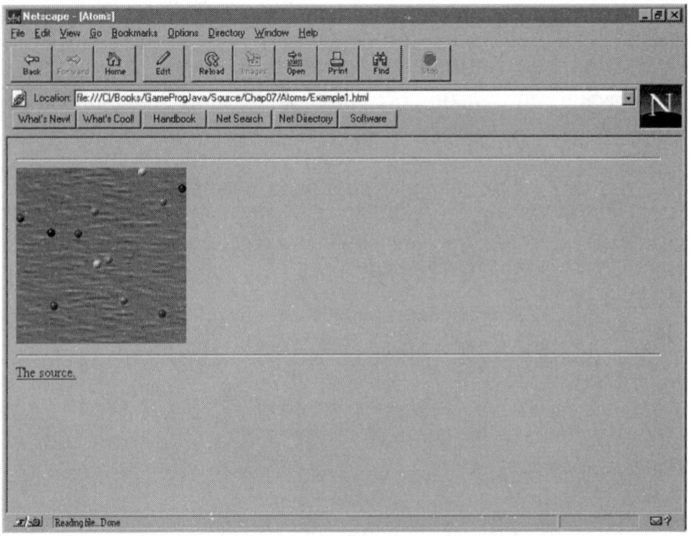

Figure 6.4.

The Atoms sample applet.

The Atoms applet uses a `SpriteVector` object to manage 12 atomic `Sprite` objects. This object, `sv`, is one of the `Atom` applet class's member variables, which look like this:

```
private Image        offImage, back;
private Image[]      atom = new Image[6];
private Graphics     offGrfx;
private Thread       animate;
private MediaTracker tracker;
private SpriteVector sv;
private int          delay = 83; // 12 fps
private Random       rand = new
  Random(System.currentTimeMillis());
```

The `Image` member variables in the `Atoms` class represent the offscreen buffer, the background image, and the atom images. The `Graphics` member variable, `offGrfx`, holds the graphics context for the offscreen buffer image. The `Thread` member variable, `animate`, is used to hold the thread where the animation takes place. The `MediaTracker` member variable, `tracker`, is used to track the various images as they are being loaded. The `SpriteVector` member variable, `sv`, holds the sprite vector for the applet. The integer member variable, `delay`, determines the animation speed of the sprites. Finally, the Random member variable, rand, is used to generate random numbers throughout the applet.

Notice that the delay member variable is set to 83. The delay member variable specifies the amount of time (in milliseconds) that elapses between each frame of animation. You can determine the frame rate by inverting the value of delay, which results in a frame rate of about 12 frames per second (fps) in this case. This frame rate is pretty much the minimum rate required for fluid animation, such as sprite animation. You'll see how delay is used to establish the frame rate later in this lesson when you get into the details of the run method.

The Atoms class's init method loads all the images and registers them with the media tracker:

```
public void init() {
  // Load and track the images
  tracker = new MediaTracker(this);
  back = getImage(getCodeBase(), "Res/Back.gif");
  tracker.addImage(back, 0);
  atom[0] = getImage(getCodeBase(), "Res/Red.gif");
  tracker.addImage(atom[0], 0);
  atom[1] = getImage(getCodeBase(), "Res/Green.gif");
  tracker.addImage(atom[1], 0);
  atom[2] = getImage(getCodeBase(), "Res/Blue.gif");
  tracker.addImage(atom[2], 0);
  atom[3] = getImage(getCodeBase(), "Res/Yellow.gif");
  tracker.addImage(atom[3], 0);
  atom[4] = getImage(getCodeBase(), "Res/Purple.gif");
  tracker.addImage(atom[4], 0);
  atom[5] = getImage(getCodeBase(), "Res/Orange.gif");
  tracker.addImage(atom[5], 0);
}
```

Tracking the images is necessary because you want to wait until all the images have been loaded before you start the animation. The start and stop methods are standard thread handler methods:

```
public void start() {
  if (animate == null) {
    animate = new Thread(this);
    animate.start();
  }
}

public void stop() {
  if (animate != null) {
    animate.stop();
    animate = null;
  }
}
```

The start method is responsible for initializing and starting the animation thread. Likewise, the stop method stops the animation thread and cleans up after it.

6

WARNING

If for some reason you think that stopping the animation thread in the stop method isn't really that big of a deal, think again. The stop method is called whenever a user leaves the Web page containing an applet, in which case it is of great importance that you stop all threads executing in the applet. So always make sure to stop threads in the stop method of your applets.

The run method is the heart of the animation thread. Listing 6.8 shows the source code for run.

Listing 6.8. The Atom class's run method.

```
public void run() {
  try {
    tracker.waitForID(0);
  }
  catch (InterruptedException e) {
    return;
  }

  // Create and add the sprites
  sv = new SpriteVector(new ImageBackground(this, back));
  for (int i = 0; i < 12; i++) {
    Point pos = sv.getEmptyPosition(new Dimension(
      atom[0].getWidth(this), atom[0].getHeight(this)));
    sv.add(createAtom(pos, i % 6));
  }

  // Update everything
  long t = System.currentTimeMillis();
  while (Thread.currentThread() == animate) {
    sv.update();
    repaint();
    try {
      t += delay;
      Thread.sleep(Math.max(0, t - System.currentTimeMillis()));
    }
    catch (InterruptedException e) {
      break;
    }
  }
}
```

The run method first waits for the images to finish loading by calling the waitForID method of the MediaTracker object. After the images have finished loading, the SpriteVector is created. Twelve different atom Sprite objects are then created using the createAtom method, which you'll learn about a little later today. These atom sprites are then added to the sprite vector. Notice that the position for each sprite is found by using the `getEmptyPosition` method of `SpriteVector`. This guarantees that the sprites won't be placed on top of each other.

After creating and adding the sprites, a `while` loop is entered that handles updating the `SpriteVector` and forcing the applet to repaint itself. By forcing a repaint, you are causing the applet to redraw the sprites in their newly updated states.

Before you move on, it's important to understand how the frame rate is controlled in the `run` method. The call to `currentTimeMillis` returns the current system time in milliseconds. You aren't really concerned with what absolute time this method is returning you, because you are only using it here to measure relative time. After updating the sprites and forcing a redraw, the `delay` value is added to the time you just retrieved. At this point, you have updated the frame and calculated a time value that is `delay` milliseconds into the future. The next step is to tell the animation thread to sleep an amount of time equal to the difference between the future time value you just calculated and the present time.

This probably sounds pretty confusing, so let me clarify things a little. The `sleep` method is used to make a thread sleep for a number of milliseconds, as determined by the value passed in its only parameter. You might think that you could just pass `delay` to `sleep` and things would be fine. This approach technically would work, but it would have a certain degree of error. The reason is that a finite amount of time passes between updating the sprites and putting the thread to sleep. Without accounting for this lost time, the actual delay between frames wouldn't be equal to the value of `delay`. The solution is to check the time before and after the sprites are updated, and then reflect the difference in the delay value passed to the `sleep` method. And that's how the frame rate is managed! This frame rate technique is so useful that you'll use it throughout the rest of the book.

The `update` method is where the sprites are actually drawn to the applet window:

```
public void update(Graphics g) {
  // Create the offscreen graphics context
  if (offGrfx == null) {
    offImage = createImage(size().width, size().height);
    offGrfx = offImage.getGraphics();
  }

  // Draw the sprites
  sv.draw(offGrfx);

  // Draw the image onto the screen
  g.drawImage(offImage, 0, 0, null);
}
```

The `update` method uses double buffering to eliminate flicker in the sprite animation. By using double buffering, you eliminate flicker and allow for speedier animations. The `offImage` member variable contains the offscreen buffer image used for drawing the next animation frame. The offGrfx member variable contains the graphics context associated with the offscreen buffer image.

In update, the offscreen buffer is first created as an Image object whose dimensions match those of the applet window. It is important that the offscreen buffer be exactly the same size as the applet window. The graphics context associated with the buffer is then retrieved using the getGraphics method of Image. After the offscreen buffer is initialized, all you really have to do is tell the SpriteVector object to draw itself to the buffer. Remember that the SpriteVector object takes care of drawing the background and all the sprites. This is accomplished with a simple call to SpriteVector's draw method. The offscreen buffer is then drawn to the applet window using the drawImage method.

Even though the update method takes care of drawing everything, it is still important to implement the paint method. As a matter of fact, the paint method is very useful in providing the user visual feedback regarding the state of the images used by the applet. Listing 6.9 shows the source code for paint.

Listing 6.9. The Atom class's paint method.

```
public void paint(Graphics g) {
    if ((tracker.statusID(0, true) & MediaTracker.ERRORED) != 0) {
        // Draw the error rectangle
        g.setColor(Color.red);
        g.fillRect(0, 0, size().width, size().height);
        return;
    }
    if ((tracker.statusID(0, true) & MediaTracker.COMPLETE) != 0) {
        // Draw the offscreen image
        g.drawImage(offImage, 0, 0, null);
    }
    else {
        // Draw the title message (while the images load)
        Font        f1 = new Font("TimesRoman", Font.BOLD, 28),
                    f2 = new Font("Helvetica", Font.PLAIN, 16);
        FontMetrics fm1 = g.getFontMetrics(f1),
                    fm2 = g.getFontMetrics(f2);
        String      s1 = new String("Atoms"),
                    s2 = new String("Loading images...");
        g.setFont(f1);
        g.drawString(s1, (size().width - fm1.stringWidth(s1)) / 2,
            ((size().height - fm1.getHeight()) / 2) + fm1.getAscent());
        g.setFont(f2);
        g.drawString(s2, (size().width - fm2.stringWidth(s2)) / 2,
            size().height - fm2.getHeight() - fm2.getAscent());
    }
}
```

Using the media tracker, paint notifies the user that the images are still loading, or that an error has occurred while loading them. This paint method is very similar to the one you saw yesterday in the `Tarantulas` class. The primary difference is the addition of drawing the title text in the `Atom` version. Check out Figure 6.5, which shows the Atoms applet while the images are loading.

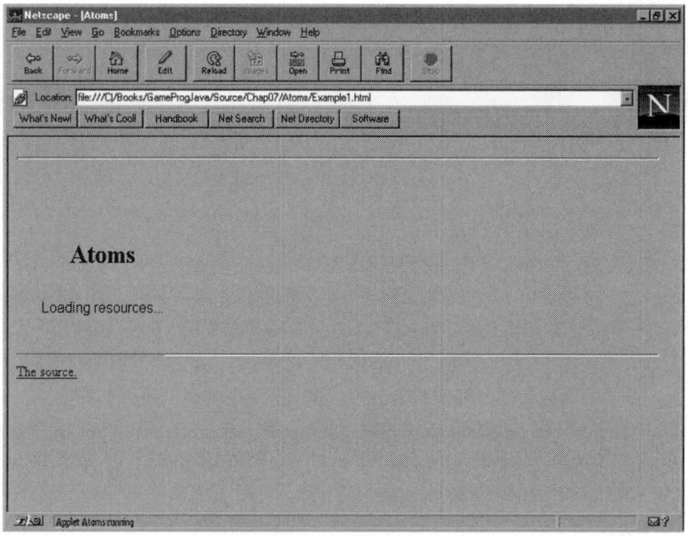

Figure 6.5.

The Atoms sample applet while the images are loading.

If an error occurs while loading one of the images, the `paint` method displays a red rectangle over the entire applet window area. If the images have finished loading, `paint` just draws the latest offscreen buffer to the applet window. If the images haven't finished loading, `paint` displays the title of the applet and a message stating that the images are still loading (see Figure 6.5). Displaying the title and status message consists of creating the appropriate fonts and centering the text within the applet window.

WARNING

You might think that the time spent waiting for images to load is an ideal time to display a flashy title screen for a game. Although this is a good time to present information to the user, remember that the whole point here is that the game images haven't finished loading, which includes any title images. Therefore, it's important to design any type of title displayed at this point as straight text and not try to display any images.

6

The last method in Atoms is `createAtom`, which handles creating a single atom sprite:

```
private Sprite createAtom(Point pos, int i) {
  return new Sprite(this, atom[i], pos, new Point(rand.nextInt()
    % 5, rand.nextInt() % 5), 0, Sprite.BA_BOUNCE);
}
```

`createAtom` takes a `Point` as its first parameter, `pos`, which determines the sprite's initial position. The second parameter, `i`, is an integer that specifies which atom image to use. `createAtom` then calculates a random velocity for the sprite using the `rand` member variable. Each velocity component for the sprite (X and Y) is given a random value between `-5` and `5`. The sprite is given a Z-order value of `0`. Finally, the sprite is assigned the `BA_BOUNCE` bounds action, which means that it will bounce when it encounters the edge of the applet window.

That's all it takes to get the sprite classes working together. It might seem like a lot of code at first, but think about all that the applet is undertaking. The applet is responsible for loading and keeping track of all the images used by the sprites, as well as the background and offscreen buffer. If the images haven't finished loading, or if an error occurs while loading, the applet has to notify the user accordingly. Additionally, the applet is responsible for maintaining a consistent frame rate and drawing the sprites using double buffering. Even with these responsibilities, the applet is still benefiting a great deal from the functionality provided by the sprite classes.

You can use this applet as a template applet for other applets you create that use the sprite classes. You now have all the functionality required to manage both cast- and frame-based animation, as well as provide support for interactivity among sprites via collision detection and sprite actions.

Summary

In today's lesson, you learned all about animation, including the two major types of animation: frame-based and cast-based. Adding to this theory, you learned that sprite animation is where the action is really at. You saw firsthand how to develop a powerful duo of sprite classes for implementing sprite animation, including a few support classes to make things easier. You then put the sprite classes to work in a sample applet that involved relatively little additional overhead.

Although it covered a lot of material, today's lesson laid the groundwork for the graphics used throughout the rest of the book. Without sprite animation, most games just wouldn't be that exciting. And without reusable Java sprite classes, implementing sprite animation in Java games would be much more difficult.

Most importantly, you learned today the fundamental animation concepts that underlie almost every Java game you'll write. Armed with the knowledge and code developed today, you are ready to move on to more advanced techniques that take you closer to writing cool Java games. More specifically, the next topic you need to cover is that of deriving your own sprite objects and working with interactions between them. You're in luck, because tomorrow's lesson covers exactly that topic by way of a really neat sample applet.

Q&A

Q What's the big deal with sprites?

A The big deal is that sprites provide a very flexible approach to implementing animation. This is important because almost every game has its own unique animation requirements. By designing a powerful sprite engine, you have a base level of animation support that can be extended to provide game-specific features.

Q What exactly is Z-order, and do I really need it?

A Z-order is the depth of a sprite relative to other sprites; sprites with higher Z-order values appear to be on top of sprites with lower Z-order values. You only need Z-order when two or more sprites overlap each other, which is in most games.

Q Why bother with the different types of collision detection?

A The different types of collision detection (rectangle, shrunken rectangle, and image data) provide different trade-offs in regard to performance and accuracy. Rectangle and shrunken rectangle collision detection provide a very high-performance solution, but with moderate to poor accuracy. Image data collision detection is perfect when it comes to accuracy, but it can bring your game to its knees in the performance department.

Q Why do I need the SpriteVector class? Isn't the Sprite class enough?

A The Sprite class is nice, but it only represents a single sprite. To enable multiple sprites to interact with each other, which most games require, you must have a second entity that acts as a storage unit for the sprites. The SpriteVector class solves this problem by doubling as a container for all the sprites as well as a communication medium between sprites.

Workshop

The Workshop section provides questions and exercises to give you a firmer grasp on the material you learned today. Try to answer the questions and at least think about the exercises before moving on to tomorrow's lesson. You'll find the answers to the questions in Appendix A, "Quiz Answers."

6

Quiz

1. What is animation?
2. What are the two main types of animation?
3. What is transparency?
4. What is flicker?
5. What is double buffering?

Exercises

1. Watch some cartoons and think about how each type of animation is being used.
2. Go see a movie and marvel at how well the illusion of movement works. I can't help it; I'm into entertainment!
3. Modify the Atoms applet so that the sprites wrap around the edges of the screen rather than bouncing.
4. Modify the Atoms applet so that the atom sprites don't bounce off each other.
5. Substitute frame animated sprites for the single frame atom sprites.

6

Day 7

Sim Tarantula: Creepy Crawly Sprites

On Day 6, you developed a suite of very powerful and easy to use sprite classes. You saw them in action in an applet that demonstrated their basic functionality. Today, you expand on that knowledge by extending the sprite classes to fit a more applied sample applet. More specifically, you derive new sprite classes to help build a tarantula simulation applet.

Today's lesson is completely devoted to the development of this applet, which makes great use of the sprite classes. You learn all about sprite actions and how to use them to add new sprites and kill existing sprites. You also learn how to incorporate multiple frame animation images into derived sprites to give them a sense of direction.

More than anything, you learn how to apply the sprite classes to problems requiring unique solutions. This is the one skill that is essential in creating Java games. So let's get busy!

Extending the Sprite Class

The concept of extending the Sprite class to fit a particular situation is crucial in Java game development. It is also important from an object-oriented design point of view and will ultimately save you a great deal of time and code testing. When you derive sprites from the Sprite class, you can reuse all the code in Sprite, while adding additional code to carry out more specific chores.

However, not all sprites derived from Sprite have to be specific to a particular game. You might need some functionality that is not included in Sprite and that might be needed by various other sprite objects in a more general sense. In this case, you are better off to create an intermediate class that is derived from Sprite. You can then derive game-specific classes from this class.

An example of this idea is a directional sprite. The Sprite class, although feature packed, includes no support for a sprite having direction. Some examples of sprites that would require direction are tanks and monsters—basically, anything that has a distinguishable front, back, and sides. If you were to use the Sprite class to create a monster, you would be able to move the monster and even give it a frame animation, but you would have no way to show it facing the direction it is moving in. Clearly, this would look pretty strange.

The solution is to derive a directional sprite that adds the functionality necessary to provide a sense of direction. Then you can derive the monster sprite from the directional sprite and instantly give it direction. From then on, any other game-specific directional sprites can simply be derived from the generic directional sprite class and gain all the same benefits. This is object-oriented programming at its best!

Designing a Directional Sprite

Because you'll need it for the Sim Tarantula applet later in today's lesson, go ahead and design a directional sprite class. The directional sprite class needs to encapsulate all the behavior necessary to provide a direction of movement.

The first step in designing the directional sprite is to determine how to model the different directions. Because you won't attempt to render the sprite image at different directions on the fly, it's important to realize that each direction requires its own image. In the case of a frame-animated directional sprite, each direction requires an array of images. You have to decide on a limited set of directions that the sprite can have, because it would be very costly in terms of resources to provide images for the sprite at many different directions. Figure 7.1 shows a discrete set of directions that apply well to directional sprites.

Figure 7.1.

Discrete directions for a directional sprite.

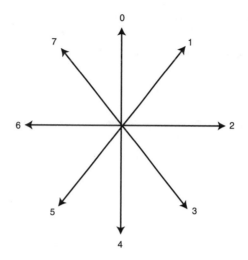

Of course, providing more directions would yield smoother rotating effects for the sprite. However, it would also up the ante a great deal in terms of resources. Remember that each direction brings with it the overhead of an image or array of images. And all those images must be transferred over a potentially low-bandwidth Internet connection. In Java programming, you must always think about the fact that the applet and resources have to be transmitted over the Internet to the user's computer. At times like this, you need to look at the design from the game player's perspective: Are smoother directional sprites worth waiting 10 minutes for the images to transfer? I seriously doubt it!

Now that you've settled on a workable set of directions for the directional sprite, you need to consider what aspects of the original Sprite class are affected by the addition of directions. Probably the most obvious change has to do with the sprite image. Now, instead of a single image, you must provide an image for each possible direction. In the case of a frame-animated directional sprite, you must provide an array of images for each direction.

The other major change brought on by the directional sprite relates to velocity. The velocity of a directional sprite is tightly linked to the direction because the sprite must be facing the direction it is traveling. This means that you need to alter the velocity whenever you change the direction, and vice versa. You'll see that this is not a problem, because you can just override the method that deals with setting the velocity.

The DirectionalSprite Class

With all the design issues laid out, it's time to move on to the Java implementation of the DirectionalSprite class. The following are the member variables defined in DirectionalSprite:

7

```
protected static final int[][] velDirs = {
  {0, -1}, {1, -1}, {1, 0}, {1, 1},
  {0, 1}, {-1, 1}, {-1, 0}, {-1, -1} };
protected Image[][] image;
protected int      direction;
```

The first member variable, velDirs, is a two-dimensional array of integers. This array holds values that are used to calculate the sprite's velocity based on a given direction. When the direction of the sprite is changed, the velocity is multiplied by an X and Y component from the velDirs array. Figure 7.2 shows how the X and Y multiplier values in velDirs correspond to the different directions of the sprite.

Figure 7.2.

Velocity multipliers for the different sprite directions.

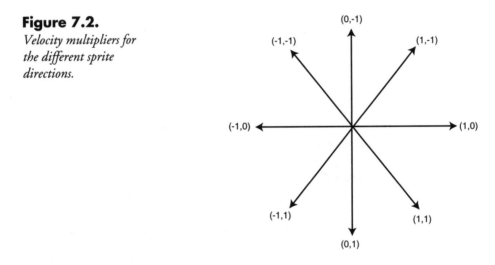

The other two member variables in DirectionalSprite, image and direction, are storage members for the directional images and the current direction. Notice that image is a two-dimensional array of Image objects, which reflects the frame animation support in DirectionalSprite.

DirectionalSprite has two constructors, similar to the original Sprite class:

```
public DirectionalSprite(Component comp, Image[] img, Point pos,
  Point vel, int z, int ba, int d) {
  super(comp, img[d], pos, vel, z, ba);
  image[0] = img;
  setDirection(d);
}

public DirectionalSprite(Component comp, Image[][] img, int f,
  int fi, int fd, Point pos, Point vel, int z, int ba, int d) {
  super(comp, img[d], f, fi, fd, pos, vel, z, ba);
  image = img;
  setDirection(d);
}
```

7

The first constructor creates a directional sprite without frame animation, and the second constructor supports frame animation, as is evident by the extra parameters. Notice that the setDirection method is called to initialize the direction of the sprite, rather than a simple assignment being made to the direction member variable. This is because the direction impacts both the velocity and image of the sprite. You see how this works later in today's lesson when you get into the setDirection method.

The getDirection method is a simple access method that returns the current direction:

```
public int getDirection() {
  return direction;
}
```

The setDirection method involves a little more work, as the following code shows:

```
public void setDirection(int dir) {
  // Set the direction
  if (dir < 0)
    dir = 7;
  else if (dir > 7)
    dir = 0;
  direction = dir;

  // Change the velocity
  velocity.x *= velDirs[dir][0];
  velocity.y *= velDirs[dir][1];

  // Set the image
  setImage(image[dir]);
}
```

setDirection first ensures that the direction is within the directional bounds (0 to 7). Notice that setDirection takes care to wrap the direction around if it goes beyond a boundary; this gives the sprite the capability to rotate freely. The velocity is then modified using the velDirs directional velocity multipliers. Finally, the new direction image is set with a call to setImage.

The setVelocity method is overridden in DirectionalSprite because changing the velocity should cause a change in the direction. Check out the following code:

```
public void setVelocity(Point vel) {
    velocity = vel;

    // Change the direction
    if (vel.x == 0 && vel.y == 0)
      return;
    if (vel.x == 0)
      direction = (vel.y + 1) * 2;
    else if (vel.x == 1)
      direction = vel.y + 1;
    else if (vel.x == -1)
      direction = -vel.y + 6;
  }
```

7

In setVelocity, velocity is first assigned its new value. The direction is then altered based on the new velocity by way of a few comparisons and equations. If the function of these equations isn't obvious to you at first, just think about what task they are handling. The task is to obtain a direction in the range 0 to 7 from a given velocity. Because no single equation can do this, I worked out a fairly concise way of calculating the direction based on the velocity. There's nothing magical about it; it's just a matter of closely analyzing the different values.

You now have a fully functional directional sprite class that can be reused in any applet from now on. Speaking of reusing the DirectionalSprite class, let's start working on the tarantula simulator.

Designing Sim Tarantula

Before jumping into the Java code of any applet, it's important to decide to some degree what you want the applet to do. This is very important because it gives you a clear goal and a strategy toward implementing the various classes that make up a complete applet. By using this approach, you save a lot of time rewriting code, and you end up with a cleaner set of classes the first time around.

Writing Java games requires a similar design approach. In the design phase of a Java game, you must determine what sprites the game needs, as well as how they interact with each other. The only potential difference in designing a game is that there are aspects of games that have to be played and then tweaked based on feel. This trial and error approach is hard to avoid in some cases because the subtleties of games are often the most fun.

Having said all that, let's take a stab at designing a simple tarantula simulator, Sim Tarantula. Although it's not technically a game, Sim Tarantula contains nearly all of the components of a game—just about everything except user interaction.

First, what objects does a tarantula simulator contain? By defining the objects used in the applet, you are indirectly defining the applet itself. Well, no doubt it will have tarantulas, and preferably some kind of background. Because tarantulas often live in the desert, it only makes sense to use a desert background. Additionally, tarantulas clearly have a front and a back, so it makes sense to model them as directional sprites. This is important because you want a tarantula to always face the direction in which it is walking; otherwise, it will look like the tarantula is sliding across the desert floor rather than walking.

Next, you might wonder where tarantulas come from. Of course, eggs! Rather than create fully grown tarantulas, it would be much more interesting to have them hatch from eggs and grow into larger tarantulas. This is a perfect place to display a frame animation of a tarantula hatching from an egg and growing up into an adult tarantula.

Then what? At this point, the full-grown tarantulas can walk around, explore things, and talk amongst themselves if they like. They can even lay more eggs, which eventually results in more tarantulas. But sooner or later, they start getting old. And like all creatures, at some point they must die. Sounds like another cool place for an animation. A frame animation showing a tarantula getting more and more frail until it just withers away should do the trick.

You now have enough information to make a pretty neat little tarantula simulator. At this point, it makes sense to break down the design into sprites so that you'll have an idea of what classes need to be written. Based on what you have so far, Sim Tarantula requires the following sprites:

- ☐ Spiderling
- ☐ Tarantula
- ☐ Spidercide

A spiderling is a baby tarantula, and the spiderling sprite basically models the birth of a tarantula from the egg. This sprite is really just a frame-animated sprite that is used to show the birth of a tarantula. The tarantula sprite models a fully grown tarantula. It is a frame-animated directional sprite and can walk around freely and create new spiderlings. The spidercide sprite models the death of a tarantula. It is a frame-animated sprite that shows a tarantula growing weaker and weaker until it finally disappears.

Overall, these sprites probably sound pretty reasonable to you. However, you haven't addressed one thing, and that is the issue of how the sprites are created and destroyed. The only sprite out of these three that the applet ever needs to create directly is the spiderling sprite. This is because the other two sprites should be created automatically. For example, the tarantula sprite should be created automatically when the spiderling finishes its animation. Similarly, the spidercide sprite should be created automatically when the tarantula is ready to die.

That covers creating the sprites, but how about destroying them? In this case, the applet isn't responsible for destroying any of the sprites. The spiderling sprite should kill itself whenever it finishes its animation and creates the tarantula sprite. Similarly, the tarantula sprite should kill itself when it creates the spidercide sprite. And last but not least, the spidercide sprite should kill itself when it finishes its animation. Just in case you've had trouble following any of this, check out Figure 7.3, which shows the life cycle of the Sim Tarantula sprites.

Now you understand when each sprite is created and destroyed, but how in the world do sprites create and destroy each other in the first place? The answer is *sprite actions*. When you use sprite actions, you have full control over creating and destroying sprites from within a sprite. You even have the option of creating custom actions for derived sprites that can make them do anything you want. Sprite actions are probably the most powerful aspect of using sprites, and you've already written support for them into the sprite classes in the last lesson.

7

Figure 7.3.
The life cycle of the
sprites in Sim Tarantula.

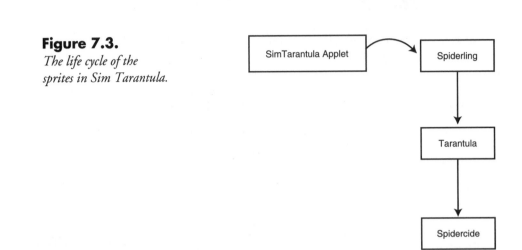

NEW TERM A *sprite action* is a mechanism that allows sprites to interact with each other. For example, using sprite actions, a sprite can create new sprites or kill existing sprites.

By now, you'll probably agree that the design of Sim Tarantula is far enough along to move on to the applet. I couldn't agree more!

Sample Applet: Sim Tarantula

The Sim Tarantula applet contains most of the elements of a complete Java game, including extensive support for derived sprites. Figure 7.4 shows the Sim Tarantula applet in action.

Figure 7.4.
The Sim Tarantula
sample applet.

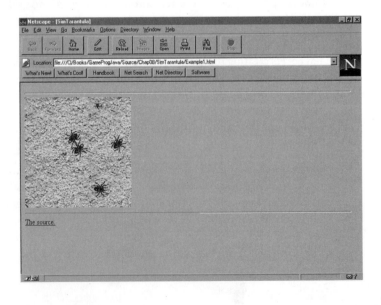

Sim Tarantula first places a number of spiderlings that eventually grow into tarantulas. These tarantulas then roam around dropping new spiderlings until they die. This process continues until all of the tarantulas die. Because the creation of spiderlings and the death of tarantulas occur randomly, the applet has the potential of running indefinitely. On the other hand, all the tarantulas could potentially die off, leaving an empty landscape.

Now that you've seen Sim Tarantula in action, let's look under the hood and figure out how everything works.

The Sprite Classes

The core of the Sim Tarantula applet is the extended sprite classes. The first of these classes is the Spiderling class, which handles displaying an animation of a tarantula hatching from an egg. The Spiderling class shows an animation and then creates a new tarantula and kills itself. The Spiderling class has a single constructor, whose code follows:

```
public Spiderling(Component comp, Point pos) {
  super(comp, image, 0, 1, 20, pos, new Point(0, 0), 40,
    Sprite.BA_DIE);
}
```

Notice that, unlike the Sprite class, the constructor for Spiderling only takes a couple of parameters. This simplification is handy because it enables you to create spiderlings in the applet without having to supply a bunch of information. This is a common technique that you will use on game-specific sprites throughout the rest of the book.

The initResources method is used to initialize the resources used by the spiderling:

```
public static void initResources(Applet app, MediaTracker tracker,
  int id) {
  for (int i = 0; i < 6; i++) {
    image[i] = app.getImage(app.getCodeBase(), "Res/Spling" +
      i + ".gif");
    tracker.addImage(image[i], id);
  }
}
```

Resources initialized by initResources could include anything from images to sound and music. In this case, the only resources used by Spiderling are images. It's important that initResources is defined as static. This means that initResources applies to all instances of the Spiderling class, which results in all Spiderling objects referencing the same images. Furthermore, this makes the loading of resources smoother because you can load the resources at the beginning of the applet before you even create any Spiderling objects. This is another tactic that will be used frequently throughout the rest of the book.

7

WARNING

Because the `Spiderling` class is completely dependent on its resources (images), the `initResources` method must be called before creating or using any `Spiderling` objects. The same rule applies to all other sprites you develop that use the `initResources` method to initialize their resources.

The overridden `update` method in `Spiderling` takes care of incrementing the spiderling frame animation:

```
public BitSet update() {
  BitSet action = new BitSet();

  // Die?
  if (frame >= 5) {
    action.set(Sprite.SA_KILL);
    action.set(Sprite.SA_ADDSPRITE);
    action.set(Tarantula.SA_ADDTARANTULA);
    return action;
  }

  // Increment the frame
  incFrame();

  return action;
}
```

An important thing to notice is how `update` kills the `Spiderling` object and creates a new `Tarantula` object. This is carried out simply by checking the current animation frame and returning the correct sprite action. The `update` method makes use of a custom sprite action, `SA_ADDTARANTULA`, which is defined in the `Tarantula` class. You learn about the `Tarantula` class in a moment.

NOTE

Notice that even though the `SA_ADDTARANTULA` sprite action is used to add tarantula sprites, the standard sprite action `SA_ADDSPRITE` must also be used in conjunction with it. This is true because the `SA_ADDSPRITE` action signals that a sprite is to be added, and the `SA_ADDTARANTULA` action specifies the specific type of sprite (a tarantula sprite).

The `addSprite` method is the other overridden method in `Spiderling` and handles adding a new `Tarantula` object when the spiderling dies:

```
protected Sprite addSprite(BitSet action) {
  // Add spider?
  if (action.get(Tarantula.SA_ADDTARANTULA))
```

```
      return new Tarantula(component, new Point(position.x, position.y));
   return null;
}
```

`addSprite` checks for the `SA_ADDTARANTULA` action flag and creates the new tarantula if it is set. The newly created `Tarantula` object is then returned so that it can be added to the sprite list.

The next extended sprite class used in Sim Tarantula is the `Tarantula` class, which you might have suspected models a tarantula. The following are the member variables defined in the `Tarantula` class:

```
public static final int SA_ADDTARANTULA = 3,
                        SA_ADDSPIDERLING = 4,
                        SA_ADDSPIDERCIDE = 5;
public static Image[][] image;
protected static Random rand = new Random(
  System.currentTimeMillis());
```

Probably the most important aspect of the `Tarantula` class is the addition of the custom sprite actions. These three actions define a mechanism to add `Tarantula`, `Spiderling`, and `Spidercide` objects. Notice that the actions are assigned increasing integer values beginning with 3. This is extremely important because the standard sprite actions defined in the `Sprite` class are already assigned the values 0, 1, and 2. If you recall, the sprite actions are actually flags used in a `BitSet` object to pass actions back and forth between individual sprites and the sprite list.

The `Image` member variable, `image`, is simply used to hold the array of images for the sprite. The `Tarantula` class also contains a `Random` object member variable, `rand`. This member variable is defined as static and is used to provide random numbers for all `Tarantula` objects. It is seeded with the current system time, which is a useful way to help guarantee randomness.

The constructor for `Tarantula` is very simple and alleviates having to pass a bunch of specific parameters:

```
public Tarantula(Component comp, Point pos) {
  super(comp, image, 0, 1, 2, pos, new Point(1, 1), 50,
    Sprite.BA_WRAP, 0);
}
```

The tarantula is given a bounds action of `BA_WRAP`, which means that it can roam off one side of the applet window and back onto the other side.

Similar to the one in `Spiderling`, the `initResources` method for `Tarantula` loads all the images used by the class:

```
public static void initResources(Applet app, MediaTracker tracker,
  int id) {
  image = new Image[8][2];
  for (int i = 0; i < 8; i++) {
    for (int j = 0; j < 2; j++) {
      image[i][j] = app.getImage(app.getCodeBase(),
```

7

```
            "Res/Tarant" + i + j + ".gif");
        tracker.addImage(image[i][j], id);
      }
    }
}
```

The update method is where most of the action takes place in Tarantula. Listing 7.1 shows the source code for the update method.

Listing 7.1. The Tarantula class's update method.

```
public BitSet update() {
    // Randomly change direction
    if ((rand.nextInt() % 10) == 0) {
      velocity.x = velocity.y = 1;
      setDirection(direction + rand.nextInt() % 2);
    }

    // Call parent's update()
    BitSet action = super.update();

    // Give birth?
    if (rand.nextInt() % 250 == 0) {
      action.set(Sprite.SA_ADDSPRITE);
      action.set(Tarantula.SA_ADDSPIDERLING);
    }

    // Die?
    if (rand.nextInt() % 250 == 0) {
      action.set(Sprite.SA_KILL);
      action.set(Sprite.SA_ADDSPRITE);
      action.set(Tarantula.SA_ADDSPIDERCIDE);
    }

    return action;
  }
```

The update method first handles giving the tarantula its ability to roam by randomly altering the direction. The superclass update method is then called so that all the default handling can take place. The update method then randomly decides whether a new Spiderling object should be created. If so, the SA_ADDSPRITE and SA_ADDSPIDERLING flags are set. Similarly, update randomly decides whether a Spidercide object should be created. If so, the SA_KILL, SA_ADDSPRITE, and SA_ADDSPIDERCIDE flags are set. The SA_KILL flag takes care of killing the Tarantula object itself, while the other two cause the new Spidercide object to be created.

The last method in Tarantula is addSprite, which handles creating Spiderling and Spidercide objects that are to be added to the sprite list:

```
protected Sprite addSprite(BitSet action) {
  // Add spiderling?
  if (action.get(Tarantula.SA_ADDSPIDERLING))
```

```
      return new Spiderling(component, new Point(position.x,
        position.y));

  // Add spidercide?
  else if (action.get(Tarantula.SA_ADDSPIDERCIDE))
    return new Spidercide(component, new Point(position.x,
      position.y));

  return null;
}
```

The addSprite method checks the sprite action flags and creates a new sprite, if necessary. addSprite then makes sure to return the newly created sprite so that it can be added to the sprite list.

Last but not least is the Spidercide class, which models a dying tarantula with a simple frame animation. The Spidercide class is very similar to Spiderling, because they both act effectively as temporary animations. Listing 7.2 contains the source code for the Spidercide class.

Listing 7.2. The Spidercide class.

```
public class Spidercide extends Sprite {
  protected static Image[] image = new Image[4];

  public Spidercide(Component comp, Point pos) {
    super(comp, image, 0, 1, 20, pos, new Point(0, 0), 30,
      Sprite.BA_DIE);
  }

  public static void initResources(Applet app, MediaTracker tracker,
    int id) {
    for (int i = 0; i < 4; i++) {
      image[i] = app.getImage(app.getCodeBase(), "Res/Spcide" +
        i + ".gif");
      tracker.addImage(image[i], id);
    }
  }

  public BitSet update() {
    BitSet action = new BitSet();

    // Die?
    if (frame >= 3) {
      action.set(Sprite.SA_KILL);
      return action;
    }

    // Increment the frame
    incFrame();

    return action;
  }
}
```

7

You can undoubtedly see a lot of similarities between Spidercide and Spiderling. As a matter of fact, the only significant difference between the two is that the Spidercide class doesn't add new sprites. Of course, it also provides its own unique frame images. Otherwise, you've seen all this code before in the Spiderling class, so I won't go over it again.

There is actually one other sprite-related class in Sim Tarantula that you need to learn about before moving on to the applet class. I'm referring to the TarantulaVector class, which is derived from SpriteVector and provides features specific to the Sim Tarantula sprite classes. Listing 7.3 contains the source code for TarantulaVector.

Listing 7.3. The TarantulaVector class.

```
public class TarantulaVector extends SpriteVector {
  public TarantulaVector(Background back) {
    super(back);
  }

  public int add(Sprite s) {
    // Only allow up to 10 sprites at once
    if (size() <= 10)
      return super.add(s);
    return -1;
  }

  protected boolean collision(int i, int iHit) {
    // Do nothing!
    return false;
  }
}
```

The TarantulaVector class probably has a lot less code than you might have guessed, because the majority of the derived functionality in Sim Tarantula is carried out in the three sprite classes you just covered. You really only need to have the TarantulaVector class for two reasons: limiting the maximum number of sprites and eliminating collision actions.

Limiting the number of sprites that can be added to the sprite list is necessary because the performance of the applet starts dragging if you get too many tarantulas running around. Also, it becomes very difficult to see what is happening if too many sprites are on the screen at one time. The solution is an overridden version of the add method, which simply checks to see how many sprites are currently in the list and only adds new sprites if it is under the limit.

Getting rid of collision actions isn't absolutely necessary, but it helps make the animation look a little more realistic. You might recall that the default collision method in Sprite causes two sprites that collide to bounce off each other. In the case of tarantulas, it actually looks better having them just walk over each other, so you simply supply a collision method that returns false and all is well.

At this point, you have all the support classes necessary to move on to the applet itself. You'll see that the applet has little responsibility in regard to the specifics of Sim Tarantula, because the derived sprite classes basically take care of themselves. This is a direct benefit of using an object-oriented design approach.

The SimTarantula Class

The SimTarantula class models the applet itself and takes care of all the dirty work related to setting up the sprite classes. Because the overhead of managing the sprite classes is very similar, much of the code in the SimTarantula class is the same as that in the Atoms class you developed yesterday. Knowing that, it makes more sense to focus on the code in SimTarantula that is new, such as the init method:

```
public void init() {
  // Load and track the images
  tracker = new MediaTracker(this);
  back = getImage(getCodeBase(), "Res/Back.gif");
  tracker.addImage(back, 0);
  Tarantula.initResources(this, tracker, 0);
  Spiderling.initResources(this, tracker, 0);
  Spidercide.initResources(this, tracker, 0);
}
```

The init method takes care of initializing all the resources for the different sprites. This is done by calling the static initResource method for each. A MediaTracker class is passed in so that the image resources can be tracked.

The run method is the workhorse for SimTarantula and is somewhat similar to the run method implemented in the Atoms class. Listing 7.4 contains the source code for the run method in SimTarantula.

Listing 7.4. The SimTarantula class's run method.

```
public void run() {
  try {
    tracker.waitForID(0);
  }
  catch (InterruptedException e) {
    return;
  }

  // Create and add some spiderlings
  tv = new TarantulaVector(new ImageBackground(this, back));
  for (int i = 0; i < 5; i++) {
    Point pos = tv.getEmptyPosition(new Dimension(
      Spiderling.image[0].getWidth(this),
      Spiderling.image[0].getHeight(this)));
```

continues

Listing 7.4. continued

```
      tv.add(new Spiderling(this, pos));
  }

  // Update everything
  long t = System.currentTimeMillis();
  while (Thread.currentThread() == animate) {
    tv.update();
    repaint();
    try {
      t += delay;
      Thread.sleep(Math.max(0, t - System.currentTimeMillis()));
    }
    catch (InterruptedException e) {
      break;
    }
  }
}
```

The run method creates the TarantulaVector object and passes an ImageBackground object into its constructor. This gives Sim Tarantula a desert background image and makes the animation a lot more realistic. Five Spiderling objects are then created and added to the tarantula vector. This is all it takes to get the simulation underway.

NOTE

If you recall, the TarantulaVector class takes a Background object as its only constructor parameter. However, in SimTarantula the TarantulaVector object is constructed using an object of type ImageBackground. This is a very neat usage of the object-oriented design of the sprite and background classes. You can use a completely different type of background simply by passing a different type of Background derived object into the TarantulaVector constructor.

The rest of the SimTarantula class is basically the same as Atoms, with the exception of different text in the applet title that is displayed while the images are loading. With that, you have a complete tarantula simulator applet with lots of cool derived sprite objects that interact with each other.

Summary

Although you didn't cover a lot of new territory in theory, you made huge strides in this lesson in regard to practical sprite usage. You started off by deriving a powerful new sprite class that gives sprites a sense of direction. You followed up on this by designing a simple tarantula simulator and putting it together piece by piece. Although the tarantula simulator isn't technically a game, it is about as close as you can get in terms of deriving new sprites that interact with each other. With this knowledge, you are empowered to create sophisticated applets with more complex sprites that can work together to do more than just give the illusion of movement.

You might be thinking at this point that it's time to jump into writing a complete Java game. Although you are technically almost ready, the next lesson changes the pace a little by introducing you to handling user input in games. By learning how to handle user input, you'll clear a major hurdle on your way to writing full-blown Java games.

Q&A

Q Why derive a directional sprite?

A A directional sprite is a sprite with a more specific purpose. In object-oriented programming, any time you have an object that extends another object, you should derive from the original object and add the new functionality. In this case, the `DirectionalSprite` class inherits all the functionality of the original `Sprite` class, while adding its own specific features.

Q Can the `DirectionalSprite` class be used to model sprites with more than eight directions?

A Unfortunately, no. The `DirectionalSprite` class is specifically designed to support exactly eight directions. It could be redesigned to be more general, in which case you would probably need to change the constructor to accept a parameter specifying the number of directions.

Q Why do I have to use sprite actions to do something as simple as adding a new sprite to the sprite list?

A Because you are trying to add a sprite from within another sprite. Sprites have no concept of the sprite list, so they don't know how to add sprites. The sprite actions define a communication protocol between the sprites and the sprite list that enables sprites to indirectly manipulate the list.

Q Why are the spiderlings and spidercides implemented as sprites?

A Because they are frame animations that need to be able to interact with the tarantula sprites. More generally, they are separate conceptual objects that are well suited for the sprite model provided by the `Sprite` class. Remember that just because an object isn't moving and bouncing around doesn't mean that it isn't a good candidate for a sprite.

7

Workshop

The Workshop section provides questions and exercises to help you get a handle on the material you learned today. Try to answer the questions and at least briefly ponder the exercises before moving on to tomorrow's lesson. You'll find the answers to the questions in Appendix A, "Quiz Answers."

Quiz

1. How are directions modeled in the DirectionalSprite class?
2. How do the velocity multipliers in the DirectionalSprite class work?
3. How do the tarantulas determine when to give birth to new spiderlings?
4. How do the tarantulas determine when to die?
5. Why do you need to derive the TarantulaVector class, as opposed to just using the SpriteVector class?

Exercises

1. Modify DirectionalSprite so that it can be used to model sprites with any number of directions.
2. Modify Sim Tarantula to use the new DirectionalSprite class.
3. Think about how cool (and scared) I felt when I saw a real tarantula in the wild while riding my mountain bike.
4. Write a Food class to model food that the tarantulas can eat.
5. Modify the TarantulaVector class to detect collisions between the tarantulas and the food.
6. Modify the Tarantula class to extend the life of the tarantulas when they eat food.
7. Design your own graphics for the sprites and background to create a different type of simulation. SimSasquatch maybe?

In Review

You covered a great deal of material this week! You went from learning about the fundamentals of Internet gaming to writing your own animated spider simulator in Java. Let's take a look at exactly what you learned so that you can prepare for next week's lesson.

Day 1

On your first day as an aspiring Java game programmer, you learned about the current status of games on the Internet. You saw some neat Web sites for trying out Internet games, but more importantly, you saw how great the appeal is for Internet games. Hopefully, you also saw how great the opportunity is for game designers and programmers to move games to the Internet.

1

2

3

4

5

6

7

Day 2

On Day 2, you learned about Java and how its advanced features impact game programming. Although Java is still in its infancy in many ways, it is very clear that the groundwork already exists for creating compelling Internet games. You learned that the Java language and runtime system are ideally suited for the needs of the next generation of globally networked games.

Day 3

It's hard to talk about Java without mentioning object-oriented programming. Day 3 presented a discussion of object-oriented programming concepts and how they are implemented in the Java language. This discussion of OOP wasn't meant as a rehash of standard Java knowledge; rather, it was presented to serve as the conceptual backbone for much of the code design throughout the book. This lesson provides the background on OOP techniques that are a necessity in Java game development.

Day 4

Day 4's lesson focused on graphics and how they are used in games. You learned about graphical images and the formats supported by Java. You also learned about a variety of graphics tools and utilities, as well as how to create, edit, and find graphics for games on the Web.

Day 5

Day 5 marked your first foray into Java game programming. Although you didn't actually create a game, you started looking at code and getting more technical with some of the aspects of Java that are important for games. You learned how to work with Java graphics primitives and graphical images in the GIF image format. You also learned about the Media Tracker and how it is used to track images being transferred across an Internet connection.

Day 6

Day 6's lesson presented the most crucial Java game programming information for the entire book—sprite animation. At the heart of most of the games throughout the book lies the sprite animation engine, which you developed entirely in this lesson. You began by learning some background on what animation is, along with the various types of animation and how they are used. You then implemented a set of Java sprite animation classes, along with a test applet called Atoms.

Day 7

What better way to finish off your first week of Java game programming than with an animated spider simulator? Day 7 presented you with the development of a complete applet, Sim Tarantula, showing off more advanced uses of the sprite animation classes. Sim Tarantula is about as close as you can get to writing a complete game without actually doing so. After this lesson, you are definitely ready to move on to writing some real games. Don't worry, because next week's lesson wastes little time getting you ready for a full-featured game!

WEEK

2

At a Glance

If you thought you learned a lot last week, buckle up because this week you learn a great deal more about Java game programming, including the development of two complete sample games. You begin with a conceptual look at user input and its role in gaming, followed by the Java specifics of handling user input. You then move on to developing your first complete Java game—Traveling Gecko. You follow this game by learning the basics of sound and the Java support for sound. With sound fresh on your mind, you develop your second complete game—Scorpion Roundup. You finish the week by taking a look at some techniques for debugging Java games.

You cover the following topics this week:

- ☐ User Input in Games
- ☐ Handling User Input with Java

- [ ] Traveling Gecko: Blistering Desert Fun
- [ ] The Basics of Sound
- [ ] Playing Sound with Java
- [ ] Scorpion Roundup: Action By Moonlight
- [ ] Squishing Bugs in Java Games

Day 8

User Input in Games

Just in case you had a hard weekend, you begin this week with a pretty easy lesson. Today you learn about user input in games, including the input devices supported by Java and how they are used in gaming scenarios. You'll be spared the details of how to actually communicate with input devices in Java until tomorrow's lesson. Nevertheless, today's lesson covers some important issues in regard to game design from a user input perspective.

Today's lesson serves as a good primer for tomorrow, when you learn about the specific Java programming techniques necessary for handling user input in games. For today, though, just relax and enjoy a break from the source code!

The following topics are covered in today's lesson:

☐ Gaming and user input
☐ User input devices

Gaming and User Input

NEW TERM *User input* is the means by which the user interacts with a game.

Considering the fact that user input encompasses the entire communications between a player and a game, you would think that designing an intuitive, efficient interface for user input would be at the top of the list of key game design elements. However, that isn't always the case. With all the hype these days surrounding real-time texture-mapped 3D graphics engines and positional 3D audio in games, effective user input support is often overlooked. In fact, user input is perhaps the most overlooked aspect of game design, which is truly a tragedy. It's a tragedy because user input support in a game directly impacts the playability of the game; and when the user input isn't effective, the play suffers.

You see, I'm from the old school of game players, and I still remember paying homage to the gods of gaming with my hard earned allowance in arcades, well before there was an option of playing anything other than Pong at home. In return for my quarter offerings, the game gods usually provided me with incredibly fun games that usually had to survive on their playability alone. Because the hardware at that time simply couldn't provide a very high level of graphic and sound intensity, the game developers were forced to make up for it with game play. Of course, they didn't consider their focus on playability as making up for anything; with the limited graphics and sound capabilities at the time, they didn't have an option.

Let me give you a quick example of what I'm talking about in regard to playability and user input. One of my all-time favorite games is Ring King, which is a boxing game for the Nintendo Entertainment System (NES). Ring King is definitely considered "old" by current gaming standards—possibly even ancient. Compared to current games, it has weak graphics, animation, and sound. However, I still play the game simply because it plays so well. And that playability is largely based on how the game handles user input; it allows for very subtle timing when you punch and dodge, which goes a long way in a boxing game! Since then, I've tried to find a modern replacement for Ring King, but I've had no luck. When I get beyond the fancy graphics and sound, I start missing the responsiveness of the controls in my old favorite. I'm still looking, though.

Lest you think I'm being overly critical of current games, plenty of recent games have incredible user input support, along with awesome graphics and sound. However, an equal number of recent games have killer graphics and sound, but little substance when it comes to playability and user input. These types of games might be visually stunning and fun to listen to, but they rarely have any lasting appeal beyond the initial "Wow!"

Now, let me step down from the soap box and get to the real point, which is that you should carefully plan the user input for your games just like you carefully plan the graphics, sound, and game logic. This doesn't mean only deciding between supporting a keyboard or a mouse for the user interface. It means putting some real thought into making the user interface as

8

8

intuitive as possible. You want the controls for the game to feel as natural as possible to the player.

User Input Devices

NEW TERM *Input devices* are the physical hardware, such as mice and keyboards, that allow a user to interact with a game.

Input devices all perform the same function: converting information provided by the user into a form understandable by the computer. Input devices form the link between the user and your game. Even though you can't directly control the input device hardware, you can certainly control how it is interpreted in your game.

Although some really neat input devices are available for PCs and Macintoshes, such as flightsticks and digital joysticks, you're working with Java, so you have to think in terms of supporting multiple platforms and therefore a fairly limited amount of input devices. As a matter of fact, the current set of input devices supported by Java consists of two devices— the keyboard and the mouse.

NOTE Trackballs have also grown in popularity as input devices recently. Trackballs are functionally very similar to mice and are often treated just like mice from a software perspective. Fortunately, Java doesn't discern between trackballs and mice, so the mouse support in Java indirectly supports trackballs as well.

It might sound limiting to not be able to support joysticks in Java, but it is simply a fact of life that joysticks aren't considered a "standard" input device by the computer community at large. Arguably, it would be nice to be able to support joysticks as an optional input device, but you'll simply have to hope for the support in a future release of Java. Even without joystick support, however, creative user input strategies can still be implemented. Personally, I like using either the keyboard or mouse for most games, rather than a joystick. But I'm kind of strange in that respect!

NOTE Sun has announced plans for extensions to the Java language that will include broader multimedia support. It's not clear whether joysticks and other game-oriented input devices will be supported in these extensions, but there is no reason that they couldn't be supported. We'll just have to wait and see.

The Keyboard

The keyboard has been the computer input device of choice since its inception. Although mice, joysticks, flightsticks, and many other user input devices have brought extended input capabilities for the game player, none is as established as the keyboard. At the bare minimum, you can always count on a game player having a keyboard.

Usage

The keyboard is a surprisingly useful input device for a wide range of games. The sheer amount of keys alone gives the keyboard appeal for games that require a wide variety of user input. Even more useful in the keyboard is the natural feel of pressing keys for games requiring quick firing and movement. This usefulness is evident in the amount of arcade games that still use buttons, even when powerful digital joysticks are readily available. Keys (or buttons) simply are easier to use in many games, including those with many input combinations.

When assessing the potential use of the keyboard in a game, try to think in terms of the most intuitive user interface possible. For example, any game involving the player moving an object around would benefit from using the arrow keys. A good example is DOOM, which makes creative use of a keyboard-specific feature that greatly enhances the playability of the game. The left and right arrow keys, when used alone, rotate the player left and right in the game world. However, when the Shift key is held down, the same left and right arrow keys cause the player to *strafe*, meaning that the player moves sideways without changing direction. This seemingly small enhancement to the keyboard controls goes a long way when playing the game.

When you're deciding on specific keys to use for keyboard controls in your game, consider the potential limitations on players using other platforms or hardware configurations. For example, I primarily use a Windows 95 PC equipped with a Microsoft Natural keyboard. If you aren't familiar with these keyboards, they are split down the middle for ergonomic reasons. If you don't use one of these keyboards, it might not occur to you that key combinations near the center of the keyboard will be separated a few inches for people like me. So, remember that if you use the G and H keys (or other middle keys) in your game, and it plays well for you, it might not work out so well for players with different keyboards.

This might sound kind of picky, but part of Java programming is trying to make everyone happy. Remember that Java games can be enjoyed by a wide range of computer users. You should make it a goal to do everything in your power to appease all of them. Think of it this way: How many times in the past have you had the opportunity to write one set of source code and have it work on such a wide range of computer systems? I have personally been involved with cross-platform multimedia development using C++, and it's not very fun. My advice is to embrace Java and its support for multiple platforms, and be open-minded when it comes to making decisions that affect users of other platforms!

8

8

Now, where were we? Keyboards! The most common keys used on the keyboard in games are the arrow keys. If you're writing an action game, you might also have keys for firing and selecting between weapons. When you're deciding on the keys to use, keep in mind things like the creative usage of the Shift key in DOOM. If you can limit the number of primary game control keys by making use of a secondary key such as Shift, you've made the game controls that much easier to use.

Rapid Fire

A common feature in action games is rapid fire, which involves firing multiple times while a key is being held down. I don't want to burden today's lesson with any source code, but I would like to briefly cover how rapid fire could be implemented in Java using standard keyboard support. As you will learn tomorrow, key presses in Java are handled as events. For now, don't worry too much about what an event is, except that it is something you can write code to respond to. The importance is that an event occurs for each key press, which means that you have the opportunity to respond to each key press (and key release).

You don't, however, have the opportunity to respond to keys being held down, which means that there is no direct way to implement rapid fire. Alas, there is a fairly painless work-around! The solution is to set a boolean member variable when a key is pressed, and then fire the bullets in an event loop based on this boolean variable being true. You receive a key release event when the user lets go of the key, in which case you simply set the boolean variable back to false. You control the speed of the rapid fire by altering the speed of the event loop or by using a separate delay counter.

The Mouse

Although the keyboard is firmly in place as the most necessary of user input devices, the graphical nature of the Web establishes the mouse, or a similar pointing device, as a standard input device as well. The mouse, however, doesn't share the wide range of input applications to games that the keyboard has. This stems from its primary usage as a point-and-click device; if you haven't noticed, lots of games don't follow the point-and-click paradigm.

Usage

In regard to gaming, the usefulness of the mouse is dependent totally on the type of game and, therefore, the type of user interaction dictated by the game. However, as quickly as some people write off the mouse as being a useless interface in some games, others praise the fine control it provides. A good example is DOOM. Personally, I think the keyboard is much more responsive than the mouse and the keyboard enables me to get around faster and with more control. But I have friends who feel lost playing the game without a mouse.

Clearly, this is a situation in which the game designers saw a way to provide support for both the keyboard and mouse. With the exception of the most extreme cases, this should be your goal as well. Different game players like different things, and the safest solution is to hedge your bets and support all input devices whenever possible. By following this simple rule, you can develop games that can be appreciated and enjoyed by a broader group of game players.

Interpreting Movement

Similar to the keyboard, Java support for the mouse is event-driven. You'll learn more about the details of mouse events tomorrow, but right now I want to cover the different interpretations of mouse movement. The standard Java mouse event handlers provide you with the current position of the mouse whenever the mouse is moved. This position is referred to as the absolute position of the mouse.

NEW TERM *Absolute position* is the specific on-screen location of the mouse.

Figure 8.1 shows an example of absolute mouse position.

Figure 8.1.

Absolute mouse position.

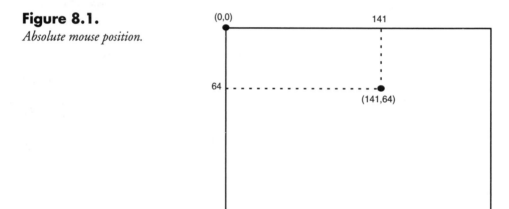

The other type of position that is important when examining mouse movement is the relative position of the mouse.

NEW TERM *Relative position* is the position of the mouse relative to its prior position.

Relative mouse position is more useful in games because you are usually concerned with whether the user moved the mouse left or right, instead of whether the mouse is at position (34, 272), for example. Figure 8.2 shows an example of relative mouse position.

Figure 8.2.

Relative mouse position.

8

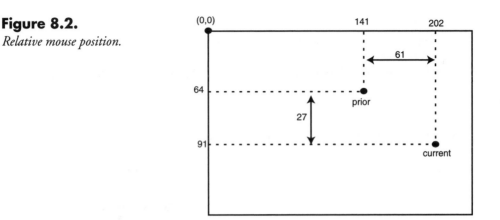

Even though Java provides no direct support for relative mouse movement, you can easily calculate a relative position by saving the prior position and comparing the two. In this scenario, you would maintain the prior mouse position in a member variable, such as a `Point` object. The mouse movement event handler calculates the relative mouse position as the differences between the X and Y values of the current mouse position and the prior mouse position stored in the member variable. These differences can then be used to determine how an object in a game is moved. For example, a positive X difference in relative position would correspond to an object being moved to the right.

Relative positioning is useful in a wide variety of games—basically, any game in which you control something by specifying a change in movement rather than an absolute location to move to. A good example is a flight simulator, in which you control small changes in the direction and altitude of the plane, rather than modifying its exact position in the sky. An example of a game that would work better with absolute mouse positioning is a Hogan's Alley type game, in which the mouse's movement maps directly to the movement of a gun sight used to shoot bad guys.

Summary

Today you learned about user input in games, including some useful tips and problems to watch out for when designing the user input support in your own games. You also learned about the two user input devices supported by Java, the keyboard and mouse, along with some suggestions about how to use them. You learned how rapid fire can be implemented using Java keyboard support, and you finished up with the two fundamental types of mouse positioning and how they are used in games.

Although somewhat brief, today's lesson covered some important issues when it comes to making determinations about user input in games. The goal of today's lesson is mainly to encourage you to put some thought into how you design the user input support in your games. Tomorrow you get to put these design ideas to work by learning exactly how to handle user input in Java.

Q&A

Q Will Java ever support more input devices, such as joysticks?

A It's hard to say for sure, but Sun has promised more extensive multimedia support in a future release of Java. Because joysticks are generally considered multimedia input devices, support for them might very well appear in a future release.

Q Are there any games that wouldn't require keyboard support?

A Sure. Any game that requires extensive point-and-click style input, such as a card game, would probably be fine without any keyboard support. However, if you can figure out a way to add keyboard controls, by all means go for it.

Q Is it possible to mix keyboard and mouse controls?

A Of course! This actually hits on an interesting point not covered in today's lesson: Many games work great by combining mouse and keyboard controls. A good example is the strafing feature in DOOM, which also works with the mouse; it is activated by holding down the Shift key while moving the mouse left or right.

Workshop

The Workshop section provides questions and exercises to help you get a better feel for the material you learned today. Try to answer the questions and at least think about the exercises before moving on to tomorrow's lesson. You'll find the answers to the questions in Appendix A, "Quiz Answers."

Quiz

1. What are the two types of mouse movement?
2. If you had to choose between supporting the keyboard or the mouse, which would you choose?
3. How is interrupt 16h used to handle key presses?

Exercises

1. Play some commercial games and pay attention to what input devices are supported and how.

2. Find out the limitations of input devices on computer systems other than the type you have. For example, are some keys in different locations or missing altogether?

3. Clean the roller mechanism inside your mouse; you need the mouse in tip-top shape for the rest of this week's lessons!

8

Day 9

Handling User Input with Java

Now that you have an idea about the role that user input plays in games, you're ready to learn the specifics of how user input works in Java. This lesson is devoted to the handling of user input in Java, including the supported input devices and the methods used to trap input events. You also learn about the event-driven structure of Java event handling and how it applies to input events.

This lesson clearly establishes the fact that Java user input handling is both powerful and simple. A handful of methods is really all it takes to deal with user input in a Java game. You get to see this firsthand by building a Java applet with keyboard and mouse input support. Let's get started.

Event-Driven Programming

Before getting into the details of how user input is handled in Java, it's important that you understand how event-driven programming works. This is important because user input in Java is heavily based on the event-driven architecture that makes up the heart of Java. In Java, an *event* is defined quite literally as something that happens that you might want to know about. For example, when a Java component gains the input focus, an event occurs because it might be important for your applet to know about the focus change.

NEW TERM An *event* is something that happens that you might want to know about and possibly react to.

In the event-driven world of Java, the flow of your program follows events external to your applet, as opposed to following an internally linear program flow. This is an important point because it means that a Java applet is in a constant state of responding to events. The most visible events are things such as mouse clicks and key presses, which are known as *input events*. You provide methods that respond to these events, which are called *event handlers*.

NEW TERM An *input event* is an event generated by user manipulation of an input device such as the mouse or keyboard.

NEW TERM *Event handlers* are special methods that are used to respond or react to events.

Because of the inherent graphical nature of Java applets, it will eventually become obvious to you why the event-driven programming model is not only more convenient, but downright necessary. With the potential of having multiple applets on a single Web page, along with on-the-fly system configuration changes and a multitude of other things going on, a procedural programming model would be much more difficult to manage. The event-based model provides a more sound solution to the problems inherent in a system with a graphical interface, such as Java.

All events in Java are processed within the AWT windowing toolkit package, and they are tightly linked to AWT components. A component is basically a generic abstraction for a Java window. You might recall that Java applets are themselves a specific type of component, which means that they inherit the same event-processing features built into the Component superclass.

NEW TERM A *component* is a generic abstraction of a window in Java.

Java Input Events

As you just learned, user input in Java is handled through an event-driven architecture. When the user interacts with an input device, it results in an input event being dispatched to the component with the input focus. In most cases, this component is the applet window. An input event is a special type of event that notifies an applet that something has occurred on an input device. An example of an input event is a movement of the mouse.

Input events are crucial in Java games because they provide a means of handling user responses. Without being able to monitor user responses, Java games wouldn't be too exciting. User response handling is not only important for providing an interface to the user for playing a game; it also establishes much of the feel of a game. Simply altering the means by which you provide user response support can dramatically alter the play of a game. This is an important point, one that you'll deal with later in this lesson when you develop the Flying Saucer sample applet.

Java user event responses come in two varieties, which correspond to the input devices supported by Java. The two types of input events supported by release 1.0 of Java are as follows:

☐ Keyboard events
☐ Mouse events

Keyboard events are events generated by a key press on the keyboard. Any time the user presses a key, a keyboard event is generated that can be trapped and handled by the applet with the input focus. Actually, a key press generates two events: a key down event and a key up event. You'll learn more about these two types soon.

Mouse events are generated by mouse clicks and movements. Every mouse click and mouse movement generates a corresponding mouse input event. Like key presses, mouse clicks actually come as a series of events: a mouse click down event and a mouse click up event. A mouse event is also specifically targeted at mouse dragging. Mouse dragging occurs when the mouse is moved with the button down. Applets that want to respond to mouse clicks and movement simply have to process these events and take action accordingly. You learn more about processing mouse events a little later in this lesson.

NOTE

You might have noticed in the discussion of mouse events the mention of the mouse *button*, as opposed to the mouse *buttons*. This is intentional because Java only supports a single mouse button. This might seem limiting to users on some platforms, such as Windows, but keep in mind that Java is designed to support as many platforms as possible. Considering the fact that some platforms (such as Macintosh) have mice with a single button, it makes sense for Java to support only a single button.

AWT Event Handling

Before getting into the specific event handlers for keyboard and mouse events, let's look at how events are handled in a general sense in Java. The Java AWT provides the Event class for encapsulating all types of events that can occur within the system. The Event class models a generic event and has constants defined within it to represent specific events. The Event class is used primarily by the handleEvent method of Component. The handleEvent method is the default event handler for all events, and is defined as follows:

```
public boolean handleEvent(Event evt)
```

Notice that handleEvent takes an Event object as its only parameter. handleEvent uses this Event object to determine what type of event has occurred. It then calls a more specific event handler method to deal with the specific event. For example, if a key is pressed, the Event object's id member variable is set to KEY_PRESS, which is a constant defining the key press event. handleEvent checks the value of id and, upon finding it equal to KEY_PRESS, calls the keyDown handler method. Listing 9.1 shows the key press handling portion of the handleEvent method in the 1.0 release of Java.

Listing 9.1. The key press portion of the handleEvent method.

```
public boolean handleEvent(Event evt) {
  switch (evt.id) {
    ...
  case Event.KEY_PRESS:
    return keyDown(evt, evt.key);
    ...
  }
  return false;
}
```

The handling of other system events is very similar to that of the KEY_PRESS event. You could easily override handleEvent to provide custom routing of event handlers, but it is rarely necessary. Although you might not ever need to intervene with the default event handling provided by handleEvent, it is nevertheless important to understand how it works.

Keyboard Events

Java keyboard events are generated when the user presses or releases a key. Two standard keyboard event handler methods are supported by the Component class: keyDown and keyUp. These two methods are defined as follows:

```
public boolean keyDown(Event evt, int key)
public boolean keyUp(Event evt, int key)
```

The keyDown method is called in response to the user pressing a key, and the keyUp method is called in response to the user releasing a key. Both methods are passed an Event object and an integer key value parameter. The key value parameter, key, specifies which key was pressed or released. The Event object parameter contains extra information relating to the keyboard event, such as whether the Shift key was held down when the key was pressed.

The Event object contains constants representing the different keys that can be specified in the key parameter. Table 9.1 shows a list of the more useful key constants.

Table 9.1. Useful key constants for games.

Constant	Key
UP	Up arrow
DOWN	Down arrow
LEFT	Left arrow
RIGHT	Right arrow
HOME	Home
END	End
PGUP	Page Up
PGDN	Page Down

To check whether the key pressed or released is one of these keys, you override keyDown or keyUp and compare the value of key to one of the constants. Listing 9.2 contains an example of overriding keyDown to check for the user pressing one of the arrow keys.

Listing 9.2. Handling arrow key presses in the keyDown method.

```
public boolean keyDown(Event evt, int key) {
  switch (key) {
  case Event.LEFT:
    // left arrow key pressed
    break;
  case Event.RIGHT:
    // right arrow key pressed
    break;
  case Event.UP:
    // up arrow key pressed
    break;
  case Event.DOWN:
    // down arrow key pressed
    break;
  }
  return true;
}
```

This `keyDown` method shows that handling different key presses is as easy as providing a `switch` statement with `case` clauses for each key. Although the example here used the `keyDown` method for handling key presses, the `keyUp` method works in the same fashion.

If you need more details about the key that was pressed or released, you can use the `Event` object passed into the `keyDown` and `keyUp` methods. The typical usage of the `Event` object in regard to key processing is to check for modifier keys. Modifier keys are keys that can be pressed in conjunction with other input events, such as the Shift and Control keys. The following are the three methods in `Event` used to check the status of modifier keys:

```
public boolean shiftDown()
public boolean controlDown()
public boolean metaDown()
```

All of these methods return boolean values specifying whether or not the key in question is being held down. Checking the status of the modifier keys is necessary sometimes in applets that make heavy use of the mouse. For example, you might have a drawing applet that performs a different function if the Shift key is held down and the mouse is moved. You probably won't need the modifier keys in Java games, but it is still important to know how they work. Who knows, you might think of an interesting way to incorporate them into a game.

Mouse Events

Mouse events occur when the user moves the mouse or clicks the mouse button. A handful of methods exist for handling mouse events, such as the following methods:

```
public boolean mouseUp(Event evt, int x, int y)
public boolean mouseDown(Event evt, int x, int y)
public boolean mouseMove(Event evt, int x, int y)
public boolean mouseDrag(Event evt, int x, int y)
public boolean mouseEnter(Event evt, int x, int y)
public boolean mouseExit(Event evt, int x, int y)
```

All of these methods are passed an `Event` object and two integer parameters representing the X and Y position of the mouse pointer. The `mouseUp` and `mouseDown` methods are called when the user presses and releases the mouse button. The `mouseMove` method is called when the mouse is moved. The `mouseDrag` method is very similar to the `mouseMove` method—the only difference being that `mouseDrag` is called when the mouse is moved with the button held down. The `mouseEnter` and `mouseExit` methods are used to track when the mouse enters and exits the applet window.

You can use the `x` and `y` parameters passed into the mouse event handler methods to perform any processing based on the position of the mouse. The following code snippet contains an example of overriding the `mouseMove` method to output the mouse position to standard output:

9

```java
public boolean mouseMove(Event evt, int x, int y) {
  System.out.println("Mouse position = (" + x + ", " + y + ")");
  return true;
}
```

Similar to the keyboard event handlers, you can use the Event object passed in the mouse event handlers to find out additional information such as the status of modifier keys.

Sample Applet: Flying Saucer

Now that you have a good idea of how to process user input events in Java, let's take a look at a sample applet that uses this newfound knowledge. The Flying Saucer applet uses the sprite classes and event handler methods to implement a user-controllable flying saucer. Figure 9.1 shows what Flying Saucer looks like. The complete source code, executable, and images for the Flying Saucer applet are included on the accompanying CD-ROM.

Figure 9.1.

The Flying Saucer sample applet.

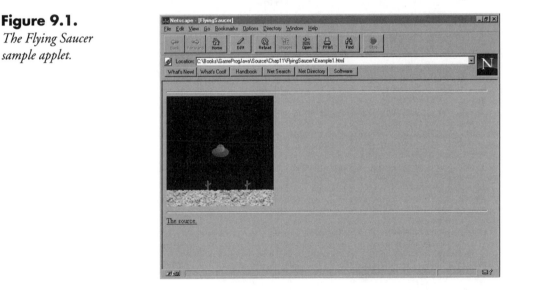

The FlyingSaucer class models the applet itself and takes care of all the details related to setting up the sprite classes and handling the user input events. Similar to the other applet classes you've developed that use sprites, FlyingSaucer contains familiar support for the sprite classes. In fact, the only significantly new code in the FlyingSaucer class is the code for handling user input.

Before getting into the specifics of the user input handlers, however, take a look at two of the member variables defined in the FlyingSaucer class:

```
private Sprite theSaucer;
private int    lastKey;
```

The theSaucer member variable is a Sprite object that holds the flying saucer sprite. It is necessary to keep up with this sprite outside of the sprite list because you need to be able to alter its position and velocity based on user input events. The lastKey member variable is used to hold the value of the last key pressed. This variable is used to provide finer control over the flying saucer, as you'll see later in this lesson.

The keyDown method handles all the details of supporting keyboard control of the saucer. Listing 9.3 shows the source code for the keyDown method.

Listing 9.3. The FlyingSaucer class's keyDown method.

```
public boolean keyDown(Event evt, int key) {
  // Change the saucer velocity based on the key pressed
  Point vel = theSaucer.getVelocity();
  switch (key) {
  case Event.LEFT:
    vel.x = -4;
    if (lastKey == Event.LEFT)
      vel.y = 0;
    break;
  case Event.RIGHT:
    vel.x = 4;
    if (lastKey == Event.RIGHT)
      vel.y = 0;
    break;
  case Event.UP:
    vel.y = -4;
    if (lastKey == Event.UP)
      vel.x = 0;
    break;
  case Event.DOWN:
    vel.y = 4;
    if (lastKey == Event.DOWN)
      vel.x = 0;
    break;
  default:
    vel.x = vel.y = 0;
  }
  theSaucer.setVelocity(vel);
  lastKey = key;
  return true;
}
```

The keyDown method first gets the current velocity of the saucer and checks to see which key was pressed. It then alters the saucer's velocity according to the directional arrow key pressed. The lastKey member variable is then checked to see whether this is a repeat key press. If so, the tangential velocity component is cleared. For example, if the left arrow key is held down, the Y velocity component is cleared. This has the result of causing the saucer to change from moving in a diagonal direction to moving in a pure X or Y direction if you hold a key down, which gives the keyboard controls a better feel. Try it out for yourself.

The `mouseDown` and `mouseDrag` methods are used to handle mouse input events and position the saucer at an absolute location:

```
public boolean mouseDown(Event evt, int x, int y) {
  theSaucer.setPosition(new Point(x - (saucerSize.width / 2),
    y - (saucerSize.height / 2)));
  return true;
}

public boolean mouseDrag(Event evt, int x, int y) {
  theSaucer.setPosition(new Point(x - (saucerSize.width / 2),
    y - (saucerSize.height / 2)));
  return true;
}
```

Both of these methods simply reposition the saucer at a location centered on the current mouse position, which enables you to click and drag the saucer around with the mouse. This might not be an ideal usage of the mouse in most game scenarios, but it shows how the mouse can be used to control a sprite, which can be useful.

Note

You might be thinking that the duplicate code in the `mouseDown` and `mouseDrag` methods goes against good programming practice. You're right! The truth is that I didn't want to confuse things by having these methods call a third method, which is typically the way you avoid duplicate code in a situation like this. You might also think that `mouseDrag` could just call `mouseDown` and simply pass its parameters along. Although this technique would work in this particular case, it's generally not a good idea to directly call event handler methods yourself, primarily because the `Event` parameter means different things to different event handlers.

Summary

In this lesson, you learned about Java events and the event-driven architecture necessary to support them. More specifically, you learned about Java input events, including the input devices capable of generating them and how they are handled by the Java AWT library.

You saw examples of using the input event handler methods to capture and respond to keyboard and mouse events. You then finished up the lesson with a sample applet using the sprite classes that implements a user-controllable flying saucer supporting both keyboard and mouse input. This sample applet brought you yet another step closer to implementing a complete game. As a matter of fact, you're now ready to embark on your first complete Java game; the next lesson focuses on developing your first full-blown Java game, Traveling Gecko.

Q&A

Q What's the big deal with event-driven programming?

A Event-driven programming provides a powerful methodology for handling the complexities inherent in a graphical system. By modeling every action in the system as an event with a corresponding handler, the complexities are broken down into individually serviceable items.

Q What are Java input events?

A They are any events generated by the user manipulating an input device such as the mouse or keyboard.

Q What is the purpose of the `handleEvent` method?

A The `handleEvent` method acts as a router method for all events. All events must pass through `handleEvent`, which in turn calls the appropriate event handler method.

Q If the user has more than one mouse button, can I detect when the user presses one of the extra buttons?

A No, Java only supports single-button mice. This is to eliminate the creation of extra button features that wouldn't be available to users (such as Macintosh users) with one button on their mice.

Workshop

The Workshop section provides questions and exercises to help strengthen your grasp on the material you learned today. Try to answer the questions and at least put some thought into the exercises before moving on to tomorrow's lesson. You'll find the answers to the questions in Appendix A, "Quiz Answers."

Quiz

1. What is an event?
2. How do you determine whether the user is holding down the Shift key while moving the mouse?

3. How can you detect when the mouse has been moved outside the applet window?

4. How is the saucer controlled in the Flying Saucer applet?

Exercises

1. Think of some things that can take place in a Java applet that might generate events.

2. Think of some popular games and how the user input is handled for each. Do they support the mouse? If so, how?

3. Add a hyperspace feature to the Flying Saucer applet. A hyperspace feature would result in the saucer moving to a random location if a certain key, such as the spacebar, is pressed.

4. Change the saucer in the Flying Saucer applet to a frame-animated sprite.

9

Day 10

Traveling Gecko: Blistering Desert Fun

On Day 9, you learned all about handling user input in Java. In this lesson, you combine what you learned about user input with your knowledge of the sprite classes to create your first complete Java game, Traveling Gecko. In doing so, you learn and apply new techniques for extending the sprite classes.

Today's lesson presents and solves the major technical issues involved in putting together a complete Java game. By developing a complete game, your core Java game programming skills come full circle. You'll see that putting together a complete game isn't really that much more complex than the sample sprite applets you've already worked on. After you finish this lesson, you'll have the fundamental Java game programming constructs firmly in place so that you can move on to more advanced topics.

Designing Traveling Gecko

As you learned back in Day 7, "Sim Tarantula: Creepy Crawly Sprites," it's very important to think through a game design as thoroughly as possible before writing any code. So, before you even consider editing a Java source file, be sure to think about the game design in both general and specific terms. With that in mind, let's break the Traveling Gecko sample game into its logical components.

The Traveling Gecko game is modeled roughly on the classic Atari 2600 Frogger game. In the original Frogger game, you guide a frog through traffic and then across a river using floating logs to get across. Traveling Gecko takes a similar approach, in that the goal is to maneuver an animal from one place to another while dodging dangers along the way. However, the setting for Traveling Gecko is the desert southwest, and your character is a gecko on the move. Your journeying little gecko only wants to get across a particularly small stretch of desert, but he has to contend with a variety of predators to do so. The predators include Gila monsters, scorpions, rattlesnakes, and tarantulas.

Sprites

Based on the game description thus far, you probably already have in mind some sprites that the game will need. Let's go ahead and break the game down into sprites, because that's where most of the substance of the game is located. Obviously, the most important sprite is the gecko sprite itself, which needs to be able to move based on user input. The gecko sprite is the heart of the game and must be designed with care.

Because the gecko is capable of being killed by the predators, you'll also need an animation of the gecko dying—a geckocide sprite. If you recall, you used a similar approach (spidercide sprite) when developing the Sim Tarantula applet on Day 7. The geckocide sprite simply shows an animation of the gecko dying so that it doesn't just disappear when it dies.

Moving along, it's fairly obvious that you'll also need sprite objects for the predators. Although each one has basically the same functionality, let's go ahead and think of them as different sprite objects, because you might decide to add unique behavior to one of them later. You should have some special logic for handling a collision between the predators and the gecko, because this contact results in the gecko's death.

Before you finish itemizing the sprites, take a moment to think about the specifics surrounding the gecko's path across the desert. Taking an approach similar to Frogger's, the gecko must travel from the bottom of the screen to safety at the top. However, it seems too easy to simply have him go from the bottom of the screen to the top with no other obstacles than the predators. Frogger has specific locations at the top of the screen where the frog must go. Let's take a similar approach here. By placing large rocks at the top and bottom of the screen, you can provide openings at which the gecko can start and finish. This makes sense too, because the openings in the rocks make good hiding places for the gecko.

If you're now thinking that the rocks would make good additions to the sprite inventory for Traveling Gecko, then pat yourself on the back! If not, don't feel too bad; it might be because you think they could just be made part of the background. That's true, but there would be a big problem in detecting collisions between the gecko and the rocks. The rocks are there for a reason—to limit the gecko's movement. And the only way to limit the gecko's movement is to detect a collision between him and a rock and not let him move if he's colliding with a rock. Without making the rocks sprites, you would have to add a bunch of special case code to a derived SpriteVector class to see whether the gecko is colliding with them. Adding code to a derived SpriteVector class isn't the problem, though; the problem is duplicating the collision detection functionality you've already written.

NOTE

The discussion about the rock sprite brings up a good point in regard to game objects: Practically any graphical object in a game that can be interacted with or handled independently of the background should be implemented as a sprite. Remember that sprites are roughly analogous to cast members in a theatrical play. To carry things a bit further, you can extend the usage of sprites to also include the props used in a play. This is essentially the role rocks play in the Traveling Gecko game: props!

The rocks are the last sprites you'll need to write for the game. To summarize what you have thus far, Traveling Gecko requires sprites modeling the following objects:

- ☐ Gecko
- ☐ Geckocide
- ☐ Gila monster
- ☐ Scorpion
- ☐ Rattlesnake
- ☐ Tarantula
- ☐ Rock

The gecko sprite models the player and is controlled by the player's user input responses. The geckocide sprite is used to show a dying gecko and comes in the form of a simple frame animation. The Gila monster, scorpion, rattlesnake, and tarantula sprites model the predators who are trying to ruin the gecko's trip. Remember that there has to be some method of killing the gecko based on a collision with these predators. This is an issue you'll deal with later in this lesson, when you get into writing the Java code. Finally, the rock sprite models rocks that block the gecko's movement, thereby making it more difficult for him to get across the desert safely.

Game Play

Now that you have an idea of what sprite classes you need to write, let's take a look at the game itself and how it will play. First, it wouldn't be much fun if the game ended as soon as you were killed by a predator. So let's give the player four geckos (lives) to play with; the game isn't over until all four are killed.

Although it is certainly fulfilling to help out a gecko in need, it would also be nice to reward the player with some type of point system. Let's give the player 25 points each time the gecko makes it safely across the desert. Then the player's good will for saving a gecko's life is given a numeric value that can be viewed with pride!

Because every game ultimately ends when all four geckos are killed, you also need to provide the player with a way to start a new game. This is an ideal situation for a button; the player simply clicks the button to start a new game.

This finishes the game design for Traveling Gecko. You now have all the information you need to get into the specifics surrounding the applet and support classes. What are you waiting for?

Sample Applet: Traveling Gecko

The Traveling Gecko applet is your first complete Java game and makes the most of the indispensable sprite classes you've come to know so well. Figure 10.1 shows the Traveling Gecko applet in the middle of a heated game.

Traveling Gecko begins by creating the gecko, rocks, and predators. You then use the keyboard to control the gecko and attempt to guide him safely into the rock opening at the top right of the screen. The score is displayed in the upper left corner of the screen. Immediately to the right of the score is the number of remaining gecko lives, which are displayed graphically as tiny geckos.

The different predators all roam around the desert background at different speeds hoping to make a quick meal out of your trusting gecko. If one of them gets lucky, a geckocide object is created to show the dying gecko. The number of remaining lives is then decremented.

10

Figure 10.1.

The Traveling Gecko sample applet.

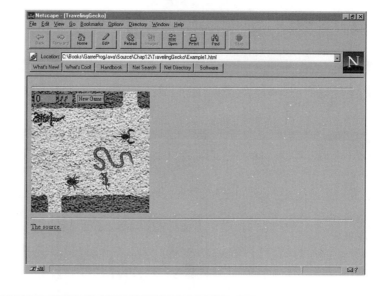

Watch out for those pesky scorpions; they're quite fast!

If you guide the gecko safely across, you receive 25 points and the chance to help him across again. I know, one would think that the gecko would be thankful for making it across once and not want to try again, but that's not the case! If you're able to help him across a few times, you'll notice that the predators start calling in reinforcements to make things more difficult.

If you manage to lose all four of your geckos to the predators, the game ends and you see a message indicating that the game is over. Figure 10.2 shows Traveling Gecko when a game has just ended.

At this point, all you have to do is click the New Game button with the mouse, and everything starts over. If you haven't checked it out yet, now might be a good time to grab the accompanying CD-ROM and try the game out for yourself. The complete source code, executable, and images for the Traveling Gecko game are included on the CD-ROM. If you just can't wait to find out all the gory details, then by all means skip the CD-ROM and read on!

The Sprite Classes

As you probably guessed, the heart of the Traveling Gecko applet is the extended sprite classes. The first of these classes is the Gecko class, which models the gecko that is controlled by the player. The Gecko class is derived straight from Sprite. You might think that it would make more sense to derive Gecko from DirectionalSprite (see Day 7), because a gecko clearly should face and move in different directions. This is logical thinking, but the gecko's movement is limited to up, down, left, and right. The DirectionalSprite class is geared more toward objects that can spin around and move in different directions, including diagonal directions.

Figure 10.2.

A Traveling Gecko game that has come to an end.

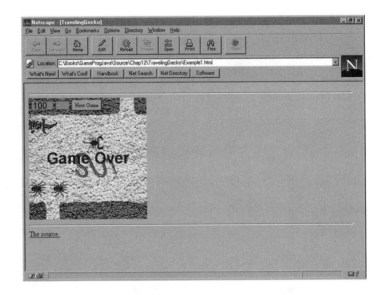

However, there is a drawback to not deriving the Gecko class from DirectionalSprite: The gecko can't face in the direction it is moving. That is why the gecko is always facing upward, regardless of its movement. This is a little unrealistic because most geckos probably don't sidestep, but it makes things easier to implement. This is one of those cases in which you sometimes have to make sacrifices in detail for the sake of making the code simpler.

The Gecko class contains the following custom sprite actions that are used to add the predators:

```
public static final int SA_ADDGILAMONSTER = 3,
                        SA_ADDSCORPION = 4,
                        SA_ADDRATTLER = 5,
                        SA_ADDTARANTULA = 6;
```

Looking at these sprite actions, it might seem a little strange to allow the gecko to add predators. However, you'll see in a moment that adding new predators is based on the gecko making it safely across the desert, which can only be detected from within the Gecko class.

The constructor for Gecko is pretty simple:

```
public Gecko(Component comp) {
  super(comp, image, 0, 1, 0, new Point(42, 232), new
    Point(0, 0), 20, Sprite.BA_STOP);
}
```

Notice in the constructor that the BA_STOP bounds action is specified, which keeps the gecko from being able to wrap around the sides of the game window.

The setCollision method is used to shrink the gecko's collision rectangle so that collision detection isn't quite so sensitive:

```
protected void setCollision() {
  collision = new Rectangle(position.x + 3, position.y + 3,
    position.width - 6, position.height - 6);
}
```

Shrinking the gecko's collision rectangle is important because having one of the legs of the gecko collide with a predator shouldn't be enough to get him into trouble. By shrinking the collision rectangle, you require more contact for the gecko to qualify as a free lunch.

The update method in Gecko does most of the work. Listing 10.1 contains the source code for the update method.

Listing 10.1. The Gecko class's update method.

```
public BitSet update() {
  BitSet action = super.update();

  // Toggle the frame and clear the velocity
  if (velocity.x != 0 || velocity.y != 0) {
    frame = 1 - frame;
    setVelocity(new Point(0, 0));
  }

  // Has he made it?
  if (position.y < 8) {
    // Update the score and reposition the gecko
    TravelingGecko.score += 25;
    position.x = 42;
    position.y = 232;

    // See if we should add another bad guy
    if (TravelingGecko.score % 100 == 0) {
      Random rand = new Random(System.currentTimeMillis());
      switch(rand.nextInt() % 4) {
      case 0:
        // Set flag to add a Gila monster
        action.set(Sprite.SA_ADDSPRITE);
        action.set(Gecko.SA_ADDGILAMONSTER);
        break;
      case 1:
        // Set flag to add a scorpion
        action.set(Sprite.SA_ADDSPRITE);
```

continues

Listing 10.1. continued

```
        action.set(Gecko.SA_ADDSCORPION);
        break;
    case 2:
      // Set flag to add a rattler
      action.set(Sprite.SA_ADDSPRITE);
      action.set(Gecko.SA_ADDRATTLER);
      break;
    case 3:
      // Set flag to add a tarantula
      action.set(Sprite.SA_ADDSPRITE);
      action.set(Gecko.SA_ADDTARANTULA);
      break;
    }
  }
}

return action;
}
```

The update method first calls the superclass update method to handle all the standard sprite updating. It then toggles the gecko's animation frame and clears the velocity. The animation frame is toggled because there are only two frames, 0 and 1. Because there are only two frames, you can just toggle them rather than increment the current frame. The velocity has to be cleared because of the way you're handling user input. When the user presses an arrow key to move the gecko, the gecko's velocity is set accordingly. But you only want the gecko to move once for each key press. The solution is to update the gecko, allowing his position to be altered based on the velocity, and then clear the velocity.

A check is then performed to see whether the gecko made it across the desert. Because the rocks block him from getting to the top of the screen in all places except the opening, you simply check his vertical position to see whether he made it. If so, the score is updated and he is repositioned back at the start. Notice that the score is referenced from the TravelingGecko class. It is declared as public static in TravelingGecko so that other objects can get to it without having access to a TravelingGecko object. Technically, this goes against standard object-oriented design practice, but the reality is that it would be very difficult to give access to the score variable using only access methods. You learn about the TravelingGecko class a little later in this section.

The update method then decides whether or not to add a new predator. This determination is based on the score: For every 100 points, a new predator is added. A predator is randomly chosen and the appropriate sprite action flags are set to trigger the creation.

The last method in Gecko is addSprite, which handles creating the predator sprite objects:

```
protected Sprite addSprite(BitSet action) {
  // Add new bad guys?
```

```
    if (action.get(Gecko.SA_ADDGILAMONSTER))
      return new GilaMonster(component);
    else if (action.get(Gecko.SA_ADDSCORPION))
      return new Scorpion(component);
    else if (action.get(Gecko.SA_ADDRATTLER))
      return new Rattler(component);
    else if (action.get(Gecko.SA_ADDTARANTULA))
      return new Tarantula(component);

    return null;
  }
```

The addSprite method checks the sprite action flags and creates the appropriate predator. addSprite then makes sure to return the newly created sprite so that it can be added to the sprite list.

Before getting to the predator classes, let's look at the Geckocide class. Listing 10.2 contains the complete source code for the Geckocide class.

Listing 10.2. The Geckocide class.

```
public class Geckocide extends Sprite {
  protected static Image[] image = new Image[4];

  public Geckocide(Component comp, Point pos) {
    super(comp, image, 0, 1, 5, pos, new Point(0, 0), 10,
      Sprite.BA_DIE);
  }

  public static void initResources(Applet app, MediaTracker tracker,
    int id) {
    for (int i = 0; i < 4; i++) {
      image[i] = app.getImage(app.getCodeBase(), "Res/Gekcide" +
        i + ".gif");
      tracker.addImage(image[i], id);
    }
  }

  public BitSet update() {
    BitSet action = new BitSet();

    // Die?
    if (frame >= 3) {
      action.set(Sprite.SA_KILL);
      return action;
    }

    // Increment the frame
    incFrame();

    return action;
  }
}
```

The Geckocide class is very similar to the Spidercide class developed in Day 7, except that it displays graphics for a dying gecko. It provides a simple frame-animated sprite that kills itself after one iteration. This functionality is implemented in the update method, which checks the frame member variable to see whether the animation is finished.

The predator classes (GilaMonster, Scorpion, Rattler, and Tarantula) are all very similar to each other and contain relatively little code. Listing 10.3 shows the source code for the GilaMonster class.

Listing 10.3. The GilaMonster class.

```java
public class GilaMonster extends Sprite {
  public static Image[] image;

  public GilaMonster(Component comp) {
    super(comp, image, 0, 1, 4, new Point(comp.size().width -
      image[0].getWidth(comp), 45), new Point(-1, 0), 30,
      Sprite.BA_WRAP);
  }

  public static void initResources(Applet app, MediaTracker
    tracker, int id) {
    image = new Image[2];
    for (int i = 0; i < 2; i++) {
      image[i] = app.getImage(app.getCodeBase(),
        "Res/GilaMon" + i + ".gif");
      tracker.addImage(image[i], id);
    }
  }

  protected void setCollision() {
    collision = new Rectangle(position.x + 3, position.y + 3,
      position.width - 6, position.height - 6);
  }
}
```

The GilaMonster class uses two images to show a simple animation of a Gila monster kicking its legs. The constructor specifies a fixed horizontal velocity that, when combined with the frame animation, gives the effect of the Gila monster walking. Admittedly, having only two frame animations creates some limitation in how effective the illusion of walking is in this case. But remember that you're trying to avoid using tons of graphics that take up precious time loading over the Internet.

The three other predator classes (Scorpion, Rattler, and Tarantula) are almost identical to GilaMonster, with the changes being the velocities, the images loaded in initResources, and the amount that the collision rectangle is shrunken. Based on the code for GilaMonster, you might be wondering why it's even implemented as a derived sprite class. It doesn't really add any new functionality; you could just as easily create a Gila monster using the Sprite class. The truth is that all the predator classes are created as more of a convenience than a necessity. Allowing the classes to manage their own image resources via initResources, as well as having self-contained constructors that don't take a bunch of parameters, improves organization.

This goes against typical object-oriented design because the classes don't technically add any new functionality. However, the clean packaging of the classes and their improved ease of use makes them justifiable in this case. You might think that I'm taking a lot of liberties by encouraging you to break the rules that are so crucial in object-oriented languages such as Java. That's not entirely true. The real skill in object-oriented programming is in knowing when to apply OOP techniques and when to leverage them against more simple solutions, as you've done here.

The Rock class is the last of the Sprite derived classes used in Traveling Gecko. Listing 10.4 contains the source code for the Rock class.

Listing 10.4. The Rock class.

```
public class Rock extends Sprite {
  public static Image[] image;

  public Rock(Component comp, int i) {
    super(comp, image, i, 0, 0, new Point((i % 2 == 0) ? 0 :
      comp.size().width - image[i].getWidth(comp), (i < 2) ?
      0 : comp.size().height - image[i].getHeight(comp)),
      new Point(0, 0), 40, Sprite.BA_STOP);
  }

  public static void initResources(Applet app, MediaTracker tracker,
    int id) {
    image = new Image[4];
    for (int i = 0; i < 4; i++) {
      image[i] = app.getImage(app.getCodeBase(),
        "Res/Rock" + i + ".gif");
      tracker.addImage(image[i], id);
    }
  }

  public BitSet update() {
    return (new BitSet());
  }
}
```

The Rock class is somewhat similar to the predator classes in that it doesn't add much functionality. However, you have a very useful reason for creating a Rock class, as opposed to just creating rocks as Sprite objects. That reason has to do with an optimization related to the update method. If you recall, the update method is called for every sprite in the sprite list to allow the animation frame and position to be updated. Rocks have no animation frames and the positions are fixed. Therefore, you can speed things up a little by overriding update with a "do nothing" version. Because speed is a crucial issue in games, especially Java games, seemingly small optimizations like this can add up in the end.

NOTE

The trick that is used to help improve speed in the Rock class's update method brings up a good point in regard to game programming: Don't be afraid to override unneeded methods with "do nothing" versions. Every little bit of execution overhead that you can eliminate will ultimately improve the performance of a game. If you see a way to cut a corner in a derived class simply by overriding a parent class method, go for it! Just remember to wait and look for these types of shortcuts after the code is already working.

The only other sprite-related class to deal with in regard to Traveling Gecko is the derived SpriteVector class, TGVector. You need the TGVector class to handle the collisions between the sprites. Listing 10.5 contains the source code for the TGVector class.

Listing 10.5. The TGVector class.

```
public class TGVector extends SpriteVector {
  private Component component;

  public TGVector(Background back, Component comp) {
    super(back);
    component = comp;
  }

  protected boolean collision(int i, int iHit) {
    Sprite s = (Sprite)elementAt(i);
    Sprite sHit = (Sprite)elementAt(iHit);
    if (sHit.getClass().getName().equals("Rock"))
      // Collided with rock, so stay put
      return true;
    else if (sHit.getClass().getName().equals("Geckocide"))
      // Collided with geckocide, so do nothing
      return false;
    else if (s.getClass().getName().equals("Gecko")) {
      // Kill or reposition it
      Point pos = new Point(s.getPosition().x, s.getPosition().y);
      if (--TravelingGecko.lives <= 0)
        removeElementAt(i--);
      else
        s.setPosition(new Point(42, 232));
```

10

```
      // Collided with bad guy, so add geckocide
      if (add(new Geckocide(component, pos)) <= i)
        i++;
    }
    return false;
  }
}
```

As you can see, the only overridden method in `TGVector` is `collision`, which is called when a collision occurs between two sprites. The sprite hit in the collision is first checked to see whether it is a `Rock` object. If so, `true` is returned, which causes the sprite that is doing the hitting to stay where it is and not use its updated position. This results in the gecko being stopped when he runs into a rock.

The sprite being hit is then checked to see whether it is a `Geckocide` object, in which case `collision` returns `false`. This results in allowing the sprite that is doing the hitting to continue on its course, and basically results in a null collision. The purpose of this code is to make sure that `Geckocide` objects don't interfere with any other objects; they are effectively ignored by the collision detection routine.

The real work begins when the hitting sprite is checked to see whether it is a `Gecko` object. If so, you know that the gecko has collided with a predator, so the number of lives is decremented. The `lives` variable is like `score` because it is a public static member of the `TravelingGecko` applet class. If `lives` is less than or equal to zero, the game is over and the `Gecko` object is removed from the sprite list. If `lives` is greater than zero, the gecko is repositioned back at the starting position. To the player, it appears as if a new gecko has been created, but you're really just moving the old one. Because a gecko has died in either case, a `Geckocide` object is created.

At this point, you've seen all the supporting sprite classes required of Traveling Gecko. The last step is to see what tasks the applet class itself is responsible for.

The `TravelingGecko` Class

The `TravelingGecko` class drives the applet and takes care of higher-level issues such as dealing with user input. Much of this class consists of animation overhead that you're already familiar with, so let's skip ahead to the more interesting aspects of `TravelingGecko`.

The `init` method adds a new twist by creating the New Game button. It also handles initializing all the resources for the different sprites. The code for the `init` method is shown in Listing 10.6.

Listing 10.6. The `TravelingGecko` **class's** `init` **method.**

```
public void init() {
  // Create the UI
  if (ngButton == null) {
    ngButton = new Button("New Game");
    add(ngButton);
  }

  // Load and track the images
  tracker = new MediaTracker(this);
  back = getImage(getCodeBase(), "Res/Back.gif");
  tracker.addImage(back, 0);
  smGecko = getImage(getCodeBase(), "Res/SmGecko.gif");
  tracker.addImage(smGecko, 0);
  Gecko.initResources(this, tracker, 0);
  Geckocide.initResources(this, tracker, 0);
  Rock.initResources(this, tracker, 0);
  GilaMonster.initResources(this, tracker, 0);
  Scorpion.initResources(this, tracker, 0);
  Rattler.initResources(this, tracker, 0);
  Tarantula.initResources(this, tracker, 0);
}
```

The update method is where a lot of interesting things take place in `TravelingGecko`. Listing 10.7 shows the source code for the update method.

Listing 10.7. The `TravelingGecko` **class's** `update` **method.**

```
public void update(Graphics g) {
  // Create the offscreen graphics context
  if (offGrfx == null) {
    offImage = createImage(size().width, size().height);
    offGrfx = offImage.getGraphics();
    scoreMetrics = offGrfx.getFontMetrics(scoreFont);
  }

  // Draw the sprites
  tgv.draw(offGrfx);

  // Draw the score
  offGrfx.setFont(scoreFont);
  offGrfx.drawString(String.valueOf(score), 10, 5 +
    scoreMetrics.getAscent());

  // Draw the number of lives
  for (int i = 0; i < (lives - 1); i++)
    offGrfx.drawImage(smGecko, 65 + i *
      (smGecko.getWidth(this) + 1), 10, this);

  // Draw the game over message
  if (lives <= 0) {
```

```
    Font        f = new Font("Helvetica", Font.BOLD, 36);
    FontMetrics fm = offGrfx.getFontMetrics(f);
    String      s = new String("Game Over");
    offGrfx.setFont(f);
    offGrfx.drawString(s, (size().width - fm.stringWidth(s)) / 2,
      ((size().height - fm.getHeight()) / 2) + fm.getAscent());
  }

  // Draw the image onto the screen
  g.drawImage(offImage, 0, 0, null);
}
```

After drawing the sprites, the update method draws the score using the drawString method. The small gecko images are then drawn to represent the number of remaining lives. If the number of lives is less than or equal to zero, the Game Over message is drawn. Finally, the offscreen buffer image is drawn to the screen.

Traveling Gecko only supports keyboard input, primarily because there isn't a good way to use the mouse in a game like this. The keyboard input in the TravelingGecko class is handled in the keyDown method, which follows:

```
public boolean keyDown(Event evt, int key) {
  // Change the gecko velocity based on the key pressed
  switch (key) {
  case Event.LEFT:
    gecko.setVelocity(new Point(-8, 0));
    break;
  case Event.RIGHT:
    gecko.setVelocity(new Point(8, 0));
    break;
  case Event.UP:
    gecko.setVelocity(new Point(0, -8));
    break;
  case Event.DOWN:
    gecko.setVelocity(new Point(0, 8));
    break;
  }
  return true;
}
```

The keyDown method simply sets the velocity of the gecko sprite based on which one of the arrow keys is being pressed. Notice that the magnitude of the velocity is set to 8, which means that the gecko moves eight pixels on the screen for each key press.

The action method is used to handle the user clicking the New Game button:

```
public boolean action(Event evt, Object arg) {
  if (evt.target instanceof Button)
    if (((String)arg).equals("New Game"))
      newGame();
  return true;
}
```

10

If the `action` method detects that a button has been clicked, the `newGame` method is called to start a new game. Speaking of the `newGame` method, here it is:

```
void newGame() {
  // Set up a new game
  lives = 4;
  score = 0;
  tgv = new TGVector(new ImageBackground(this, back), this);
  gecko = new Gecko(this);
  tgv.add(gecko);
  for (int i = 0; i < 4; i++)
    tgv.add(new Rock(this, i));
  tgv.add(new GilaMonster(this));
  tgv.add(new Scorpion(this));
  tgv.add(new Rattler(this));
  tgv.add(new Tarantula(this));
}
```

The `newGame` method does everything necessary to set up a new game; the `lives` and `score` member variables are initialized, the sprite list is re-created, and all the sprites are added back to the list. Notice that a reference to the gecko sprite is stored away in the `gecko` member variable so that it can be accessed in `keyDown` to move the gecko.

That finishes up the details of your first Java game, Traveling Gecko! I encourage you to study this game in detail and make sure that you follow what is happening with the sprites. Then you can try your hand at enhancing it and adding any new features you can dream up.

Summary

Congratulations, you made it through your first complete Java game! In this lesson, you made the journey from concept to reality on a pretty neat game that uses just about everything you've learned in the book thus far. Once again, you saw the power of the sprite classes because the majority of the game takes place within them. You also saw how easy it is to provide keyboard support within the context of a real game.

Even though you finished your first Java game in this lesson, you still have a way to go on your path toward becoming a Java game programming whiz. The good news is that you're in a nice position, having a complete game under your belt. Your next challenge is how to incorporate sound into Java games, which is covered in the next section of the book. You'll learn that sound adds a much needed dimension to games in Java.

Q&A

Q Why model the rocks as sprites? Aren't they really just part of the background?

A Logically, you could think of the rocks as part of the background, in that they don't do much beyond limiting the gecko's movement. But that one action, limiting the gecko's movement, is the whole reason that the rocks have to be implemented as sprites. If the rocks were just drawn on the background, there would be no straightforward way to detect collisions between them and the gecko.

Q Why derive different classes for all the predators?

A Although it isn't strictly necessary to derive different classes for the predators, it is very convenient and makes for good organization because the images used by each predator are linked to the predator class. It is also nice to have constructors with fewer parameters for each predator.

Q How does the `collision` method in `TGVector` know which types of sprites have collided with each other?

A The `collision` method uses the name of the sprite class to determine what type of sprite it is. This is accomplished by using the `getClass` method to get a `Class` object for the sprite, and then the `getName` method to get the class name as a `String` object. When you have the string name of a sprite class (`"Gecko"`, for example), it's easy to take different actions based on the types of sprites that are colliding.

Q Why are the score and number of lives member variables declared as public static in the `TravelingGecko` class?

A Because they must be modifiable from outside the `TravelingGecko` class. More specifically, the `Gecko` class needs to be able to increment the score when the gecko makes it across the screen, and the `TGVector` class needs to be able to decrement the number of lives when the gecko collides with a predator and dies.

Workshop

The Workshop section provides questions and exercises to help you get a better feel for the material you learned today. Try to answer the questions and at least ponder the exercises before moving on to tomorrow's lesson. You'll find the answers to the questions in Appendix A, "Quiz Answers."

Quiz

1. What classic arcade game is Traveling Gecko based on?
2. How is the player rewarded for his kind help in guiding the gecko safely across the hazardous desert?
3. How are the keyboard controls for the gecko implemented?
4. How well would a real gecko fare in the same situation?
5. How do you know when the New Game button has been pressed?

Exercises

1. Change the Gecko class so that the gecko faces in the direction in which he's traveling.
2. Make the destination opening in the rocks vary in position. Hint: Use smaller images for the rocks and more rock sprite objects that can be tiled and rearranged on the screen.
3. Vary the speeds of the predators based on the difficulty level (score).
4. Extend the predator classes to allow them to travel in either horizontal direction. This could vary with each new game.
5. Do some research on geckos and see whether I'm right about them faring pretty well in this situation.

10

Day 11

The Basics of Sound

On Day 10, you created your first complete game, Traveling Gecko, which contained most of the core components found in commercial games. However, it was missing one particularly important component—sound. In today's lesson, you remedy this problem by learning about sound and how to create it for your games. You don't get into too many of the technical details surrounding sound in Java; you'll learn all about that in tomorrow's lesson. The focus of today's lesson is on the overall usage of sound and how to create your own sound effects.

There was a time when a game without sound might have been acceptable. I'm here to tell you that you're now living in a different time! Although Traveling Gecko is a neat game, it seems somewhat lacking without any sound effects or music. Game players have come to expect realistic sound that works hand in hand with the graphics to convey a greater sense of realism. Sound is such an integral part of computer games that you should consider it a necessary part of your design—as necessary as graphics. Understanding that, let's get started on today's lesson!

The following topics are covered in today's lesson:

- ☐ The physics of sound
- ☐ Digital sound fundamentals
- ☐ The AU sound format
- ☐ Using sound in games
- ☐ Sound utilities
- ☐ Creating and editing sounds
- ☐ Finding sounds

The Physics of Sound

Before getting into the specifics of sound and how to create your own, a little background on digital sound is in order. By understanding how sounds are modeled in Java, and in software in general, you gain more insight into what functionality is provided in the standard Java audio implementation. You learn all about Java audio support in tomorrow's lesson.

The first issue to tackle is understanding the physics behind sound waves. A sound wave is a mechanical wave moving through a compressible medium such as air. A sound wave is actually a result of the pressure of air expanding and contracting. In other words, a sound wave is a series of traveling pressure changes in the air. You hear sound because the traveling sound wave eventually gets to your ears, where the pressure changes are processed and interpreted by your eardrums. The softness or loudness of a sound is determined by the amount of energy in the wave. Because sound waves lose energy as they travel, you hear sounds louder up close and softer from a distance. Eventually, sound waves travel far enough to be completely absorbed by the air or some other less compressible medium such as a wall in your house.

NEW TERM   A *sound wave* is a mechanical wave moving through a compressible medium such as air.

When I refer to the energy of a sound wave, I'm really talking about the amplitude of the wave. Amplitudes of sound waves are usually measured in decibels (dB). Decibels are a logarithmic unit of measurement, meaning that 80dB is 10 times louder than 79dB. This type of measurement is used because it reflects the hearing characteristics of the human ear. The threshold of human hearing is 0dB, which means that anything less is too soft to be heard by humans. Likewise, the threshold of pain is 120dB, which is the amplitude level at which humans experience physical pain. Prolonged exposure to sound this loud can cause permanent hearing damage, not to mention an annoying ringing sensation. This typically isn't a problem in computer games!

When a sound wave is converted to an electrical signal (by a microphone, for example), the amplitude is represented by a voltage. The amplitude of the voltage directly corresponds to the amplitude of the physical sound wave. As the amplitude of the wave varies, so does the corresponding voltage. In fact, the varying amplitude of a sound wave over time is all that is needed to reproduce a sound. Figure 11.1 shows a sound wave plotted as a voltage (amplitude) varying over time.

Figure 11.1.
A sound wave plotted as voltage versus time.

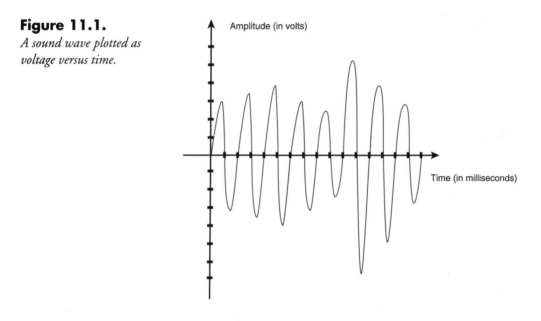

Digital Sound Fundamentals

When a microphone converts sound waves to voltage signals, the resulting signal is an analog (or continuous) signal. Because computers are digital machines, it is necessary to convert this analog signal to a digital signal for a computer to process. Analog to digital (A/D) converters handle the task of converting analog signals to digital signals, which is also referred to as *sampling*. The process of converting an analog signal to a digital signal doesn't always yield exact results. How closely a digital wave matches its analog counterpart is determined by the frequency at which it is sampled, as well as the amount of information stored at each sample.

NEW TERM   *Sampling* is the process of converting an analog audio signal to a digital audio signal.

To sample a sound, you just store the amplitude of the sound wave at regular intervals. Figure 11.2 shows how an analog sound wave is converted to a digital wave by sampling the sound at regular intervals. Notice in Figure 11.2 that the digital representation of the analog sound wave is not a very good one. Taking samples at more frequent intervals causes the digital signal to more closely approximate the analog signal and, therefore, sound more like the analog wave when played.

Figure 11.2.

An analog sound wave and its digital representation.

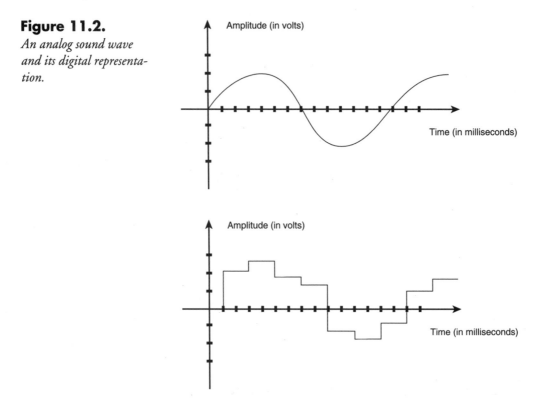

When sampling sounds, the rate (frequency) at which the sound is sampled is very important, as well as how much data is stored for each sample. The unit of measurement for frequency is Hertz (Hz), which specifies how many samples are taken per second. In Java 1.0, the only supported sound frequency is 8,000 Hz, which means that there are 8,000 samples per second. Although it sounds like a lot, this frequency actually results in a fairly low-quality sound. To understand why, consider the fact that the frequency for CD-quality audio is 44,000 Hz.

NOTE

The limitations on sound quality imposed by Java are really a reflection of the underlying AU sound format, which is discussed in the next section. When Java widens its support for other sound formats in a future release, these limitations will likely disappear.

The amount of data stored per sample determines the number of discrete amplitudes that a digital signal can represent. The wider the range is of amplitudes represented by the digital signal, the closer the original wave is approximated. In Java 1.0, the sample data width is limited to 8 bits. A wave sampled at 8 bits has 256 different discrete amplitude levels (2^8). Again, compare this to CD-quality sound, which uses 16 bits per sample and therefore has 65,536 different discrete amplitude levels (2^{16}).

The AU Sound Format

The AU sound format is currently the only sound format supported by Java. The *AU* name stands for ULAW, which specifies the type of encoding used to store each sample. The format is specific to Sun and NeXT computer systems, and it specifies that sounds be 8,000 Hz mono 8-bit ULAW encoded. This is a pretty low-quality sound format, especially when compared to what other formats provide.

However, within the context of the Web, the AU format is acceptable for now. This is mainly because of the ever-present bandwidth problem associated with the transfer of data over the Internet. Restricting sounds to a compact format such as AU guarantees that all sounds incur relatively low transmission times.

However, don't expect this situation to last long. Sun is already promising more complete multimedia support in a future release of Java, which will no doubt include support for more sound formats. At that point, it will be up to Web developers to balance the scale between sound quality and bandwidth delays.

Using Sound in Games

Aside from the programming issues surrounding sound in Java, which you learn about tomorrow, integrating sound into Java games consists primarily of creating or finding the right sound effects and music to fit your needs. You'll be happy to know that creating sound effects for games is often one of the most creative and fun aspects of game development, because there are very few rules. Which aspects of a game you want to associate sounds with are totally up to you. Along with that, you have complete freedom over the sounds you create and use.

Well, almost complete freedom. Actually, two limitations are imposed on sounds in games. The first limitation is communication bandwidth, which keeps you from being able to use lots of long sounds. This limitation exists because it takes time to transmit resources used by a Java game, such as graphics and sounds, over the Internet. To keep game players from having to wait an inordinate amount of time for resources to load, you should try to keep the quantity and size of sounds used by your games within reasonable limits.

11

The second limitation, which is a little less obvious, is that you can't use copyrighted sounds without written permission from the owner of the copyright. For example, sounds sampled from copyrighted movies or audio recordings can't be used without permission. It is technically no different than using copyrighted software without permission or a licensing agreement. So be careful when sampling sounds from copyrighted sources.

WARNING

Some seemingly public domain sound collections are actually copyrighted and can get you into trouble. Most of these types of collections come in the form of an audio CD containing a variety of sound effects. Be sure to read the fine print on these CDs, and make sure you can legally reuse the sounds or get explicit permission from the publisher.

Beyond these two limitations, you are free to do whatever you want with sounds in your game creations. Let's take a look at how you can begin experimenting with sound.

Sound Utilities

To be able to create and modify your own sounds, you need some type of software sound editing utility. Sound editing utilities usually provide a means of sampling sounds from a microphone, CD-ROM, or line input. From there, each utility varies as to what degree of editing it provides. Some sound editing utilities include very advanced signal processing features, in addition to the relatively standard amplification and echoing features.

The most important component of a good sound editor in regard to Java games is the capability to save sounds in the AU format. It doesn't matter how cool the sounds are if you can't play them with Java. Another key feature is the capability to zoom in and clip sounds down to exactly the portions you want to use. Because the length of sounds is of the utmost importance in Java games, you should always clip sounds down to the absolute minimum length possible.

The rest of this section focuses on some popular shareware sound editors that you can use to edit sounds for Java games. They all support the AU sound format and provide some degree of sound effects processing. There are also equally, or more, feature-packed commercial sound utilities out there, but I want to keep the focus on shareware because you can easily download shareware and try it out.

Cool Edit

Cool Edit, by Syntrillium Software, is a sound editor for Windows 95 that is loaded with features. Its creators have suggested thinking of it as a paint program for audio. Just as a paint program enables you to create images with colors, brush strokes, and a variety of special effects, Cool Edit enables you to "paint" with sound: tones, pieces of songs with voices and other noises, sine waves and sawtooth waves, noise, or just pure silence. Cool Edit provides a wide variety of special effects for manipulating sounds, such as reverberation, noise reduction, echo and delay, flanging, filtering, and many others.

You can get information about Cool Edit and download the latest version from the Syntrillium Software Web site, which is located at `http://www.netzone.com/syntrillium`. Figure 11.3 shows the Syntrillium Software Web site.

Figure 11.3.

The Syntrillium Software Web site.

Sound Exchange (SoX)

Sound Exchange (also known as SoX), by Lance Norskog, is the self-proclaimed Swiss army knife of sound editors because it provides a minimal interface but a lot of features. It functions more as a sound converter rather than a sound editor and is available for both UNIX and DOS PCs. It provides support for converting between many different sound formats, along with sampling rate conversion and some sound effects. The complete source code for SoX is also available, so if you're adventurous enough, you could port it to another platform. As if you don't have enough to keep you busy learning Java game programming!

You can get information about Sound Exchange and download the latest version from the Sound Exchange Web site, which is located at `http://www.spies.com/Sox`. Figure 11.4 shows the Sound Exchange Web site.

Figure 11.4.

The Sound Exchange
sound utility Web site.

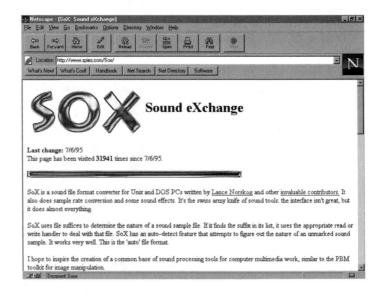

Sound Machine

Sound Machine, by Rod Kennedy, is a Macintosh sound editor with lots of conversion and sound effects features. Mr. Kennedy is also working on some interesting Netscape plug-ins that will interact with Sound Machine. Pretty neat!

You can get information about Sound Machine and download the latest version from the Sound Machine Web site, which is located at

```
http://online.anu.edu.au/RSISE/teleng/Software/SoundMachine/welcome.html
```

Figure 11.5 shows the Sound Machine Web site.

Sound Hack

Sound Hack, by Tom Erbe, is another Macintosh sound utility with a wide variety of neat features. Unlike Sound Machine, however, Sound Hack is more of a sound processor, and it leans toward more esoteric sound processing features. For example, Sound Hack includes processing effects such as pitch shifting, binaural filter spatialization, and spectral mutation, among others. If you have no idea what these features are, just grab a copy of Sound Hack and try them out for yourself!

You can get information about Sound Hack (including online documentation) and download the latest version from the Sound Hack Web site, which is located at `http://shoko.CALARTS.EDU/~tre/SndHckDoc`. Figure 11.6 shows the Sound Hack Web site.

Figure 11.5.
The Sound Machine sound editor Web site.

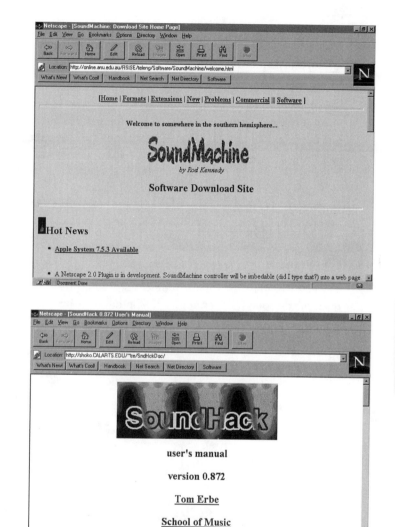

Figure 11.6.
The Sound Hack sound processor Web site.

11

Creating and Editing Sounds

After you've decided on a sound utility, you're ready to start creating and editing sounds. The first decision to make is how you will create the sounds. For example, are you planning to record sounds yourself with a microphone or sample sounds from a stereo cassette deck or VCR? The microphone is probably the easiest route, because many multimedia computers come equipped with one. It's also the most creative route. However, you might already have some sounds in mind from a prerecorded cassette, CD, or movie, which means that you need to look into connecting an external sound source to your computer. This is covered in detail a little later in today's lesson.

Regardless of where you sample sounds from, the process of getting a sampled sound cleaned up for use in a game is basically the same. After you've sampled a sound, play it back to make sure that it sounds okay. It's likely that the sound will be either too loud or too soft. You can judge whether the volume of the sound is acceptable by looking at the waveform displayed in the sound editor. If the sound amplitude goes beyond the top or bottom of the waveform display, you know it's definitely too loud. If you can barely hear it, it's probably too soft. To remedy this problem, you can either adjust the input level for the sound device and resample the sound or try to use amplification effects provided by the sound utility.

NEW TERM   The *waveform* of a sound is the graphical appearance of the sound when plotted over time.

The best way to fix the volume problem is to adjust the input level of the sound device and resample the sound. For example, in Windows 95 you can easily adjust the microphone or line input level using the Volume Control application (see Figure 11.7).

Figure 11.7.

The Windows 95 Volume Control application.

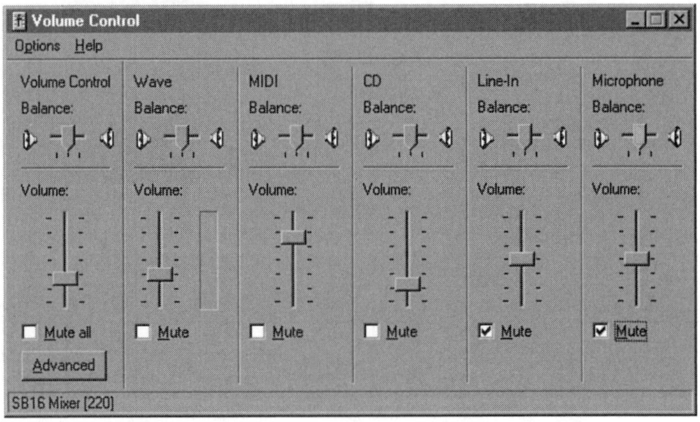

After you have the volume of the sound at a level you like, you need to clip the sound to remove unwanted portions of the sound. *Clipping* a sound involves zooming in on the waveform in a sound editor and cutting out the silence that appears before and after the sound. This helps shorten the length of the sound and prevents unnecessary latency.

NEW TERM   *Clipping* is the process of removing unneeded parts of a sound, such as silence at the beginning and end.

NOTE

Latency is the amount of time between when you queue a sound for playing and when the user actually hears it. Latency should be kept to a minimum so that sounds are heard when you want them to be heard without any delay. Unnecessary silence at the beginning of a sound is a common cause of latency problems. The other, less controllable, cause is the audio mixing support in Java itself.

When you have a sound clipped, it should be ready for prime time! You might want to check out the kinds of effects that are available with the sound utility you are using. Some simple effects range from reverse to echo, with more advanced effects including fading and phase shifts. It's all up to your imagination and your discerning ears!

Recording with a Microphone

If you are recording sounds with a microphone, you can get much better results by covering the microphone with soft foam, like the kind found on some portable earphones. Some microphones already have foam covers. The foam cover greatly reduces the hiss caused by blowing on the microphone. It seems that no matter how careful you are, you always end up blowing into the microphone a little. This causes a noisy hiss unless you have the microphone covered. You can tape tissue over the microphone if you can't find any foam.

After you have the microphone set up for recording, prepare to throw convention aside and get creative. It's really amazing what can be done with a microphone and a little reckless abandon! You can come up with some pretty neat sound effects just by being creative with everyday household items. Let's take a few examples.

If you need gunshots or simple explosions, try tapping the microphone on a table. You can get different sounds by hitting it harder or softer and by trying different surfaces. Please don't hold me responsible if you beat your microphone to death on a table, though! You'll notice that harder surfaces generate sharper sounds. Because most gunshot sounds are repeated often, it's nice to have them as short and sweet as possible. The sharp sounds generated by a hard surface work pretty well for this.

If you're looking for more realistic explosions that actually fade out, you're going to have to perform a little. Hold your hand around the microphone and make a rough, blowing sound into your hand. After a little practice, you can get pretty realistic explosion sounds with this method. Just make sure no one's around when you're practicing!

If you need mechanical sounds, look no farther than your kitchen appliances. You probably don't want to drag your whole computer into the kitchen, which means you'll be limited to portable appliances. However, that still leaves a lot of opportunities. My juicer makes sounds that easily could pass for some interesting futuristic weapons. How about opening a bottle of soda? Sounds an awful lot like hydraulic brakes, doesn't it? Or maybe the huff or puff of a big alien?

What if you need some background sounds? I know I could open my window on many nights and record the sound of crickets chirping all night long. Although less dramatic, cricket sounds can add a lot to the realism of a night scene in a game. That is, until dogs start barking!

The goal here isn't to go through an exhaustive description of every possible thing you can use to create sounds. I mainly just want to spark your imagination so that you can start thinking about what you can do with things that are readily available. That's the beauty of creating games. You can turn otherwise ordinary things into interesting elements of a game. Think about all the things you hear on a daily basis. Then go through your house and make notes of what sounds you could create with different items. You'll find that this process can be a lot of fun. It's even better after you've incorporated the sounds into a game and people ask where the sounds came from.

Sampling from External Sound Sources

Another very useful method for finding sound effects for games is to sample sounds from external sound sources such as VCRs and CD players. Before I say any more, let me reiterate that it is illegal to distribute sounds sampled from movies or copyrighted CDs or cassettes without getting permission.

Sampling sounds from external sound sources requires a little more work than recording them with a microphone, but not much. Basically, the extra work is in connecting the external sound source to your computer. You connect external sound sources via a line input on your computer; most multimedia computer systems these days have a line input for receiving analog audio. For example, Soundblaster sound cards on PCs have a line input jack that can be used to connect a stereo cassette deck or VCR. To see whether your computer has a line input jack, look at the back of your computer. If you have speakers hooked up, they are probably plugged in very close to the line input jack. Look for one or more jacks labeled *input*. On PCs equipped with Soundblaster family sound cards, the word *input* usually accompanies the input jack. Input jacks are usually the same type of mini connectors used for headphones on a portable Walkman.

After you determine where the line input jack is located, plug in the line out cable from the sound device from which you want to sample sounds. The only problem is that the connectors are usually of differing types. The type of connector used by most audio equipment—including cassette decks, CD players, and VCRs—is called an RCA connector. You need to go to an electronics store and buy a cable that allows you to connect the RCA sound device to the mini input jack on your computer. You might also want to pick up an RCA extension cable so that you don't have to stack the sound device on top of your monitor!

When you get the cables squared away, plug the RCA end into the line output of the sound device, and the mini end into the input jack on the back of your computer. Then fire up the sound utility and get ready for some fun. From this point on, it's pretty much the same as recording sounds using a microphone, except that the sound device is generating the sound rather than you. The sound utility doesn't really care where the sound is coming from; it knows only to look at the input jack and grab whatever sound information is there.

If a sound doesn't sound right after you sample it, it's probably because you have the cable plugged into the microphone input rather than the line input. Try switching inputs (if you have another one) and trying again. If it sounds okay this time, you're set. If not, don't worry because there are work-arounds.

If you only have a microphone input, you need to make an adjustment to record sounds from other input devices because microphone inputs are designed to deal only with low-amplitude signals. The signals from other sound devices can easily overwhelm a microphone input jack. The solution is to somehow alter the incoming signal so that it comes in at around a microphone level. The easiest fix is to lower the input level of the sound source in software. An example of this is using the Volume Control application in Windows 95.

If you aren't so lucky to be able to fix things in software, you can adjust the output level of the sound device by passing it through an audio mixer. If you don't have an audio mixer handy, your best bet is to buy an attenuator connector. Attenuator connectors adjust the signal level down to a level that will work for a microphone input. You can find attenuator connectors at most electronics stores.

New Term An *attenuator* is an electronic device or circuit that lowers the magnitude of an electric signal. In the case of audio signals, an attenuator results in a decrease in volume.

After you have the technical difficulties out of the way, you can focus on the creative end of sampling sounds. When it comes to movies, I tend to favor war movies for finding gunshots and explosions, for obvious reasons. Science fiction movies are great for space sounds and other weird effects. The range of sounds that can be found in movies is practically unlimited.

One advantage of sampling sounds from movies is that they typically are of very high quality. Companies exist that do nothing more than create sounds for movies. For this reason, movies provide probably the richest variety of sounds available. Typically, every sound you hear in a movie has been carefully placed there. The problem, of course, is that they are protected by copyright law, which means that you can't just run around ripping sounds out of movies and putting them into your games.

Finding Sounds

If you've decided that you don't have what it takes to create your own sounds, you still have options. In this case, you need to seek an outside source for your sounds. The best source for finding prerecorded sounds is in sound archives on the Web. Many different sound archives are out there with a vast amount of sounds to choose from. Many are even available already in the AU sound format. Even if you get sounds from a sound archive, be very careful about the copyright issues surrounding using them.

A good starting point for finding sounds is the World Wide Web Virtual Library, which maintains an Audio page with links to sound archives. This Audio Web site is located at

```
http://www.comlab.ox.ac.uk/archive/audio.html
```

Figure 11.8 shows what the WWW Virtual Library Audio Web site looks like.

Figure 11.8.

The World Wide Web Virtual Library Audio Web site.

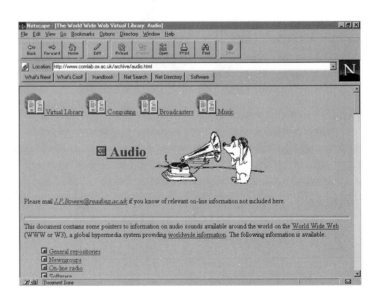

Summary

Today you took a step away from the details of Java coding to learn about sound and how it can be created for games. You began with the physics of sound and followed it up with the basics of digital sound representation and the AU sound format supported by Java. You then saw where you could get some shareware sound utilities that enable you to record and edit your own sounds. You finished up by learning about creative outlets for creating your own sounds, both from scratch and also from existing sources.

I hope today's lesson gave you a break from technical programming details, along with providing a creative surge for you to go out and create some interesting sounds. My main goal was to remind you that games are all about fun—and not just from a player's perspective. The more you enjoy the process of creating games, the more fun they will probably end up being. Sound creation is only one of the aspects of game development that can be both challenging and fun.

Just in case you forgot that this book is about Java, tomorrow's lesson turns your attention toward the specifics of playing sound in Java. Don't worry; it's a lot easier than you might suspect!

Q&A

Q **What's the difference between sampled sound and sampled music?**

A Technically, there is no difference; they are both sampled as digital audio and stored in the AU sound format. However, sampled music is usually designed to be relatively short in length and sampled so that it can be looped repeatedly to sound like a longer piece of music. The trick then is to sample music sounds so that they end similarly to how they begin, thereby smoothing out the looping effect.

Q **Can I record sounds from an audio CD in an internal CD-ROM drive?**

A Certainly! As a matter of fact, this is an ideal scenario because you bypass the whole issue of connecting an external sound device through an input jack. Typically, this simply involves adjusting the volume of the CD-ROM appropriately and sampling just as if you were using the microphone.

Q **What if I find a bunch of neat sounds but they are stored in a different sound format, such as WAV?**

A You need to convert them to the AU sound format to be able to use them with Java. This is usually as easy as loading them into a sound utility and saving them as an AU file type.

Workshop

The Workshop section provides questions and exercises to help strengthen your grasp of the material you learned today. Try to answer the questions and at least go over the exercises before moving on to tomorrow's lesson. You'll find the answers to the questions in Appendix A, "Quiz Answers."

Quiz

1. What is a sound wave?
2. What is an analog to digital converter used for in regard to sampling sounds?
3. What is the sampling frequency for the AU sound format?
4. What is latency?

Exercises

1. Find a sound utility capable of recording and editing sounds. You'll need it!
2. Try your hand at creating some sounds of your own with a microphone.
3. Sample some sounds from an external sound device, making sure to get the volume level settings correct.
4. Try applying some special effects in the sound utility to your newly sampled sounds.

Day 12

Playing Sound with Java

On Day 11, you learned all about sound and how it is used in computer games, as well as how to find and record your own sounds. However, you didn't learn anything about how to actually implement sound in Java. Sure, you might have sampled a bunch of neat sounds, but they aren't of much use until you understand how to play them in a real applet.

Today you learn all about sound and how it works in Java. You find out all the not-so-gory details about how sound is represented in Java, along with the classes and methods used to load and play sounds. It turns out that the current release of Java has pretty limited support for sound. Nevertheless, more than enough audio support is there to liven up Java games. You finish up today's lesson by using the sound support in Java 1.0 to build a pretty neat applet that plays multiple sound effects.

The following topics are covered in today's lesson:

- ☐ Java sound support
- ☐ Sample applet: WildAnimals

Java Sound Support

The current sound support in Java comes in the form of a class and a few methods in the `Applet` class. The `AudioClip` class, which is part of the applet package, models a digital audio sound clip in the AU file format. You learn about this class next. You learn about the methods supporting sound in the `Applet` class later in today's lesson.

The AU file format, which you learned about in yesterday's lesson, is currently the only sound format supported by Java. If you recall, it is designed around 8,000 Hz mono 8-bit ULAW encoded audio clips. This is a fairly low-quality sound format, and it severely limits Java in providing professional audio capabilities. However, in the current context of the Web, just being able to play AU audio clips in Java is plenty for many applets.

As far as games go, the quality of the sound isn't always as crucial as you might think. Many sound effects (animal noises, for example) don't require very high-quality audio. You find this out firsthand in this lesson when you implement an applet using various animal sound effects.

The `AudioClip` Class

The `AudioClip` class models a sound clip in Java. It is an abstract class, so you can't directly create instances of it. The only way to create `AudioClip` objects is by calling one of the `getAudioClip` methods of the `Applet` class. You'll learn more about that in a moment. But first, take a look at the methods in the `AudioClip` class.

```
public abstract void play()
public abstract void loop()
public abstract void stop()
```

As you can see, these methods are very high-level and quite simplistic. You can't ask for a much easier interface than just calling `play` to play an audio clip and `stop` to stop an audio clip. The only twist is the `loop` method, which plays an audio clip repeatedly in a loop until you explicitly call `stop` to stop it. The `loop` method is useful when you have an audio clip that needs to be repeated, such as a music clip or a footstep sound.

None of the methods in `AudioClip` require parameters; the `AudioClip` object is entirely self-contained. For this reason, there isn't a lot to learn about using the `AudioClip` class. By simply understanding the three methods implemented by the `AudioClip` class (`play`, `loop`, `stop`), you are practically already a Java sound expert!

Before your ego gets too inflated, remember that you still haven't learned the details of how to create an `AudioClip` object. As I mentioned a little earlier, you use one of the `Applet` class's `getAudioClip` methods to create and initialize an `AudioClip` object. The two versions of `getAudioClip` are as follows:

```
public AudioClip getAudioClip(URL url)
public AudioClip getAudioClip(URL url, String name)
```

NOTE

I mentioned earlier that you can't create an `AudioClip` object directly because `AudioClip` is an abstract class. Because the class is abstract, you might be wondering how an `AudioClip` object can be created at all. Technically, it is impossible to ever create an object based on an abstract class. However, in the case of `AudioClip`, you use the `getAudioClip` method to get a platform-specific `AudioClip` derived object. In other words, `getAudioClip` acts as a native method that returns a native class derived from `AudioClip`. The method and class are native because sound support varies so widely on different platforms. The purpose of the `AudioClip`, therefore, is to standardize the interface for the native audio clip classes, which results in a general, platform-independent programming solution.

The only difference between these two `getAudioClip` methods is whether or not the URL parameter contains a complete reference to the name of the audio clip. In the first version, it is assumed that the URL contains the complete name; the second version uses the name in a separate `name` parameter. You will typically use the second version, because you can easily retrieve the base URL of the applet or the HTML document in which the applet is embedded. You do this by using either the `getCodeBase` or the `getDocumentBase` method of `Applet`, like this:

```
AudioClip clip1 = getAudioClip(getCodeBase(), "sound1.au");
AudioClip clip2 = getAudioClip(getDocumentBase(), "sound2.au");
```

The `getCodeBase` method returns the base URL of the applet itself, whereas `getDocumentBase` returns the base URL of the HTML document containing the applet. It is usually smarter to use `getCodeBase` to specify the base URL for loading resources used by a Java applet. The reason for this is that it is often useful to organize Java applets into a directory structure beneath the HTML documents in which they appear. Furthermore, you usually reference images and sounds either from the same directory where the applet is located or from a subdirectory beneath it.

12

I like to organize images and sounds used by an applet in a directory called Res, beneath the directory containing the actual Java classes. This isolates the executable part of an applet from the resource content used by the applet, resulting in a more organized file structure.

Alternatives to Using AudioClip

In the audio discussion thus far, I might have led you to believe that you must use an AudioClip object to play sounds in Java. This isn't entirely true! The truth is that you are only required to create an AudioClip object if you want to play looped sounds. For normal (nonlooped) sounds, you have the option of using one of the play methods in the Applet class instead of using an AudioClip object. The definitions for the play methods implemented in Applet are as follows:

```
public void play(URL url)
public void play(URL url, String name)
```

These play methods take exactly the same parameters taken by the getAudioClip methods. In fact, the play methods in Applet actually call getAudioClip to get an AudioClip object and then use the AudioClip object's play method to play the sound. In this way, the Applet play methods basically provide a higher level method of playing audio. This is evident in Listing 12.1, which shows the Java 1.0 source code for the Applet play methods.

Listing 12.1. The Java 1.0 Applet class's play methods.

```
public void play(URL url) {
  AudioClip clip = getAudioClip(url);
  if (clip != null) {
    clip.play();
  }
}

public void play(URL url, String name) {
  AudioClip clip = getAudioClip(url, name);
  if (clip != null) {
    clip.play();
  }
}
```

The Applet play methods both create a temporary AudioClip object and then use it to play the sound by calling its play method. This provides an even higher level of interface to playing nonlooped sounds than the AudioClip class provides.

12

Sample Applet: WildAnimals

Now that you are a Java sound expert (at least in theory), it's time to put your newfound knowledge to work in a sample applet. Because this book is ultimately about writing games, it's important for you to never compromise in making your applets as entertaining as possible. For this reason, the applet you're going to develop to demonstrate sound is a little more than a simple sound player. As a matter of fact, it's quite wild! Figure 12.1 shows a screen of the WildAnimals applet, which uses the Java `AudioClip` class to generate some entertaining results. The source code, executable, images, and sounds for WildAnimals are located on the accompanying CD-ROM.

Figure 12.1.

The WildAnimals sample applet.

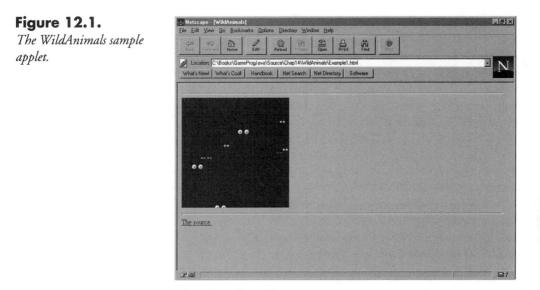

12

The screen shot of WildAnimals doesn't quite convey the real purpose of the applet. So, at this point, I encourage you to run it for yourself from the CD-ROM to get the real effect. Just in case you're the impatient type and choose to skip the wild animal experience, I'll fill you in on what's happening. WildAnimals randomly plays a variety of wild animal sounds to go with the eyes that are staring at you from the darkness.

Now that you know what it does, let's take a look at the implementation of WildAnimals. The `WildAnimals` class really only defines one member variable beyond the variables required for animation that you've already seen in prior applets:

```
private AudioClip[] clip = new AudioClip[5];
```

This array of `AudioClip` objects is used to store the wild animal sounds.

The init method in WildAnimals initializes the audio clips by calling the getAudioClip method:

```
public void init() {
    // Load and track the images
    tracker = new MediaTracker(this);
    Eyes.initResources(this, tracker, 0);

    // Load the audio clips
    clip[0] = getAudioClip(getCodeBase(), "Res/Crow.au");
    clip[1] = getAudioClip(getCodeBase(), "Res/Hyena.au");
    clip[2] = getAudioClip(getCodeBase(), "Res/Monkey.au");
    clip[3] = getAudioClip(getCodeBase(), "Res/Tiger.au");
    clip[4] = getAudioClip(getCodeBase(), "Res/Wolf.au");
}
```

After the audio clips are initialized in init using getAudioClip, they are ready to be played.

The eyes you see in the applet are implemented as sprites, which you'll learn about later in today's lesson. These sprites are created in the run method, which also creates and initializes the sprite list. Listing 12.2 contains the source code for the run method.

Listing 12.2. The WildAnimals class's run method.

```
public void run() {
    try {
        tracker.waitForID(0);
    }
    catch (InterruptedException e) {
        return;
    }

    // Create and add the sprites
    sv = new SpriteVector(new ColorBackground(this, Color.black));
    for (int i = 0; i < 8; i++) {
        sv.add(new Eyes(this, new Point(Math.abs(rand.nextInt() %
            size().width), Math.abs(rand.nextInt() % size().width)),
            i % 2, Math.abs(rand.nextInt() % 200)));
    }

    // Update everything
    long t = System.currentTimeMillis();
    while (Thread.currentThread() == animate) {
        // Update the animations
        sv.update();
        repaint();

        // Play an animal sound
        if ((rand.nextInt() % 15) == 0)
            clip[Math.abs(rand.nextInt() % 5)].play();

        try {
            t += delay;
            Thread.sleep(Math.max(0, t - System.currentTimeMillis()));
```

12

```
    }
    catch (InterruptedException e) {
      break;
    }
  }
}
```

Beyond creating the sprites for WildAnimals, the run method also handles playing the random animal sounds. This is carried out by using the nextInt method of the Random object to get a random number between -15 and 15. This random number is checked to see whether it is equal to 0, in which case a sound is played. This creates a 1-in-31 chance of a sound being played each time through the update loop. There is no magic surrounding the range of the random numbers; it was determined by trying out different values. When a sound is to be played, nextInt is used again to randomly select which sound to play. That's all there is to playing the random sounds.

That covers all the unique aspects of the WildAnimals class. However, you still haven't seen how the eye sprites are implemented. The Eye class implements a blinking eye sprite that can be either small or large. It uses a static two-dimensional array of Image objects to store the frame animations for the blinking eye in each size. Like all derived Sprite classes you've seen, the images are initialized in the initResources method:

```
public static void initResources(Applet app, MediaTracker tracker, int id) {
  for (int i = 0; i < 4; i++) {
    image[0][i] = app.getImage(app.getCodeBase(), "Res/SmEye" + i + ".gif");
    tracker.addImage(image[0][i], id);
    image[1][i] = app.getImage(app.getCodeBase(), "Res/LgEye" + i + ".gif");
    tracker.addImage(image[1][i], id);
  }
}
```

Figure 12.2 shows what the animation images for the eye look like.

The Eye class contains two member variables, blinkDelay and blinkTrigger, for managing the rate at which it blinks:

```
protected int blinkDelay,
              blinkTrigger;
```

blinkDelay determines how long the eye waits until it blinks again, and blinkTrigger is the counter used to carry out the wait. They are both initialized to the blink delay parameter passed into the constructor of Eye:

```
public Eyes(Component comp, Point pos, int i, int bd) {
  super(comp, image[i], 0, 1, 2, pos, new Point(0, 0), 0, Sprite.BA_WRAP);
  blinkTrigger = blinkDelay = bd;
}
```

12

Figure 12.2.

The images used by the Eye *class.*

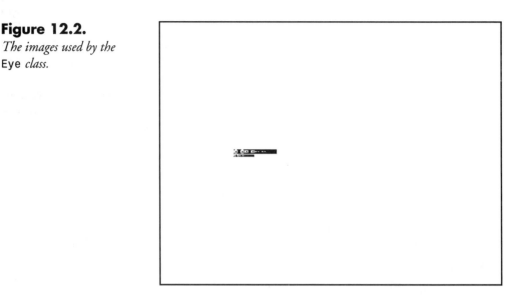

The only overridden method in Eye is incFrame, which handles incrementing the animation frame:

```
protected void incFrame() {
  if ((frameDelay > 0) && (--frameTrigger <= 0) &&
    (--blinkTrigger <= 0)) {
    // Reset the frame trigger
    frameTrigger = frameDelay;

    // Increment the frame
    frame += frameInc;
    if (frame >= 4) {
      frame = 3;
      frameInc = -1;
    }
    else if (frame <= 0) {
      frame = 0;
      frameInc = 1;
      blinkTrigger = blinkDelay;
    }
  }
}
```

It is necessary to override incFrame so that you can add the blinking functionality. This is done by decrementing blinkTrigger and seeing whether it has reached zero. If so, it's time to blink! Notice that the blink is still dependent on the frame delay, which is very important. This is important because you don't want an added feature, such as blinking, to interrupt a basic function of the sprite, such as the frame delay.

The `incFrame` method does one other thing worth pointing out. If you think about it, a blink must consist of going through the frame animations forward (to close the eye) and then backward (to open the eye again). The standard implementation of `incFrame` in `Sprite`, which you saw last week, always goes in a constant direction—that is, forward or backward as determined by the sign of the `frameInc` member variable. In `Eye`'s `incFrame`, you want the frame animations to go forward and then backward without having to fool with `frameInc`. The `if-else` clause in `incFrame` solves this problem beautifully.

That finishes up the WildAnimals sample applet. It proves that sound in Java is not only fun, but it is also easy to implement!

Summary

Today you learned all about how sound is used in Java. You started off by learning how Java supports sound through the `AudioClip` class and a few methods in the `Applet` class. You then progressed to building a complete applet using sound to create somewhat of a virtual wilderness at night. It showed you how easy it is to add sound to Java applets. It also was a good example of how the sprite classes can be used in new and creative ways.

You now have all the background necessary to add sound to any Java applet you write, including games. Speaking of games, it's almost time for you to write another one. But that will have to wait until tomorrow!

Q&A

Q Do I have to do anything special to mix sounds in Java?

A No. The Java sound support automatically handles mixing sounds that are being played at the same time. This might seem trivial, but it is actually a very nice feature.

Q How do I play MIDI music in Java?

A Right now, you can't. The current version of Java (1.0) doesn't provide any support for MIDI, but hopefully it will appear in a later release. Sun has promised more extensive multimedia features in the near future. For now, you can record music as an audio clip and then loop it; more on this tomorrow.

Q In the WildAnimals applet, how can I make the eyes blink faster?

A Decrease the blink delay parameter passed into the constructor. More specifically, decrease the number used in the modulus operation after the call to `nextInt`.

12

Q How can I add more animals to the WildAnimals applet?

A The first step is to record or find more animal sounds and copy them to the Res
directory. You then need to increase the size of the clip array of AudioClip objects
and load the new sounds in init using the getAudioClip method. Finally, in the
call to play in the run method, increase the number used to index into the clip
array (it is currently 5).

Workshop

The Workshop section provides questions and exercises to help you get a better feel for the
material you learned today. Try to answer the questions and at least think about the exercises
before moving on to tomorrow's lesson. You'll find the answers to the questions in Appendix
A, "Quiz Answers."

Quiz

1. Are any other sound formats supported by Java besides the AU format?
2. Why should you use the getCodeBase method to get a base URL for a sound rather
   than the getDocumentBase method?
3. When would you need to use an AudioClip object rather than the play method in
   the Applet class?
4. How do you stop a looped sound after it has started playing?

Exercises

1. Draw or find an image containing some animals and use it as the background.
   Hint: Use the ImageBackground class instead of the ColorBackground class when
   creating the SpriteVector.
2. Try out different values for the blink delay of the eyes.
3. Add more animal sounds.
4. Modify the Eye class so that the eyes look like the animals are walking around.

Day **13**

Scorpion Roundup: Action By Moonlight

Yesterday you saw how sound is supported in Java. You also wrote a fairly simple applet to demonstrate how sound can be used in a creative way. Today you go a step further by creating your second complete game, including sound effects and music. The entire lesson today is devoted to the design and development of this game, which will provide you with another invaluable Java game creation experience.

The game you develop today is called Scorpion Roundup, and it uses the all too familiar sprite classes to implement its animation and sprite interactions. It uses the `AudioClip` class you learned about in yesterday's lesson to represent both sound effects and music. Unlike the Traveling Gecko game you developed a few days ago, which used the keyboard exclusively for user input, Scorpion Roundup uses the mouse as the user input device. You'll see why when you get into the game.

The following topics are covered in today's lesson:

- ☐ Designing Scorpion Roundup
- ☐ Sample applet: Scorpion Roundup

Designing Scorpion Roundup

Unlike Traveling Gecko, Scorpion Roundup isn't directly modeled after any other game. Before getting into how the game plays, you need some background on the premise surrounding the game, because it is based on a very real concept that is pretty interesting.

Scorpions are fairly popular as pets. Not quite as popular as dogs or cats, but what do you expect? They are also useful in captivity for retrieving their poison, which is used in developing antivenin medicine for people and pets stung by them. They are also used to make souvenirs; just visit Sky Harbor Airport in Phoenix, Arizona, and you'll see plenty of scorpions frozen in plastic in the gift shops. The point here is that there are a variety of human uses for scorpions. And where there's a demand, there's a supply. This means that someone has to take on the job of heading out into the desert and catching the rascals.

Catching a scorpion isn't as easy as you might think, though. They are nocturnal creatures, so they only come out at night. The thought of taking off into the desert at night might not appeal to everyone, but conquering your fear of the dark desert isn't the only hurdle when hunting for scorpions: It's hard to find them at night! One of those brave souls that head into the darkness in search of scorpions figured out a neat approach to finding scorpions in the dark—using a black light. Black lights give off a greenish glow that illuminates certain objects, including scorpions. Therefore, to catch scorpions you simply head out into the darkness with a black light and a net. That's the premise of the Scorpion Roundup game. You're a scorpion hunter armed with a net, working within a landscape illuminated by a black light that shows the scorpions with their greenish glow.

WARNING

Real scorpions are caught by real professionals. For your own safety, I suggest only trying to catch the Java scorpions you meet in today's lesson!

Based on this description of the game, you might already see why the mouse is the ideal input device for the game. This is because you are controlling a net, which is a hand-held object in real life. The best way to handle controlling a net with the mouse is to make the net a sprite. You also need a scorpion sprite to model the scorpions that you are trying to catch.

At this point, the game is defined enough to move into more specifics. Let's start by taking a look at the sprites in more detail.

Sprites

You've established that the game requires two types of sprites for modeling the net and the scorpions. You also know that the net sprite is to be controlled by the mouse. Basically, all you need the net sprite to do is follow the mouse around, which requires very basic sprite movement. Based on this requirement of the net sprite, it doesn't sound like you need to use a derived class for it; you don't need any functionality beyond that provided in the base Sprite class. This is a correct assumption because deriving a new class is usually only necessary when you need to add new functionality.

This means that Scorpion Roundup really only needs one derived sprite class: the Scorpion sprite class. What should this sprite do? To make the game a little more simple to implement, let's limit the scorpion sprites to traveling in horizontal directions only. The scorpions can run in either the left or right direction, which means that they can also face in either the left or right direction. You're probably thinking that the directional sprite you developed last week might work well here. Unfortunately, it won't work in this case because it was specifically designed for sprites having exactly eight directions; the scorpions in Scorpion Roundup only have two directions (left and right).

The scorpion sprite needs to be frame animated so that the scorpions look like they are moving their legs and running. You've also established that the sprite needs two directions. Anything else? Actually, there is one other thing. The goal of the game is to catch as many scorpions as possible. However, you haven't established how a game is lost; the game has no negative result when you don't catch any scorpions. One solution is to have the scorpions get away when they reach the other side of the screen, rather than wrapping around. Furthermore, you could track how many scorpions get away and end the game when a certain number of them escape. The only place to determine when a scorpion has made it across is within the Scorpion class. Therefore, the Scorpion class needs some method of determining when a scorpion has escaped and modifying a value accordingly.

Game Play

Now that you understand how the sprites work in the game, let's move on to the specifics of the game itself. You've established that the goal of the game is to use a net to catch scorpions that are running across the screen. You lose the game when you miss a certain number of scorpions. You never really win; you just try to catch as many scorpions as possible.

One thing you haven't covered is how the player is to be challenged as the game goes on. Few games remain fun without increasing the challenge as the play progresses, and Scorpion Roundup is no different. The easiest way to make the game harder is to speed up the scorpions themselves. You could also increase the speed at which the scorpions are created; more scorpions on the screen at a time mean more work for the player.

How do you establish when to increase the difficulty of the game? Well, you could just do it behind the scenes based on time or on how many scorpions have been caught. I like the latter approach because it directly increases the difficulty based on the performance of the player. The only catch is that most game players like to know when they have progressed to another difficulty level. This is easy enough to accommodate; just display the current level along with the number of scorpions caught and lost. You then increment the difficulty level when a certain number of scorpions have been caught.

Options

That wraps up the play aspects of the game, but you should consider a few other small issues related to how the player controls the game. The first one is how to start a new game. You might recall that the Traveling Gecko game you developed a few days ago used a New Game button to start new games. That approach was fine in Traveling Gecko because the button was drawn on top of one of the rocks. In Scorpion Roundup, the game appearance would suffer more by having a button drawn on top of everything. The easy way around starting a new game without using a button is to simply allow the player to start a game with a certain key press, such as the N key.

NOTE

You actually could use buttons without covering up any of the game area by using an AWT `Canvas` object as the game area, rather than the applet window. This is a good way to handle sharing the applet window between user interface controls and the game area, but it involves more complexity. I didn't want this added complexity to make the game implementation more difficult to understand.

The only other issue in Scorpion Roundup that needs to be addressed is music. Because the game uses looped music, it would be nice for the player to be able to easily turn it on and off. Using the keyboard approach again, the M key makes perfect sense as a music toggle key.

That wraps up the design phase for Scorpion Roundup. Hopefully, you're now anxious to dive into the details of implementing all these cool ideas to build a real game!

Sample Applet: Scorpion Roundup

The Scorpion Roundup applet is your second fully functional Java game and shows off the sound skills you developed in yesterday's lesson. Figure 13.1 shows a screen shot of a fast and furious game of Scorpion Roundup. The complete source code, executable, images, and sounds for Scorpion Roundup are located on the accompanying CD-ROM.

Figure 13.1.

The Scorpion Roundup sample applet in action.

Scorpion Roundup begins by creating the net sprite, which you can move around the play area with the mouse. Scorpions then begin to run across the screen. If you click on a scorpion with the net, you hear a sound indicating that you got him. If you miss, you hear a sound of the net swishing through the air. All the while, the music is playing in the background.

The current difficulty level is displayed in the upper left corner of the screen, along with the number of scorpions caught and lost. The level is incremented and a cheering sound is played each time you catch 15 new scorpions. The scorpions start running faster and appearing quicker with each increasing difficulty level.

If you let five scorpions get away, the game ends and you see a Game Over message. Figure 13.2 shows Scorpion Roundup right after the game ends.

Figure 13.2.

A Scorpion Roundup game that has come to an end.

At this point, you can simply press the N key to start a new game. If you haven't run Scorpion Roundup yet, please load the CD-ROM and try it out. If you're not the type that responds well to the word "please," then by all means skip playing the game and read on!

The Sprite Classes

The only derived `Sprite` class used in Scorpion Roundup is the `Scorpion` class, which models a horizontally running scorpion. Listing 13.1 shows the source code for the `Scorpion` class.

Listing 13.1. The `Scorpion` class.

```
public class Scorpion extends Sprite {
  public static Image[][] image;
  private static Random   rand = new Random(System.currentTimeMillis());

  public Scorpion(Component comp, int dir, int speedInc) {
    super(comp, image[dir], 0, 1, 1, new Point((dir == 0) ?
      (comp.size().width - image[dir][0].getWidth(comp)) : 0,
      60 + Math.abs(rand.nextInt() % 5) * 44), new Point((dir == 0)
      ? (-5 - speedInc) : (5 + speedInc), 0), 10,
      Sprite.BA_DIE);
  }

  public static void initResources(Applet app, MediaTracker
    tracker, int id) {
    image = new Image[2][2];
    for (int i = 0; i < 2; i++)
      for (int j = 0; j < 2; j++) {
        image[i][j] = app.getImage(app.getCodeBase(),
          "Res/Scorp" + i + j + ".gif");
        tracker.addImage(image[i][j], id);
      }
  }

  protected void setCollision() {
    collision = new Rectangle(position.x + 3, position.y + 3,
      position.width - 6, position.height - 6);
  }

  public BitSet update() {
    // See if the scorpion escaped
    BitSet action = super.update();
    if (action.get(Sprite.SA_KILL))
      ScorpionRoundup.lost++;
    return action;
  }
}
```

The `Scorpion` class uses a two-dimensional array of images to show the animations of the scorpion kicking its legs and wagging its tail in each direction. Figure 13.3 shows the images used by the `Scorpion` class.

The constructor for `Scorpion` takes parameters specifying the direction and speed increment for the scorpion, `dir` and `speedInc`. The `dir` parameter determines in which direction the

13

scorpion travels, as well as which side of the screen it starts from, and the parameter can be set to either 0 (left) or 1 (right). The speedInc parameter specifies how much to increase the scorpion's speed beyond its default speed. This parameter is how new scorpions become faster as the difficulty level of the game increases.

Figure 13.3.

The images used by the Scorpion *class.*

The update method in Scorpion is overridden to track when the scorpion makes it across the screen. This works rather indirectly, so bear with me. Notice in the constructor for Scorpion that the bounds action is set to BA_DIE. If you recall, the bounds actions determine what a sprite does when it reaches a boundary (the other side of the applet window, in this case). The BA_DIE bounds action causes the SA_KILL flag to be returned by the default sprite update method, eventually resulting in the sprite being removed from the sprite list. By looking for this flag in Scorpion's overridden update method, you can tell when the scorpion makes it across the screen unscathed. Pretty tricky, huh?

If the scorpion has made it across safely, the ScorpionRoundup.lost variable is incremented. This variable is a public static member of the ScorpionRoundup applet class that can be accessed by other classes, such as Scorpion. You'll learn more about it later in this lesson when you get into the ScorpionRoundup class.

Scorpion Roundup uses a derived version of the SpriteVector class called SRVector. Listing 13.2 contains the source code for the SRVector class.

Listing 13.2. The SRVector class.

```
public class SRVector extends SpriteVector {
  public SRVector(Background back) {
    super(back);
  }

  Sprite isPointInside(Point pt) {
    // Iterate backward through the sprites, testing each
    for (int i = (size() - 1); i >= 0; i--) {
      Sprite s = (Sprite)elementAt(i);
      if ((s.getClass().getName().equals("Scorpion")) &&
        s.isPointInside(pt))
        return s;
```

continues

Listing 13.2. continued

```
    }
    return null;
  }

  protected boolean collision(int i, int iHit) {
    // Do nothing!
    return false;
  }
}
```

The SRVector class overrides two methods in SpriteVector: isPointInside and collision. The overridden isPointInside method is necessary to distinguish between the user clicking a scorpion sprite and clicking the net sprite. Without overriding this method, you would never be able to detect when a scorpion is clicked, because the net sprite would always be in the way. This is a result of the fact that the net sprite follows the mouse around and has a higher Z-order than the scorpions (so it can always be seen). The simple solution is to look only for sprites of type Scorpion in the isPointInside method.

Because the scorpions don't need to be able to collide with each other or the net sprite, it makes sense to do nothing when a collision occurs. This is carried out by simply returning false from the collision method.

You've now seen the sprite classes used by ScorpionRoundup. It's time to check out the applet class.

The ScorpionRoundup Class

The ScorpionRoundup class takes care of all the high-level animation and sound issues, as well as handling user input. First take a look at the member variables defined in the ScorpionRoundup class:

```
private Image        offImage, back, netImage;
private AudioClip     music, netHit, netMiss, applause;
private Graphics      offGrfx;
private Thread        animate;
private MediaTracker  tracker;
private SRVector      srv;
private Sprite        net;
private int           delay = 83; // 12 fps
private Font          infoFont = new Font("Helvetica",
                      Font.PLAIN, 14);
private FontMetrics   infoMetrics;
private Random        rand = new
                      Random(System.currentTimeMillis());
```

13

```
private boolean     musicOn = true;
private static int  level, caught;
public static int   lost;
```

You might be curious about a few of these member variables. The four AudioClip member variables hold audio clips for the music and sound effects used in the game. The musicOn member variable is a boolean variable that determines whether the music is on or off. The level, caught, and lost member variables are used to store the state of the game: level is the current difficulty level, caught is how many scorpions have been caught, and lost is how many scorpions have escaped.

The init method in ScorpionRoundup is pretty straightforward—it loads and initializes all the images and sounds used by the game:

```
public void init() {
  // Load and track the images
  tracker = new MediaTracker(this);
  back = getImage(getCodeBase(), "Res/Back.gif");
  tracker.addImage(back, 0);
  netImage = getImage(getCodeBase(), "Res/Net.gif");
  tracker.addImage(netImage, 0);
  Scorpion.initResources(this, tracker, 0);

  // Load the audio clips
  music = getAudioClip(getCodeBase(), "Res/Music.au");
  netHit = getAudioClip(getCodeBase(), "Res/NetHit.au");
  netMiss = getAudioClip(getCodeBase(), "Res/NetMiss.au");
  applause = getAudioClip(getCodeBase(), "Res/Applause.au");
}
```

The stop method has been pretty standard in all the applets you've seen thus far. However, in ScorpionRoundup it has an extra line of code that stops looping the music audio clip:

```
public void stop() {
  if (animate != null) {
    animate.stop();
    animate = null;
  }
  music.stop();
}
```

The extra line of code, music.stop(), is important because it ensures that the music is stopped when the thread is stopped. Without this simple method call, the music would continue to play even after a user has left the Web page containing the game.

13

Be sure to always stop all looped sounds when the applet thread is stopped. You do this simply by calling the stop method on the AudioClip object from within the applet's stop method, as you just saw in ScorpionRoundup.

The run method in ScorpionRoundup calls the newGame method, which you'll learn about in a moment. Listing 13.3 contains the source code for the run method.

Listing 13.3. The ScorpionRoundup class's run method.

```
public void run() {
  try {
    tracker.waitForID(0);
  }
  catch (InterruptedException e) {
    return;
  }

  // Set up a new game
  newGame();

  // Update everything
  long t = System.currentTimeMillis();
  while (Thread.currentThread() == animate) {
    srv.update();
    repaint();
    try {
      t += delay;
      Thread.sleep(Math.max(0, t - System.currentTimeMillis()));
    }
    catch (InterruptedException e) {
      break;
    }
  }
}
```

After setting up a new game, the run method enters the main update loop where it updates the sprite list and forces a repaint. Speaking of updating, the update method does a few new things in ScorpionRoundup; check out Listing 13.4.

Listing 13.4. The ScorpionRoundup class's update method.

```
public void update(Graphics g) {
  // Create the offscreen graphics context
  if (offGrfx == null) {
    offImage = createImage(size().width, size().height);
    offGrfx = offImage.getGraphics();
    infoMetrics = offGrfx.getFontMetrics(infoFont);
  }

  // Draw the sprites
  srv.draw(offGrfx);

  // Draw the game info
```

13

```
offGrfx.setFont(infoFont);
offGrfx.setColor(Color.white);
offGrfx.drawString(new String("Level: " + level +
  "  Caught: " + caught + "  Lost: " + lost), 10, 5 +
  infoMetrics.getAscent());

// Is the game over?
if (lost >= 5) {
  Font        f = new Font("Helvetica", Font.BOLD, 36);
  FontMetrics fm = offGrfx.getFontMetrics(f);
  String      s = new String("Game Over");
  offGrfx.setFont(f);
  offGrfx.drawString(s, (size().width - fm.stringWidth(s)) / 2,
    ((size().height - fm.getHeight()) / 2) + fm.getAscent());

  // Stop the music
  music.stop();
}
else
  // Add a new scorpion?
  if ((rand.nextInt() % (20 - level / 2)) == 0)
    srv.add(new Scorpion(this, 1 -
      Math.abs(rand.nextInt() % 2), level));

// Draw the image onto the screen
g.drawImage(offImage, 0, 0, null);
}
```

After drawing the sprites, the update method draws the game information in the upper left corner of the applet window. The game information includes the difficulty level, the number of scorpions caught, and the number of scorpions lost. It then checks the lost member variable to see whether it is greater than or equal to 5. If so, the game has ended, so update draws the Game Over message and stops the music. If the game isn't over, update determines whether or not it should add a new scorpion. This determination is based on the current level and a little randomness.

The mouse input in the game is handled by four different methods: mouseEnter, mouseExit, mouseMove, and mouseDown. mouseEnter and mouseExit show and hide the net sprite based on the mouse being inside or outside the applet window:

```
public boolean mouseEnter(Event evt, int x, int y) {
  if (net != null)
    net.show();
  return true;
}

public boolean mouseExit(Event evt, int x, int y) {
  if (net != null)
    net.hide();
  return true;
}
```

13

Showing and hiding the net sprite based on the mouse being in the applet window visually helps tie the net to the mouse pointer. The mouseMove method simply sets the position of the net to the position of the mouse, which causes the net to follow the mouse around:

```
public boolean mouseMove(Event evt, int x, int y) {
  if (net != null)
    net.setPosition(new Point(x - 10, y - 10));
  return true;
}
```

The last of the mouse input methods, mouseDown, checks to see whether a scorpion has been caught by calling the isPointInside method:

```
public boolean mouseDown(Event evt, int x, int y) {
  if (lost < 5) {
    Sprite s = srv.isPointInside(new Point(x - 5, y - 5));
    if (s != null) {
      // Remove the scorpion and increase number caught
      srv.removeElement(s);
      if ((++caught % 15) == 0) {
        // Increase the level and play applause sound
        level++;
        applause.play();
      }
      else
        // Play the net hit sound
        netHit.play();
    }
    else
      // Play the net miss sound
      netMiss.play();
  }
  return true;
}
```

If no scorpion has been caught, the mouseDown method plays the netMiss audio clip. If a scorpion has been caught, the scorpion sprite is removed from the list, and the caught member variable is incremented. If caught is divisible by 15, level is also incremented, and the applause audio clip is played. This results in a new level being reached for every 15 scorpions that are caught.

The keyboard input in Scorpion Roundup is only used to start a new game or toggle the music on and off. The keyDown method checks for these keys and takes the appropriate actions:

```
public boolean keyDown(Event evt, int key) {
  if ((key == (int)'n') || (key == (int)'N'))
    newGame();
  else if ((key == (int)'m') || (key == (int)'M')) {
    musicOn = !musicOn;
    if (musicOn)
      music.loop();
    else
```

13

```
      music.stop();
  }
  return true;
}
```

Finally, you arrive at the `newGame` method:

```
void newGame() {
  // Set up a new game
  level = 1;
  caught = lost = 0;
  srv = new SRVector(new ImageBackground(this, back));
  net = new Sprite(this, netImage, new Point((size().width -
    netImage.getWidth(this)) / 2, (size().height -
    netImage.getHeight(this)) / 2), new Point(0, 0), 20,
    Sprite.BA_WRAP);
  srv.add(net);
  if (musicOn)
    music.loop();
}
```

The `newGame` method does everything necessary to initialize and start a new game: The `level`, `caught`, and `lost` member variables are initialized, the sprite list is re-created, and the net sprite is re-created and added back to the list. The music is also restarted.

That wraps up the details of Scorpion Roundup, your second complete Java game. You are fast becoming a Java game expert! However, before you throw the book down and start hacking away at a game of your own, make sure you fully understand how this game works. I encourage you to try your hand at enhancing it and adding some new features. For some enhancement ideas, check out the "Exercises" section at the end of this lesson.

Summary

In today's lesson, you built your second complete Java game—Scorpion Roundup. You began by learning a little background on the game, followed by fleshing out the conceptual game design. With the groundwork laid, you saw that it wasn't so bad moving on to the actual game implementation. It was still a lot of work, but it resulted in a pretty neat game that made use of mouse input, sound effects, and music.

With another complete game under your belt, you're probably feeling pretty invincible. It's a good thing too, because tomorrow you're going to shift gears and tackle an often difficult and sobering aspect of game programming—debugging. Tomorrow's lesson covers all the big issues relating to hunting down and ridding your games of bugs. But you don't need to worry about that now; go play a few games of Scorpion Roundup and relax!

13

Q&A

Q Are scorpions really popular as pets?

A Yes they are. If you're interested in adopting your own pet scorpion, the folks at Glades Herp, Inc. would be glad to help you out. They are on the Web and can be found at `http://www.tntonline.com/gherp/gherp.htm`.

Q Why are the scorpions in the game colored green?

A Because scorpion hunters use black lights to illuminate scorpions at night, thereby making them visible. The black light causes the scorpions to take on a greenish glow.

Q Why isn't the net sprite implemented as a new sprite class?

A Because it doesn't require any new functionality beyond that provided by the `Sprite` class. You should make a strong effort to only derive new classes when you specifically need to add new functionality.

Q Why is the music in Scorpion Roundup so repetitive?

A The music is implemented as a looped audio clip. Because audio clips tend to take up a lot of space and therefore take a while to transfer over an Internet connection, it is important to keep them as short as possible. Although it is short and repetitive, the music in Scorpion Roundup still manages to add an interesting dimension to the game without taking all day to transfer.

Workshop

The Workshop section provides questions and exercises to help you get a better feel for the material you learned today. Try to answer the questions and at least think about the exercises before moving on to tomorrow's lesson. You'll find the answers to the questions in Appendix A, "Quiz Answers."

Quiz

1. Which major U.S. airport is a good place to find scorpion souvenirs?

2. Why do you need the `SRVector` class?

3. Why do scorpions only come out at night?

4. Why is the music stopped in the `stop` method of the `ScorpionRoundup` class?

5. Why is the `lost` member variable in the `ScorpionRoundup` class declared as public static?

Exercises

1. Order your own pet scorpion and give it a loving home.
2. Make the net a frame-animated sprite that gives the effect of the net waving in the air.
3. Buy a black light and see whether your pet scorpion really looks green.
4. Change the sound effects and music to use your own custom audio clips.
5. Add some entirely new sound effects, such as a laughter sound when a scorpion gets away.
6. Use the Scorpion Roundup code to create an entirely new game. For example, you could change the graphics and sound, modify the code a little, and turn the game into a target shooting game. Just change the background to a picture of a sky, the net to cross-hairs, and the scorpions to clay targets. Then modify the code so that the clay targets arch through the air, and use a gunshot sound instead of the swoosh sound used for the net. You'll have a whole new game!

13

Day 14

Squishing Bugs in Java Games

Wow, you've now finished two complete Java games! You're probably feeling pretty good about your new Java game programming skills, as you should. Without putting a damper on things, keep in mind that you didn't have to worry much about bugs in those games. Actually, you did have to contend with scorpions and tarantulas, but I'm talking about programming bugs. As sobering as it might sound, I have to admit that the games had programming bugs in them prior to some heavy debugging sessions. Who knows, they might even have a few bugs now that managed to slip by. Knowing all this, it simply wouldn't be fair to teach you about game programming without covering the often dreaded issue of debugging.

Today's lesson focuses on debugging as it applies to Java game programming. As you go through today's lesson, keep in mind that bugs are a natural part of the development process; as humans, we simply are error prone. So you should embrace debugging as a necessary part of the development process and accept the fact that even your precious code will have bugs. I'll do what I can throughout today's lesson to help you develop skills that keep bugs to a minimum, but the rest is up to you.

The following topics are covered in today's lesson:

- [ ] Debugging basics
- [ ] Choosing a debugger
- [ ] Debugging strategies

Debugging Basics

Before getting into any type of discussion regarding game debugging, let's take a moment to define exactly what a bug is.

NEW TERM   A *bug* is simply a coding error that results in some unwanted action taking place in your game.

This unwanted action can vary, from a score not being updated correctly, to the user's computer going down in flames. Although the latter case is admittedly a little exaggerated (especially in Java programming), you should take bugs very seriously because they speak volumes about the quality (or lack of quality) of your game.

The concept of bugs has been an accepted part of programming for a long time now. Although all programmers strive for perfection, few are ever able to attain it. Even those that do reach that nerd nirvana typically encounter significant numbers of bugs along the way. The difference is that these programmers anticipate bugs rather than suggest that their code is immune to bugs. Therefore, the first rule in regard to debugging is to assume that bugs are in your code and that it is your responsibility to hunt them down and fix them to the best of your ability.

The issue of finding and fixing bugs is especially important in games, because game players are often very fickle. If a game does something screwy like trashing a player's score, the player will probably get frustrated and toss your game. This makes it all the more important to be vigilant in finding bugs before you release your game. Sure, you can always distribute a patch to fix a bug in a release version, but it typically leaves game players with a less than high opinion of your development ethic.

Before getting into specific debugging strategies, let's go over a few debugging basics. If you are already familiar with debugging in Java or in another language, feel free to jump to the next section. The following are three fundamental debugging techniques that you will find indispensable when finding and fixing bugs in your games:

☐ Single-stepping code
☐ Watching variables
☐ Using breakpoints

Single-Stepping Code

A very common debugger feature is the capability to single-step through code.

NEW TERM *Single-stepping* is the process of executing your code one line at a time (in single steps).

The significance of single-stepping as a debugging technique is that it provides you with a means to see exactly what code is being executed, along with the ability to trace the flow of execution through your program. Typically, single-stepping in itself isn't entirely useful; you usually combine it with another technique known as *watching* to see what happens to variables as you step through code.

> Incidentally, a *debugger* is a software tool specifically designed to help you find bugs by letting you analyze your code as it is running. The Java Developer's Kit ships with a debugger called jdb, which you learn about a little later today in the "Choosing a Debugger" section.
>
> **NOTE**

Watching Variables

NEW TERM *Watching* is a technique that involves specifying certain variables in your code as watch variables.

NEW TERM A *watch variable* is a variable whose contents you can see while code is executing in a debugger.

Of course, in the context of a program running at normal speed, watch variables don't help much. But if you watch variables as you single-step through code, you can gain lots of insight into what is happening. Very often, you will find that variables values are changing unexpectedly or being set to values that don't make sense in the context of what you thought the code was doing. This type of insight into the inner workings of your code can lead you directly to bugs. Single-stepping combined with watch variables is the standard approach to finding bugs using a debugger.

14

Using Breakpoints

Another fundamental debugging technique is that of using breakpoints.

NEW TERM   A *breakpoint* is a line of code that you specify, which halts the execution of a program.

To understand the usefulness of breakpoints, imagine that you are interested in a line of code in the middle of a program. To get to that line of code in the debugger, you would have to single-step for hours. Or you could set a breakpoint on that line and let the debugger run the program like normal. The program then runs in the debugger until it hits the breakpoint, in which case the program halts and leaves you sitting on the specified line of code. At this point, you can watch variables and even single-step through the code if you want. You also have the option of setting multiple breakpoints at key locations in your code, which is very useful when dealing with complex execution flow problems.

Debugging Strategies

Although debugging tools have come a long way since the early days of programming, the ultimate responsibility of eliminating bugs still rests squarely on your shoulders. Think of debuggers and standard debugging techniques simply as a means of helping you find bugs, but not as your sole line of bug defense. It takes a diversified arsenal of knowledge, programming practices, debugging tools, and even some luck to truly rid your games of bugs.

Debugging can almost be likened to a hunt: You know there is something out there, and you must go find it. For this reason, you need to approach debugging with a very definite strategy. Debugging strategies can be broken into two fundamental groupings: bug prevention and bug detection. Let's take a look at both and see how they can be used together to help make your games bug-free.

Bug Prevention

Bug prevention is the process of eliminating the occurrence of bugs before they have a chance to surface. Bug prevention might sound completely logical—and that's because it is. However, surprising numbers of programmers don't employ enough bug prevention strategies in their code, and they end up paying for it in the end. Keep in mind the simple fact that bug detection is a far more time-consuming and brain-aching task than bug prevention. If you haven't understood the point yet, I'm all for bug prevention as a primary way to eliminate bugs.

Think of bug prevention versus bug detection as roughly parallel to getting an immunization shot versus treating a disease after you've contracted it. Certainly, the short-term pain of getting the shot is much easier to deal with than the long-term treatment associated with a full-blown disease. This metaphor is dangerously on the money when it comes to debugging, because bugs can often act like code diseases; just when you think you've got a bug whipped, it rears its ugly head in a new way that you never anticipated.

Hopefully, I've closed the sale and you're set to employ some bug prevention in your code. Fortunately, most preventive bug measures are simple and take little extra time to implement. Unfortunately, compared to other languages, Java is fairly limited in regard to providing preventive debugging facilities. However, this fact is a little misleading because the nature of Java removes many of the bug creation opportunities available in other languages such as C and C++. For example, the `assert` mechanism is one of the most popular preventive debugging techniques in C/C++. `assert` allows you to check boolean conditions in debug versions of your programs. A primary usage of `assert` is to defend against the occurrence of null pointers. Because Java has no pointers, you can immediately eliminate the risks associated with this entire family of bugs. So, even though Java doesn't have a bug prevention facility similar to `assert`, there's no loss because in Java you can't create the bugs typically found using `assert`.

Isolated Test Methods

A good way to prevent bugs early in the development cycle is to test your code heavily as it is being developed. Of course, most programmers do indeed try out their code as they are writing it, so you're probably thinking that you perform enough testing as it is. However, the type of testing I'm talking about is a thorough test of your classes in an isolated manner. Think about it like this: If you heavily test your classes in isolation from other classes, don't you think the odds of bugs appearing when you connect everything will be lower? Furthermore, think of how much easier it is to test your classes early without having to contend with a bunch of complex interactions taking place between different classes.

My suggestion is to build a single method into each one of your classes that puts the class through a series of tests. Call the method `test` if you like, and make sure that it handles creating instances of the class using various constructors (if you have more than one), as well as calling all the methods that can be called in isolation. I know that, practically speaking, certain aspects of the class can only be tested in the presence of other classes, but that's all right; just test whatever you can.

In your `test` method, you probably want to output the values of certain member variables. Just output the results to standard output. If you are unfamiliar with using standard output, don't worry. You learn about using it for debugging later in today's lesson.

14

Exception Handling

One useful preventive debugging mechanism used in C++ is exception handling, which also shares very solid support in Java.

NEW TERM   *Exception handling* is a technique focused on detecting and responding to unexpected events at runtime.

NEW TERM   An *exception* is something (usually bad) that occurs in your program that you weren't expecting.

Unlike some other forms of preventive bug detection, however, exception handling also has a valuable place in release code.

To handle exceptions in your game code, you enclose potentially troublesome code within a try clause. A try clause is a special Java construct that tells the runtime system that a section of code could cause trouble. You then add another piece of code (a handler) in a corresponding catch clause that responds to errors caused by the code in the try clause. The error event itself is the exception, and the code in the catch clause is known as an exception handler.

The following is some exception handling code that you've seen a lot in the sample applets throughout this book:

```
try {
  tracker.waitForID(0);
}
catch (InterruptedException e) {
  return;
}
```

In this code, the exception being handled is of type InterruptedException, which specifies that the current thread was interrupted by another thread. In some cases, this might not be a problem, but the code following this particular code is dependent on images successfully loading, which is indicated by the return from the waitForID method. Therefore, it's important that the thread is not interrupted. The only problem with this exception handler is that it doesn't output any information regarding the nature of the exception. Typically, you would have code here that prints information to standard output, which you learn about a little later today in the "Standard Output" section.

This discussion of exception handling really only scratches the surface of handling runtime errors (exceptions). I strongly encourage you to learn more about exception handling and how to effectively use it. Fortunately, a lot of information has been published about exception handling in Java, so you shouldn't have much trouble finding useful references.

14

Parentheses and Precedence

One area prone to bugs is that of operator precedence. I've been busted plenty of times myself for thinking that I remembered the precedence of operators correctly when I didn't. Take a look at the following code:

```
int a = 37, b = 26;
int n = a % 3 + b / 7 ^ 8;
```

If you are a whiz at remembering things and you can immediately say without a shadow of a doubt what this expression is equal to, then good for you. For the rest of us, this is a pretty risky piece of code because it can yield a variety of different results depending on the precedence of the operators. Actually, it only yields one result, based on the correct order of operator precedence set forth by the Java language. But it's easy for programmers to mix up the precedence and write code that they think is doing one thing when it is doing something else.

What's the solution? The solution is to use parentheses even when you don't technically need them, just to be safe about the precedence. The following is the same code with extra parentheses added to make the precedence more clear:

```
int a = 37, b = 26;
int n = ((a % 3) + (b / 7)) ^ 8;
```

Hidden Member Variables

Another potentially tricky bug that is common in object-oriented game programming is the hidden member variable. A hidden member variable is a variable that has become "hidden" due to a derived class implementing a new variable of the same name. Take a look at Listing 14.1, which contains two classes: `Weapon` and `Bazooka`.

Listing 14.1. The `Weapon` and `Bazooka` classes.

```
class Weapon {
  int power;
  int numShots;

  public Weapon() {
    power = 5;
    numShots = 10;
  }

  public void fire() {
    numShots--;
  }
}
```

continues

14

Listing 14.1. continued

```
class Bazooka : extends Weapon {
  int numShots;

  public Bazooka() {
    super();
  }

  public blastEm() {
    power--;
    numShots -= 2;
  }
}
```

The Weapon class defines two member variables: power and numShots. The Bazooka class is derived from Weapon and also implements a numShots member variable, which effectively hides the original numShots inherited from Weapon. The problem with this code is that when the Weapon constructor is called by Bazooka (via the call to super), the hidden numShots variable defined in Weapon is initialized, not the one in Bazooka. Later, when the blastEm method is called in Bazooka, the visible (derived) numShots variable is used, which has been initialized by default to zero. As you can probably imagine, more complex classes with this problem can end up causing some seriously tricky and hard to trace bugs.

The solution to the problem is to simply make sure that you never hide variables. That doesn't mean that there aren't a few isolated circumstances in which you might want to use variable hiding on purpose; just keep in mind the risks involved in doing so.

Bug Detection

Even if you rigorously employ bug avoidance techniques, you will still have to contend with a certain number of bugs. It's just a fact of life that programmers make mistakes, and the sheer complexity of large programming projects often causes problems that elude us. That's all right. Just embrace the notion that you're imperfect and focus your attention on tracking down the mistakes. The point is that in addition to applying bug prevention techniques as much as possible, you must learn how to track down the inevitable bugs that will surface when you start testing your game. Let's look at a few techniques for hunting down bugs.

Standard Output

The age-old technique for tracking down bugs is to print information to standard output. This approach probably sounds pretty archaic—and in many ways it is—but if you want a quick and dirty look into what's going on in your game, it's often your best bet. This

14

technique is especially useful now, because visual Java debuggers are still rough around the edges.

Employing the standard output technique is as simple as inserting calls to System.out.println at appropriate locations in your code. You can use standard output for anything from looking at the value of variables to determining whether a method is being called; just sprinkle those println calls wherever you need them! The primary caveat to this approach is that you should attempt to place the println call in an update loop, like the loop controlling the animation in games. In this case, the println call might slow the game to a crawl simply because of the overhead involved in printing text to the standard output device.

NOTE

Speaking of standard output devices, you might be wondering exactly where standard output goes when you are running an applet inside a Web browser such as Netscape Navigator. The truth is that nobody knows! (Just kidding!) Netscape Navigator provides a console window where you can see everything that is being sent to standard output. To display this window, just look under the Options menu in Navigator and select Show Java Console.

Call Stack Trace

An indispensable tool in tracking down hard to find bugs is the method call stack. The method *call stack* is a list of the methods called to arrive at the currently executing code. By examining the call stack, you can see exactly which methods were called to get to the current piece of code in question. This information often sheds light on a problem regarding a method being called inadvertently.

You can view the call stack by calling the printStackTrace method, which is a member of the Throwable class. Because printStackTrace is a method in Throwable, you must have a Throwable object to look at the call stack. It just so happens that all exceptions are derived from Throwable, so any time you have an exception, you can view the call stack. Check out the following code:

```
try {
  int nums[] = new int[5];
  for (int i = 0; i < 10; i++)
    nums[i] = 6670;
}
catch (ArrayIndexOutOfBoundsException e) {
  System.out.println("**Exception** : " + e.getMessage());
  e.printStackTrace();
}
```

14

In this code, the array `nums` is indexed out of bounds in the `for` loop, generating an `ArrayIndexOutOfBoundsException`. The exception is logged to standard output in the `catch` clause, along with a call to `printStackTrace`. The resulting output follows:

```
**Exception** : 5
java.lang.ArrayIndexOutOfBoundsException: 5
 at TravelingGecko.init(TravelingGecko.java:32)
 at sun.applet.AppletPanel.run(AppletPanel.java:259)
 at java.lang.Thread.run(Thread.java:294)
```

Incidentally, I placed this example code in the `init` method in the Traveling Gecko game, which explains the call stack results.

Choosing a Debugger

An important decision regarding how you finally decide to debug your game is that of choosing a debugger. A debugger is an invaluable tool in ridding your game of bugs, and it can directly determine how much time you spend debugging. Therefore, you should make sure to invest your resources wisely and choose a debugger that fits your development style. Unfortunately, the third-party Java debugger market is still in its infancy, so don't expect to have lots of debuggers to choose from at this point. Nevertheless, try to keep tabs on the latest Java development tools and how they might impact your debugging.

A few third-party integrated development environments that include built-in visual debuggers are available for Java. These are very nice and usually include lots of cool features beyond the ones you just learned about; definitely look into getting a full-featured debugger if at all possible. You learn much more about Java development environments, including debuggers, on Day 21, "Assembling a Game Development Toolkit." For now, just keep in mind that choosing a debugger that fits your needs is important in determining how successfully you can rid your code of bugs. Fortunately, nearly all debuggers perform the basic debugging functions of single-stepping, supporting watch variables, and using breakpoints.

The Java Developer's Kit comes standard with a debugger (jdb) that performs basic debugging functions such as those you learned about earlier. It is a command-line debugger, which means that it has no fancy graphics or point-and-click features but it does get the job done. If you aren't ready to commit to a third-party tool, by all means try out jdb. After you get comfortable with jdb, you might find that it serves your purposes well enough.

Before you can use jdb, you need to compile your code so that it includes debugging information. The Java compiler switch for doing this is `-g`, which causes the compiler to generate debugging tables containing information about line numbers and variables.

NOTE

Some distributions of the JDK also include an alternate Java compiler called javac_g. If you have this compiler in your distribution (look in the java/bin directory), use it, because it compiles code without using some of the internal optimizations performed by the javac compiler.

Using the jdb debugger is a topic best left to the introductory books on Java. However, there is a nice online tutorial for using jdb to debug Java code on Sun's Java Web site, which is located at http://www.javasoft.com.

Summary

Today you learned about crushing bugs in Java code. You not only learned the importance of diagnosing and putting an end to bugs in games, you learned some valuable tips on how to help prevent bugs before they can even appear. You began the lesson with a somewhat formal definition of a bug, followed by some debugging basics. You then moved on to determining how to select a debugger, and you finished up with a look at some common debugging strategies.

The debugging strategies you learned about today are in no way comprehensive. The reality is that debugging is an art form involving a lot of practice, intuition, and even heartache. You will no doubt establish your own bag of debugging tricks far beyond those I've suggested here. I encourage you to be as crafty as possible when it comes to ferreting out pesky bugs!

If you think debugging puts a strain on your brain, try letting the computer think for you. Hey, that just happens to be the topic of your next lesson: artificial intelligence. But before you move on to that, there's some celebrating to do. You're finished with your second week of lessons!

Q&A

Q Where does the term "bug" come from?

A The term "bug" was coined by programming pioneer Grace Hopper back in the days when programming was performed using rudimentary hardware switches. As the story goes, a computer malfunctioned and someone noticed that a moth had gotten caught in one of the mechanical relays in the computer, keeping the relay from closing and making contact. From that time forward, programming errors were referred to as bugs.

14

Q Using watch variables, is it possible to watch an entire object at once?

A Yes, most debuggers provide a means of watching an entire object at once, just like any other variable.

Q How does Java's use of automatic garbage collection impact debugging?

A The garbage collection mechanism employed by Java, coupled with the inability to use pointers, removes a wide range of bug creation opportunities. Aside from removing the problem of dealing with null pointers, Java also alleviates having to contend with memory leaks, which are very common in C and C++. *Memory leaks are chunks of memory that are allocated but inadvertently never deleted, effectively resulting in memory loss.*

Workshop

The Workshop section provides questions and exercises to help you get a better feel for the material you learned today. Try to answer the questions and at least go over the exercises before moving on to tomorrow's lesson. You'll find the answers to the questions in Appendix A, "Quiz Answers."

Quiz

1. What is the significance of single-stepping?
2. What is an exception?
3. How does a variable become "hidden"?
4. What is a method call stack?

Exercises

1. Learn how to use the jdb debugger that comes with the Java Developer's Kit.
2. Try using breakpoints and single-stepping through some of the code in the Scorpion Roundup sample game.
3. See whether you can find any bugs in Scorpion Roundup, or for that matter in any of the sample code in the book. If you manage to find anything, be sure to e-mail me and let me know how disappointed you are that I could be such a slacker to ship bug-ridden code! My e-mail address is located in the author bio at the front of the book.

In Review

Congratulations! You survived another week. This week you learned about user input, sound, and Java debugging, in addition to writing a couple of games along the way. Let's look at what you did each day in a little more detail before you embark on your final week of Java game programming.

Day 8

On Day 8, you learned about user input and how it is used in games. You learned about the two primary input devices supported by Java (the keyboard and the mouse) and various issues associated with each. Although it was fairly brief, this lesson gave you the background necessary to understand how user input works in Java games.

Day 9

Day 9 presented the details of how Java supports user input. More specifically, it showed how to handle user input events generated by the user manipulating input devices. You began by learning about input events and how they are managed in Java by the AWT. You then learned how to trap keyboard and mouse input events, culminating in an animated sample applet—Flying Saucer.

Day 10

On Day 10, you wrote your first complete Java game—Traveling Gecko. Traveling Gecko incorporated practically everything you learned throughout the prior nine lessons, including animation and user input. In developing Traveling Gecko, you learned the importance of fully designing the game before beginning the development of Java code. This strategy served your purposes well and is emphasized throughout the rest of the book.

Day 11

In Day 11's lesson, you learned about the fundamentals of sound and how sound is used in games. You began by learning the basics of digital sound and the sound format supported by Java. You moved on to learning about how sound is used in games. You then saw some popular sound editing tools and utilities, and you finished up by learning how to create, edit, and find sounds for games.

Day 12

Day 12 presented you with the specifics of how to play sounds in Java. You learned that Java's current sound support, although still fairly rudimentary, is enough to provide pretty neat sound effects for games. You finished up the lesson by developing a sample applet, WildAnimals, that showed off Java's sound capabilities.

Day 13

Day 13 marked another major milestone in your quest to become a Java game programming expert: You wrote your second complete Java game—Scorpion Roundup. Scorpion Roundup incorporated much of the information learned thus far, including animation, user input, and sound. Hopefully, with the development of Scorpion Roundup, you started to feel more confident in your skills as a Java game programmer.

Day 14

You finished up your second week of Java game programming with a lesson on debugging. This lesson presented some basic strategies for tracking down and eliminating bugs, along with some thoughts about bugs specific to games. You'll certainly find that bugs are as unique as the games they reside in, so think of this lesson as a starting point in your journey toward bug-free Java game development.

WEEK

3

15

16

17

18

19

20

21

At a Glance

If you've made it this far, you're probably feeling pretty good about your Java game programming skills. You might even wonder how much could be left to learn. Well, I don't mean to dampen your spirits, but you still have a decent amount of stuff to cover. You have yet to touch on artificial intelligence or multiplayer network gaming, which are two very big topics. You begin your final week with a conceptual lesson on artificial intelligence, followed by a complete game utilizing AI—Connect4. You then learn about the basics of multiplayer games, along with the network support provided by Java. You combine this knowledge to create a two-player network version of Connect4—NetConnect4. You finish the week with lessons on Java code optimization and assembling a set of Java game development tools.

You cover the following topics this week:

- ☐ Teaching Games to Think
- ☐ Connect4: Human versus Machine
- ☐ The Basics of Multiplayer Gaming
- ☐ Networking with Java
- ☐ NetConnect4: Human versus Human
- ☐ Optimizing Java Code for Games
- ☐ Assembling a Game Development Toolkit

Day 15

Teaching Games to Think

Creating truly engaging games is often a matter of effectively mimicking human thought within the confines of software constructs. Because you no doubt want your Java games to be engaging, you need at least a basic understanding of how to give your games some degree of brain power. So you begin this week by tackling one of the most exciting and challenging areas of gaming: artificial intelligence.

Today's focus is understanding the fundamental theories of artificial intelligence and how they can be applied to games. If you're tired of sifting through source code, you're in luck; today, I promise to go very lightly on the use of Java code. Think of today's lesson as a theoretical journey through artificial intelligence as applied to games, complete with examples of popular commercial games and the artificial intelligence algorithms they use to keep you coming back for more. After today, you will have the fundamental knowledge required to begin implementing artificial intelligence strategies in your own games.

The following topics are covered in today's lesson:

- ☐ Artificial intelligence fundamentals
- ☐ Types of game AI
- ☐ Implementing your own AI
- ☐ AI in commercial games
- ☐ AI resources on the Web

Artificial Intelligence Fundamentals

NEW TERM *Artificial intelligence* (AI) is defined simply as techniques used on a computer to emulate the human thought process.

This is a pretty general definition for AI, as it should be; AI is a very broad research area, with game-related AI being a relatively small subset of the whole of AI knowledge. Today's goal is not to explore every area of AI, because that would take up the space of the book in itself, but rather to cover much theoretical AI territory as it applies to games.

As you might have already guessed, human thought is no simple process to emulate, which explains why AI is such a diverse area of research. Even though there are many different approaches to AI, all of them basically boil down to attempting to make human decisions within the limitations of a computer. Most traditional AI systems use a variety of information-based algorithms to make decisions, just as people use a variety of previous experiences and mental rules to make a decision. In the past, the information-based AI algorithms were completely deterministic, meaning that every decision could be traced back to a predictable flow of logic. Figure 15.1 shows an example of a purely logical human thought process. Obviously, human thinking doesn't work this way at all; if we were all this predictable, it would be quite a boring planet!

Eventually, AI researchers realized that the deterministic approaches to AI weren't sufficient to accurately model human thought. Their focus shifted from deterministic AI models to more realistic AI models that attempted to factor in the subtle complexities of human thought, such as best-guess decisions. In people, these types of decisions can result from a combination of past experience, personal bias, or the current state of emotion, in addition to the completely logical decision making process. Figure 15.2 shows an example of this type of thought process. The point is that people don't always make scientifically predictable decisions based on analyzing their surroundings and arriving at a logical conclusion. The world would probably be a better place if we did act like this, but again, it would be awfully boring!

Figure 15.1.

A completely logical human thought process.

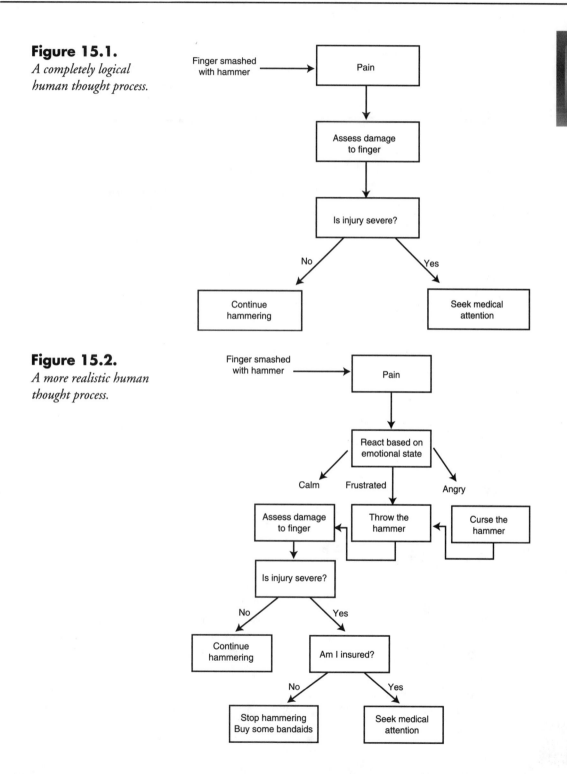

Figure 15.2.

A more realistic human thought process.

The logic flow in Figure 15.1 is an ideal scenario where each decision is made based on a totally objective logical evaluation of the situation. Figure 15.2 shows a more realistic scenario, which factors in the emotional state of the person, as well as a financial angle (the question of whether the person has insurance). Examining the second scenario from a completely logical angle, it makes no sense for the person to throw the hammer, because that only slows down the task at hand. However, this is a completely plausible and fairly common human response to pain and frustration. For an AI carpentry system to effectively model this situation, there would definitely have to be some hammer throwing code in there somewhere!

This hypothetical thought example is meant to give you a tiny clue as to how many seemingly unrelated things go into forming a human thought. Likewise, it only makes sense that it should take an extremely complex AI system to effectively model human thought. Most of the time this statement is true. However, the word "effectively" allows for a certain degree of interpretation, based on the context of the application requiring AI. For your purposes, effective AI simply means AI that makes computer game objects an engaging challenge.

More recent AI research has been focused at tackling problems similar to the ones illustrated by the hypothetical carpentry example. One particularly interesting area is fuzzy logic systems, which attempt to make "best-guess" decisions, rather than the concrete decisions of traditional AI systems.

NEW TERM   A *fuzzy logic system* is an AI system that uses "best-guess" evaluations to make decisions, which is more akin to how humans make decisions.

Another interesting AI research area in relation to games is genetic algorithms, which try to model evolved thought. A game using genetic algorithms would theoretically have computer opponents that learn as the game progresses, providing the human player with a seemingly never ending series of challenges.

NEW TERM   *Genetic algorithms* are algorithms that learn and evolve in their ability to make decisions as they are run repeatedly.

Types of Game AI

There are many different types of AI systems and even more specific algorithms implementing those systems. Even when you limit AI to the world of games, there is still a wide range of information and options from which to choose when it comes to adding AI to a game of your own. Many different AI solutions are geared toward particular types of games, with a plethora of different possibilities that can be applied in different situations.

What I'm getting at is that there is no way to just present a bunch of AI algorithms and tell you which one goes with which particular type of game. Rather, it makes more sense to give you the theoretical background on a few of the most important types of AI, and then let you

15

figure out how they might apply to your particular gaming needs. Having said all that, I've broken game-related AI down into three fundamental types: roaming, behavioral, and strategic.

NOTE The three types of AI discussed here are in no way meant to encompass all the AI approaches used in games, they are simply the most common types I've seen. So, please feel free to do your own research and expand on these; some Web sites are included at the end of today's lesson that contain very useful information about more advanced AI topics.

Roaming AI

NEW TERM *Roaming AI* refers to AI that models the movement of game objects—that is, the decisions game objects make that determine how they roam about the game world.

A good example of roaming AI is in shoot-em up space games, where aliens often tend to track and go after the player. Similarly, aliens that fly around in a predetermined pattern are also implemented using roaming AI. Basically, roaming AI is used whenever a computer-controlled object must make a decision to alter its current path, either to achieve a desired result in the game or simply to conform to a particular movement pattern. In the space shoot-em up example, the desired result is colliding with and damaging the player's ship.

Implementing roaming AI is usually very simple; it typically involves altering an object's velocity or position (the alien) based on the position of another object (the player's ship). The roaming movement of the object can also be influenced by random or predetermined pattern. There are three different types of roaming AI: chasing, evading, and patterned.

Chasing

NEW TERM *Chasing* is a type of roaming AI in which a game object tracks and goes after another game object or objects.

Chasing is the approach used in the space shoot-em up example, where an alien is chasing the player's ship. It is implemented simply by altering the alien's velocity or position based on the current position of the player's ship. The following is a sample Java implementation of a simple chasing algorithm:

```
if (aX > pX)
  aX--;
else if (aX < pX)
  aX++;
```

```
if (aY > pY)
  aY--;
else if (aY < cY)
  aY++;
```

As you can see, the X and Y position (aX and aY) of the alien is altered based on where the player is located (pX and pY). The only potential problem with this code is that it could work too well; the alien will home in on the player with no hesitation, basically giving the player no chance to dodge it. This might be what you want, but more than likely, you want the alien to fly around a little while it chases the player. You probably also want the chasing to be a little imperfect, giving the player at least some chance of out-maneuvering the alien.

One method of smoothing out the chasing algorithm is to throw a little randomness into the calculation of the new position, like this:

```
if ((rand.nextInt() % 2) == 0) {
  if (aX > pX)
    aX--;
  else if (aX < pX)
    aX++;
}
if ((rand.nextInt() % 2) == 0) {
  if (aY > pY)
    aY--;
  else if (aY < cY)
    aY++;
}
```

In this code, the alien has a one in three chance of tracking the player in each direction. Even with only a one in three chance, the alien will still tend to chase the player pretty effectively, while allowing the player a fighting chance at getting out of the way. You might think that a one in three chance doesn't sound all that effective, but keep in mind that the alien only alters its path to chase the player. A smart player will probably figure this out and change directions frequently.

If you aren't too fired up about the random approach to leveling off the chase, you probably need to look into patterned movement. But you're getting a little ahead of yourself; let's take a look at evading first.

Evading

NEW TERM   *Evading* is the logical counterpart to chasing; it is another type of roaming AI where a game object specifically tries to get away from another object or objects.

Evading is implemented in a similar manner to chasing, as the following code shows:

```
if (aX > pX)
  aX++;
else if (aX < pX)
  aX--;
```

```
if (aY > pY)
  aY++;
else if (aY < cY)
  aY--;
```

This is roughly the same code used by the chasing algorithm, with the only differences being the unary operators (++, --) used to change the alien's position. Like chasing, evading can be softened using randomness or patterned movement.

A good example of using the evading algorithm would be a computer-controlled version of the player's ship. If you think about it, the player is using the evading algorithm to dodge the aliens; it's just implemented by hitting keys rather than in a piece of code. If you want to provide a demo mode in a game like this where the computer plays itself, you would use an evading algorithm to control the player's ship.

Patterned

NEW TERM *Patterned* movement refers to a type of roaming AI that uses a predefined set of movements for a game object.

Good examples of patterned movement are the aliens in the classic Galaga arcade game, which perform all kinds of neat aerobatics on their way down the screen. Patterns can include circles, figure eights, zigzags, or even more complex movements. Another example of patterned movement is the ghosts in another classic, Pac Man, who always move toward the player (subject to the constraints of the walls and, of course, whether you've eaten a power pellet).

NOTE

In truth, the aliens in Galaga use a combined approach of both patterned and chasing movement; although they certainly follow specific patterns, the aliens still make sure to come after the player whenever possible. Additionally, as the player moves into higher levels the roaming AI starts favoring chasing over patterned movement, simply to make the game harder. This is a really neat usage of combined roaming AI. This touches on the concept of behavioral AI, which you learn about in the next section.

Patterns are usually stored as an array of velocity or position offsets (or multipliers) that are applied to an object whenever patterned movement is required of it, like this:

```
int[][] zigzag = {{1, 1}, {-1, 1}};
aX += zigzag[patStep][0];
aY += zigzag[patStep][1];
```

This code shows how to implement a very simple vertical zigzag pattern. The int array `zigzag` contains pairs of XY offsets used to apply the pattern to the alien. The `patStep` variable is an integer representing the current step in the pattern. When this pattern is applied, the alien moves in a vertical direction while zigzagging back and forth horizontally.

Behavioral AI

Although the types of roaming AI strategies are pretty neat in their own right, a practical gaming scenario often requires a mixture of all three.

NEW TERM *Behavioral AI* is another fundamental type of gaming AI that often uses a mixture of roaming AI algorithms to give game objects specific behaviors.

Using the trusted alien example again, what if you want the alien to chase some times, evade other times, follow a pattern still other times, and maybe even act totally randomly every once in a while? Another good reason for using behavioral AI is to alter the difficulty of a game. For example, you could favor a chasing algorithm more than random or patterned movement to make aliens more aggressive in higher levels of a space game.

To implement behavioral AI, you need to establish a set of behaviors for the alien. Giving game objects behaviors is pretty simple, and usually just involves establishing a ranking system for each type of behavior present in the system, and then applying it to each object. For example, in the alien system, you would have the following behaviors: chase, evade, fly in a pattern, and fly randomly. For each different type of alien, you would assign different percentages to the different behaviors, thereby giving them each different personalities. For example, an aggressive alien might have the following behavioral breakdown: chase 50% of the time, evade 10% of the time, fly in a pattern 30% of the time, and fly randomly 10% of the time. On the other hand, a more passive alien might act like this: chase 10% of the time, evade 50% of the time, fly in a pattern 20% of the time, and fly randomly 20% of the time.

This behavioral approach works amazingly well and yields surprising results considering how simple it is to implement. A typical implementation simply involves a `switch` statement or nested `if-else` statements to select a particular behavior. A sample Java implementation for the behavioral aggressive alien would look like this:

```java
int behavior = Math.abs(rand.nextInt() % 100);
if (behavior < 50)
  // chase
else if (behavior < 60)
  // evade
else if (behavior < 90)
  // fly in a pattern
else
  // fly randomly
```

As you can see, creating and assigning behaviors is open to a wide range of creativity. One of the best sources of ideas for creating game object behaviors is the primal responses common in the animal world (and unfortunately all too often in the human world, too). As a matter of fact, a simple fight or flight behavioral system can work wonders when applied intelligently to a variety of game objects. Basically, use your imagination as a guide and create as many unique behaviors as you can dream up.

Strategic AI

The final fundamental type of game AI you're going to learn about is strategic AI.

NEW TERM *Strategic AI* is basically any AI that is designed to play a game with a fixed set of well-defined rules.

For example, a computer-controlled chess player would use strategic AI to determine each move based on trying to improve the chances of winning the game. Strategic AI tends to vary more based on the nature of the game, because it is so tightly linked to the rules of the game. Even so, there are established and successful approaches to applying strategic AI to many general types of games, such as games played on a rectangular board with pieces. Checkers and chess immediately come to mind as fitting into this group, and likewise have a rich history of AI research devoted to them.

Strategic AI, especially for board games, typically involves some form of weighted look-ahead approach to determining the best move to make. The look-ahead is usually used in conjunction with a fixed table of predetermined moves. For a look-ahead to make sense, however, there must be a method of looking at the board at any state and calculating a score. This is known as *weighting* and is often the most difficult part of implementing strategic AI in a board game. As an example of how difficult weighting can be, watch a game of chess or checkers and try to figure out who is winning after every single move. Then go a step further and think about trying to calculate a numeric score for each player at each point in the game. Obviously, near the end of the game it gets easier, but early on it is very difficult to tell who is winning, simply because there are so many different things that can happen. Attempting to quantify the state of the game in a numeric score is even more difficult.

NEW TERM *Weighting* is a method of looking at a game at any state and calculating a score for each player.

Nevertheless, there are ways to successfully calculate a weighted score for strategic games. Using a look-head approach with scoring, a strategic AI algorithm can test for every possible move for each player multiple moves into the future and determine which move is the best. This move is often referred to as the "least worst" move rather than the best, because the goal typically is to make the move that helps the other player the least, rather than the other way around. Of course, the end result is basically the same, but it is an interesting way to look at a game, nevertheless.

Even though look-ahead approaches to implementing strategic AI are useful in many cases, they do have a fairly significant overhead if very much depth is required (in other words, if the computer player needs to be very smart). This is because the look-ahead depth search approach suffers from a geometric progression of calculations, meaning that the overhead significantly increases when the search depth is increased.

To better understand this, consider the case of a computer Backgammon player. The computer player has to choose two or four moves from possibly several dozen, as well as decide whether to double or resign. A practical Backgammon program might assign weights to different combinations of positions and calculate the value of each position reachable from the current position and dice roll. A scoring system would then be used to evaluate the worth of each potential position, which gets back to the often difficult proposition of scoring, even in a game, such as Backgammon, with simple rules. Now apply this scenario to a hundred-unit war game, with every unit having unique characteristics, and the terrain and random factors complicating the issue still further. The optimal system of scoring simply cannot be determined in a reasonable amount of time, especially with the limited computing power of a workstation or PC.

The solution in these cases is to settle for a "good enough" move, rather than the "best" move. One of the best ways to develop the algorithm for finding the "good enough" move is to set up the computer to play both sides in a game, using a lot of variation between the algorithms and weights playing each side. Then sit back and let the two computer players battle it out and see which one wins the most. This approach typically involves a lot of tinkering with the AI code, but it can result in very good computer players.

Implementing Your Own AI

When deciding how to implement AI in a game, you need to do some preliminary work to assess exactly what type and level of AI you think is warranted. You need to determine what level of computer response suits your needs, abilities, resources, and project timeframe.

If your main concern is developing a game that keeps human players entertained and challenged, go with the most simple AI possible. Actually, try to go with the most simple AI regardless of your goals, because you can always enhance it incrementally. If you think your game needs a type of AI that doesn't quite fit into any I've described, do some research and see whether something out there is closer to what you need. Most importantly, budget plenty of time for implementing AI, because 99 percent of the time, it will take longer than you ever anticipated to get it all working at a level you are happy with.

15

What is the best way to get started? Start in small steps, of course. Let's look at a hypothetical example of implementing AI for a strategic war game. Many programmers like to write code as they design, and while that approach might work in some cases, I recommend at least some degree of preliminary design on paper. Furthermore, try to keep this design limited to a subset of the game's AI, such as a single tank. Rather than writing the data structures and movement rules for an armored division and all related subordinate units, and then trying to work out how the lower units will find their way from point A to point B, start with a small, simple map or grid and simple movement rules. Write the code to get a single tank from point A to point B. Then add complications piece by piece, building onto a complete algorithm at each step. If you are careful to make each piece of the AI general enough and open enough to connect to other pieces, your final algorithms should be general enough to handle any conditions your game might encounter.

Getting back to more basic terms, a good way to build AI experience is to write a computer opponent for a simple board game, such as tic-tac-toe or checkers. Detailed AI solutions exist for many popular games, so you should be able to find them if you check out some of the Web sites mentioned later in today's lesson.

AI in Commercial Games

Now that you have a little theory under your belt, it's time to take a look at how the game industry is using AI. So far, adventure and strategy games are the only commercial games to have a great deal of success in implementing complex AI systems. One of the most notable series of games to implement realistic AI is the immensely popular Ultima series, by Origin Systems, Inc. The Ultima series allows the player to explore villages, complete with all walks of human life, also known as non-player characters (NPCs). The NPCs in the Ultima series are true to their expected natures, which makes the game more believable. Even more importantly, however, is how the computer-controlled humans engage the player in various circumstances, which makes the games infinitely more interesting. This degree of interactivity, combined with effective AI, results in players feeling as though they are part of a virtual world; this is typically the ultimate goal of AI in games, especially in adventure games.

Origin Systems later delivered System Shock, which added an innovative twist to the interaction between the player and the NPCs. In System Shock, the player interacts with NPCs via e-mail, which is certainly a more logical communication medium for games set in the future. This approach really hits home with those of us who rely on e-mail for our day-to-day communications.

With more powerful hardware affording new opportunities for implementing complex AI systems in games, there is a renewed interest in AI within the commercial game community. As a matter of fact, many new games that boast a wide range of AI implementations are being released. Following are some of the new commercial games making strong claims to AI support. Because these games are all new, and because most of them aren't on the market as I'm writing this, be aware that each game may change when it actually hits the shelves.

Battlecruiser: 3000AD

Battlecruiser: 3000AD, by Take 2 Interactive Software, claims to be the first commercial game to feature neural networks. Neural networks are a fairly recent area of AI research and use very complex mathematics to model communications and actions in the brain. Virtually every non-player character in Battlecruiser: 3000AD is driven by a neural network, including each of the 125 crew members on your own ship. The computer opponents also use neural networks to guide negotiations, trading, and of course, combat.

For more information about Battlecruiser: 3000AD, check out its Web page at

```
http://www.westol.com/~taketwo/battle.html
```

Cloak, Dagger, and DNA

Cloak, Dagger, and DNA, by Oidian Systems, is one of, if not *the* first game to make use of genetic algorithms. Genetic algorithms comprise an advanced branch of AI devoted to evolved thought in AI systems. Cloak, Dagger, and DNA is the first in a family of games by Oidian Systems using genetic algorithms. The game itself is somewhat similar to Risk; a map is broken down into regions, some of which contain factories. The possession of factories both brings income to the player and provides bases where you can build more units (either armies or spies). Armies are necessary to take and defend areas, and combat is calculated based on the number of units in a given area, with the defender getting a defensive bonus.

The heart of the game is its use of genetic algorithms to guide the computer opponent play. It comes with four "DNA strands," which are rules governing the behavior of the computer opponents. As each DNA strand plays, it tracks how well it does in every battle. Between battles, the user can allow the DNA strands to compete against each other (and/or the player's DNA strand) in a series of tournaments that allow each DNA strand to evolve. There are a number of rules governing how DNA strands mutate, and the user can edit these rules for a particular strand. A library of up to 50 DNA patterns can be maintained in the shareware version.

For information about Cloak, Dagger, and DNA, and to download your own copy, check out its Web page at

```
http://www.quake.net/~obrien/oidian/cddna.html
```

Destiny

Destiny, by Interactive Magic, promises to combine the best elements of Civilization, Sim City, and Descent to provide a 3-D strategy game. Interactive Magic, the same company that produced Star Rangers, Apache, and Air Warrior II, has teamed up with a company called Neuromedia, an AI development studio. Not a lot is known about Neuromedia, but they've published papers for various AI symposiums, mostly on genetic algorithms, so it's only logical to expect some degree of genetic AI in the game.

For more information about Destiny, stop by its Web page, which is located at

```
http://www.imagicgames.com/destiny.dir/destiny.html
```

Dungeon Keeper

Dungeon Keeper, by Interplay, puts you in the role of a keeper of a dungeon filled with monsters, traps, and treasure, among other things. The game is somewhat of a dungeon simulator, where you are placed in charge of a limited amount of resources and monsters and must build a dungeon room by room. If you're successful, you'll be able to bring in new recruits and continue to fight off parties of adventurers foolish enough to visit.

The AI in the game makes use of a process called "behavioral cloning" to learn from the human player's actions. The brains of the monsters themselves come from hundreds of hours of internal play by the game designers; every time an interesting trick by one of the human players proved to be repeatedly successful, it was incorporated by the designers into the monsters' AI database. In the network mode, you can even allow the game to run in the background and let the AI manage the hiring of monsters and placement of rooms and traps, solely based on information the game has learned from watching the player.

Dungeon Keeper claims to possess the "most sophisticated monster AI of any game yet," with each monster having roughly 1500 bytes dedicated to AI and personality statistics. By comparison, the AI for each character in Populous used 48 bytes. Monsters that are hurt will feel pain and try to run away, and monsters that can smell will use this ability to track players and lead other monsters to where the players are hiding.

For the latest information about Dungeon Keeper, check out Interplay's Web site at

```
http://www.interplay.com/website/homepage.html
```

Grand Prix II

According to *PC Review*, Grand Prix II, by Microprose, has computer-controlled drivers with AI based on real drivers from the sport. Each driver has a personality that determines its driving style. Cut off an aggressive driver, and you'll likely get side-swiped in revenge. The intention is to give the game more of a feel for true racing strategy, which often comes from having to deal with the many different personalities behind the wheel of each car.

For more information about Grand Prix II, stop by Microprose's Web site at

`http://www.holobyte.com/mpshp.html`

AI Resources on the Web

To keep up with the latest trends in AI, along with finding out information about traditional areas of AI research, check out some of the Web sites listed in the following sections.

World Wide Web Virtual Library

Figure 15.3 shows the AI Web page in the World Wide Web Virtual Library, which is located at

`http://www.cs.reading.ac.uk/people/dwc/ai.html`

Figure 15.3.

The Artificial Intelligence page in the World Wide Web Virtual Library.

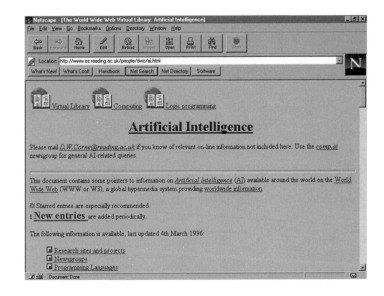

This Web page contains many useful links to other AI sites on the Web, including research projects at universities and archived messages from news groups.

15

The University of Chicago AI Lab

Figure 15.4 shows the University of Chicago Artificial Intelligence Lab Web site, which is located at

```
http://cs-www.uchicago.edu/html/groups/ai
```

Figure 15.4.

The Artificial Intelligence Lab Web site at the University of Chicago.

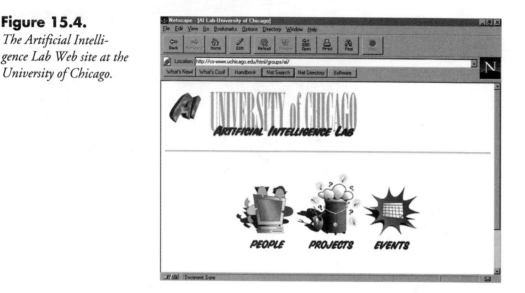

This Web site contains some interesting AI projects in the works at the University of Chicago. Although little of the information is directly related to AI in games, this is nevertheless a very neat site to gather more general information about AI and how it is being used.

Machine Learning in Games

Figure 15.5 shows the Machine Learning in Games Web site, which is located at

```
http://forum.swarthmore.edu/~jay/learn-game
```

This Web site contains a wealth of information about how to make games learn. There are many links to current projects, including algorithms and source code. You might also be able to hook up with some people at this site for more advanced questions and ideas.

Figure 15.5.

The Machine Learning in Games Web site.

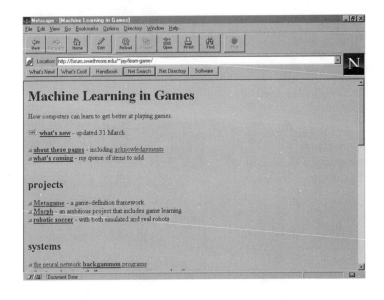

Bibliography on Machine Learning in Strategic Game Playing

Figure 15.6 shows the Bibliography on Machine Learning in Strategic Game Playing Web site, which is located at

```
http://www.ai.univie.ac.at/~juffi/lig/lig.html
```

Figure 15.6.

The Bibliography on Machine Learning in Strategic Game Playing Web site.

This is another site with a lot of useful information regarding learning in games. If you're interested in this topic at all, be sure to check it out; it has lots of interesting stuff.

15

Summary

Today you took a step back from the business of hacking Java code and learned some of the basic theory behind artificial intelligence and how it applies to games. You learned about the three fundamental types of game AI (roaming, behavioral, and strategic), along with how they are used in typical gaming scenarios. You even learned about some of the more advanced AI techniques being used in the latest commercial games. Finally, you finished up today's lesson with a few useful Web sites for furthering your knowledge of AI.

As a game programmer with at least a passing interest in AI, your AI knowledge will likely grow a great deal as you encounter situations where you can apply AI techniques. After you get comfortable with implementing the basics, you can move on to more advanced AI solutions based on prior experience and research on the Web. I hope today's lesson at least provided you with a roadmap to begin your journey into the world of the computer mind.

Now, if you think I'm going to discuss all this AI theory and then leave you hanging in regard to a real game that uses it, you are sorely mistaken. In tomorrow's lesson, you learn how to build a Connect4 game, complete with a computer player that uses a strategic AI strategy similar to what you learned about today.

Q&A

Q Everyone acts like computers are so smart, but now you make it sound like they're dumb. What gives?

A Computers, in fact, are very "dumb" when it comes to what we humans refer to as free thought. However, computers are very "smart" when it comes to mathematical calculations and algorithms. The trick with AI is to model the subtleties of human thought in such a way that the computer can do what it's good at, executing mathematical calculations and algorithms.

Q Are the three fundamental types of game AI the only choices I have when adding AI to games?

A Absolutely not; the AI types you learned about today are simply three of the most popular types I've encountered in games. By all means, explore and build on these strategies to come up with AI solutions that more closely fit your own particular needs.

Q **If my game is designed to have only human players, do I even need to worry with AI?**

A Even though games with all human players might appear to not require any AI at first, it is often useful to control many of the background aspects of the game using simple AI. For example, consider a two player head-to-head space battle game. Even though you might not have any plans for computer ships, consider adding some AI to determine how the environment responds to the players' actions. For example, add a black hole near the more aggressive player from time to time, providing that player with more hassles than the other player. Although the intelligence required of a black hole is pretty weak by most AI standards, it could still use a simple chase algorithm to follow the player around.

Q **Is it difficult to implement strategic AI?**

A Yes and no, depending on the particular game. If you're talking about adding AI to simple board games, then it isn't usually very difficult. As a matter of fact, you'll see this firsthand in tomorrow's lesson. However, once you broaden the context of strategy games to include complex strategic simulations, implementing strategic AI can get very messy.

Workshop

The Workshop section provides questions and exercises to help you get a better feel for the material you learned today. Try to answer the questions and at least think about the exercises before moving on to tomorrow's lesson. You'll find the answers to the questions in Appendix A, "Quiz Answers."

Quiz

1. What are the three types of roaming AI?
2. How does behavioral AI work?
3. What is one of the most difficult aspects of implementing strategic AI?
4. Why are we only now beginning to see commercial games exploit advanced AI strategies?

Exercises

1. Stop by some of the AI Web sites mentioned today and explore what else is out there in the world of AI.

2. Play some games with computer opponents and see whether you can tell which type of AI approach is being used.

3. Do some research on primal responses in animals, particularly insects, and develop a behavioral model based on this information.

4. Stop by some of the game Web sites mentioned today to find out more about the specifics of the AI used.

15

Day 16

Connect4: Human versus Machine

Yesterday you broke away from Java code for a little while and spent some time learning about artificial intelligence (AI) and how it is used in games. I promised you yesterday that you would spend today's lesson implementing a game complete with a computer opponent using strategic AI. I've been known to keep most of my promises, and today's lesson is no exception.

Today you develop a complete Connect4 game from scratch. Along the way, you learn about the type of AI strategy used by a game like Connect4, and then you get to work implementing it. By the end of today, you will have created your own worst nightmare: a computer opponent that can consistently beat you in a game of Connect4. You might be thinking that no stupid computer player could ever match wits with you. At this point, I'm not going to making any guarantees, but let me just say that if any money were involved, mine would be on the player with the silicon brain! Still skeptical? Well, read on and find out for yourself.

The following topics are covered in today's lesson:

☐ Designing Connect4

☐ Sample applet: Connect4

Designing Connect4

Today's entire focus is on creating a Connect4 game with a computer player that can at least give a human player a good game. After you finish the game, I think you'll agree that the computer player can do a lot more than give you a good game. In fact, I've already mentioned that the computer player will be able to beat most human players pretty consistently. But enough of that for now; you'll have plenty of time to go head-to-head against the computer later.

How to Play the Game

In case you've never played Connect4, let's briefly go over the basic rules. It is a simple game that is similar to tic-tac-toe in that the goal is to complete a continuous row, column, or diagonal series. The game is played on a rectangular "board" that contains a 7×6 array of positions. You use round pieces, similar to checker pieces, to represent each move. Figure 16.1 shows what a Connect4 board looks like.

Figure 16.1.
A Connect4 board, complete with pieces.

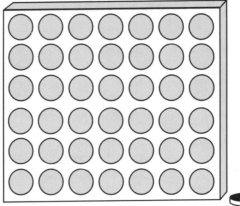

The main catch to Connect4 is that the board stands upright, with each column being slotted. So a move consists of selecting a column to drop your piece in, and then gravity takes care of the rest. This means that instead of explicitly choosing the vertical position of each move, you can only stack up the pieces vertically. This fact impacts the strategy greatly.

16

The game is won when one of the players manages to connect a horizontal, vertical, or diagonal series of four pieces. There is the chance for a tie, as in tic-tac-toe, but it is less likely, simply because of the number of ways in which the game can be won.

The Elements of the Game

Before moving into the meat of today's lesson—studying the AI necessary to create an engaging computer opponent—let's take a look at what Connect4 requires in terms of the basic game. First of all, you know that it is a board game, or at least the play is similar to that of a board game. The style of play involves the players dropping pieces into columns of the board on alternating turns. Thus, you apparently don't have much need for the sprite animation code you've relied on so heavily throughout the book. Well, technically you could animate the pieces falling down the columns, but because that would involve a decent amount of extra work, let's leave it as an exercise for later!

Because you're not going to fool with any animation, the graphics for the game are simplified a little. This is a good thing, because implementing the AI alone will keep you busy enough. The graphics for the game basically consist of drawing the board and pieces. Not bad so far. Because the computer player is likely to take time calculating its next move, it might also be nice to have a status line. The status line simply indicates the current state of the game, with a message something like "Thinking..." or "Your Turn."

Because you're not going to implement animation, there is one neat little extra you can add without too much extra work: a column selector hand. The column selector hand is displayed over the currently selected column so that the human player can tell exactly which column a piece will be dropped in. Each time the player moves the mouse, the hand is updated to reflect the selected column. The selector hand is simple to implement, and it gives the game a nice touch.

So far, the graphics requirements of the game consist of four elements:

- ☐ Board
- ☐ Pieces
- ☐ Status line
- ☐ Hand selector

Now, let's take a look at what type of user input the game needs. Because you've already decided to go with a mouse-controlled hand selector to pick the column to drop a piece in, it only makes sense to make the entire user interface for the game mouse-driven. So moving the mouse selects a column, and clicking the mouse button drops a piece in that column.

16

The AI Strategy

The only other area to cover is the type of AI strategy used by the game and how it connects to the general play of the game. As you might recall from yesterday's lesson, the most popular type of AI used in games like Connect4 is strategic AI that makes use of a depth search algorithm linked to a fixed table of rule information. This is exactly the AI strategy you use when developing the Connect4 code, but you'll learn the details of that later in this lesson.

For now, let's think of the AI in terms of the logical components required to make it work. Basically, the AI algorithm should come up with the best possible column for the computer player to drop the next piece into. Keeping that in mind, a good approach would be to break the game into two components: the AI engine that calculates the computer player's next move, and the higher-level applet itself, which uses this move to update the graphics in the game.

In this way, the human and computer players' moves are handled very similarly, which makes things much easier to deal with; each move just results in a piece being placed in a position on the game board. Another important benefit of this arrangement is that the AI engine handles all the details of figuring out whether moves are valid, along with determining whether there is a winner in the game. In this way, the engine is actually more of a general Connect4 game engine, rather than just an AI engine. Figure 16.2 shows the two Connect4 components and what kind of information they transfer to each other.

Figure 16.2.

The logical Connect4 game components.

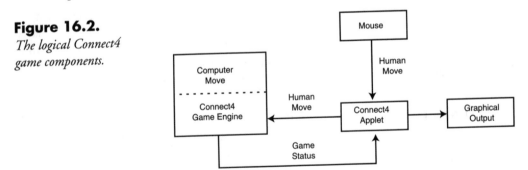

This approach results in a complete separation of the low-level algorithms necessary to drive the game from the high-level applet issues. But you still haven't learned anything about the details of the AI itself. How can the computer player possibly know what moves to make and be able to actually compete with a human player? To answer this question, you must first be able to assess the state of the game from a particular player's perspective. More specifically, you need to be able to calculate a score for a player that determines how he is faring in the game.

A player's score reflects his status in the game and basically how close he is to victory. So to calculate the score, you first need to be able to know when a game has been won. This might at first seem trivial; just look for a series of four pieces in a row, column, or diagonal, right? That's right for you or me, but teaching the computer how to look at the board and figure this out isn't quite so simple. One approach is to keep up with every possible combination of piece positions that constitutes a victory. These combinations could be stored in a table and then used as a basis to determine how close each player is to winning the game. Although this approach sounds fairly cumbersome, it's actually not too hard to implement.

With the scoring system in place, you can then use a look-ahead depth search to try out different moves for the computer player and determine the best one. The combination of the table of winning moves and the look-ahead search is what gives the computer player its "brains." Although a few more details are involved in implementing the AI for the game, this covers the major points of interest. I don't know about you, but I'm getting tired of talking about the game in general terms; let's start writing it!

NOTE

Incidentally, a look-ahead depth search is a technique that involves looking into the future of a game and trying out every possible move to determine the best one. A look-ahead depth search is a computer AI version of the common human strategy of planning moves in a game based on what the other player might do in each situation; the primary difference being that the computer is much more efficient and can evaluate a lot more possibilities.

Sample Applet: Connect4

The Connect4 applet is a complete Java Connect4 game including strategic AI for a computer player good enough to give most people fits. Figure 16.3 shows a screen shot of a game of Connect4—and, yes, I'm the one losing! The complete source code, executable, images, and sounds for Connect4 are located on the accompanying CD-ROM.

Connect4 starts out by setting up an empty game board and giving the human player the first turn. After the human player makes a move, the status message "Thinking..." is displayed while the AI engine determines the computer player's move. Figure 16.4 shows the game while the computer player is "thinking."

Figure 16.3.

The Connect4 sample applet.

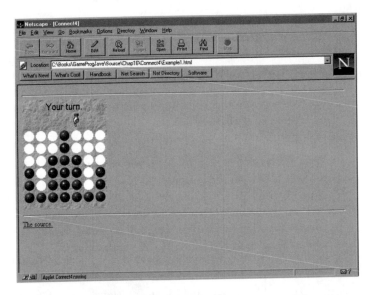

Figure 16.4.

The Connect4 sample applet during the computer player's turn.

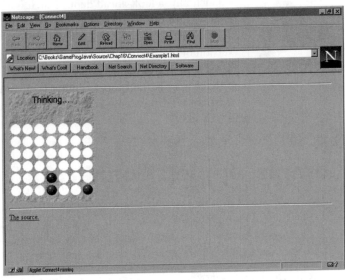

NOTE

Study has revealed that it is technically possible to always win at Connect4 if you are the player to make the first move, regardless of the other player's strategy.

16

The computer makes its move and the play shifts back to the human player. This exchange of turns continues until there is a win, loss, or tie. When the game ends, you can start a new one by clicking in the applet window. Sound effects are played during the course of the game to indicate who made which move. Sound effects are also played for making an invalid move, starting a new game, winning, and losing.

If you're curious about how well the computer player plays the game, load it up and give it a try. You might be a Connect4 whiz and teach the computer a lesson, or you might end up learning a few things!

16

The Game Engine Classes

The heart of the AI in Connect4 is the Connect4 game engine. The Connect4 game engine is composed of two classes: `Connect4Engine` and `Connect4State`. The `Connect4Engine` class provides the framework for the game engine itself, while the `Connect4State` class models the current state of a Connect4 game. Together, these two classes provide the overhead necessary to conduct a two-player game of Connect4 with either player being a human or computer player.

These engine classes implement a computer player using look-ahead depth searching AI. The intelligence of the computer player is determined by the depth of the search. Higher depth searches result in a more intelligent computer player, but at the cost of more processing time. But enough theory, let's go ahead and look into how all this stuff is implemented in the `Connect4Engine` and `Connect4State` classes!

The `Connect4Engine` class models the game engine, including the computer player AI, for the Connect4 game; it is based on implementations originally developed by Keith Pomakis and Sven Wiebus. The following are the member variables defined in `Connect4Engine`:

```
private static Random rand = new Random(System.currentTimeMillis());
private Connect4State state;
```

The `Connect4Engine` class contains a member variable, `state`, which is of type `Connect4State`. It turns out that `Connect4Engine` delegates much of the dirty work of the AI and game state upkeep to the `Connect4State` class. Even without knowing the details of the `Connect4State` class, you'll find that it's not too hard to figure out what the `Connect4State` class is doing by examining how `Connect4Engine` uses it. Nevertheless, you'll learn all the messy details of the `Connect4State` class in a little while.

`Connect4Engine` implements two methods for handling each player making a move: `makeMove` and `computerMove`. The following is the source code for `makeMove`:

```
public Point makeMove(int player, int xPos) {
  int yPos = state.dropPiece(player, xPos);
  return (new Point(xPos, yPos));
}
```

The makeMove method is called when the human player makes a move. makeMove takes a player number (player), which can be 0 or 1, and a column to drop the piece in (xPos) as parameters. The game state is updated to reflect the move, and the XY position of the move on the board is returned as a Point object. If the move is invalid (for example, the column might already be full), the y member of the Point object is set to -1. Otherwise, it has a value in the range of 0 to 6.

The computerMove method is called for the computer player to make a move. Listing 16.1 shows the source code for the computerMove method.

Listing 16.1. The Connect4Engine class's computerMove method.

```
public Point computerMove(int player, int level) {
    int bestXPos = -1, goodness = 0, bestWorst = -30000;
    int numOfEqual = 0;

    // Simulate a drop in each of the columns
    for (int i = 0; i < 7; i++) {
        Connect4State tempState = new Connect4State(state);

        // If column is full, move on
        if (tempState.dropPiece(player, i) < 0)
            continue;

        // If this drop wins the game, then cool
        if (tempState.isWinner(player)) {
            bestWorst = 25000;
            bestXPos = i;
        }
        // Otherwise, look ahead to see how good it is
        else
            goodness = tempState.evaluate(player, level, 1, -30000,
                -bestWorst);

        // If this move looks better than previous moves, remember it
        if (goodness > bestWorst) {
            bestWorst = goodness;
            bestXPos = i;
            numOfEqual = 1;
        }

        // If two moves are equally good, make a random choice
        if (goodness == bestWorst) {
            numOfEqual++;
            if (Math.abs(rand.nextInt()) % 10000 <
                (10000 / numOfEqual))
                bestXPos = i;
        }
    }

    // Drop the piece in the best column
    if (bestXPos >= 0) {
```

```
      int yPos = state.dropPiece(player, bestXPos);
      if (yPos >= 0)
        return (new Point(bestXPos, yPos));
    }
    return null;
  }
```

The `computerMove` method handles all the details of determining the best move for the computer player given the current state of the game. It takes a player number (`player`) and a level (`level`) as parameters. The `level` parameter specifies the depth of the look-ahead search and directly affects both the intelligence of the computer player and the amount of time it takes the computer player to figure out its move. All this is carried out by determining how each possible move affects the computer player's score. Most of the low-level AI work is handled by the `evaluate` method in `Connect4State`, which is called by `computerMove`. Notice that if `computerMove` isolates the best move down to two equal choices, it randomly chooses one or the other. This gives a little more human feel to the computer player.

The other three methods in `Connect4Engine` are `getBoard`, `getWinner`, and `isTie`, whose source code follows:

```java
public int[][] getBoard() {
  return state.board;
}

public boolean isWinner(int player) {
  return state.isWinner(player);
}

public boolean isTie() {
  return state.isTie();
}
```

The `getBoard` method simply returns a 7×6 array of integers representing the current state of the game board. `getWinner` and `isTie` check with the game state member object, `state`, to see whether the game has been won or tied.

That pretty much sums up the `Connect4Engine` class. With the exception of the `computerMove` method, which was a little tricky, it was pretty painless, don't you think? Well, brace yourself, because `Connect4State` is a little messier. Here are the member variables defined in the `Connect4State` class:

```java
public static final int winPlaces = 69, maxPieces = 42, Empty = 2;
public static boolean[][][] map;
public int[][]  board = new int[7][6];
public int[][]  score = new int[2][winPlaces];
public int      numPieces;
```

The first step in figuring out `Connect4State` is to understand what the member variables represent. The first three members (`winPlaces`, `maxPieces`, and `Empty`) are static final integers, which simply means that they are all constant. `winPlaces`, which specifies the number of possible winning combinations on the board, is calculated using the following equation:

```
winPlaces = 4*w*h - 3*w*n - 3*h*n + 3*w + 3*h - 4*n + 2*n*n;
```

This is a general equation that can be applied to any ConnectX-type game. In the equation, w and h represent the width and height of the game board, and n represents the number of pieces that must be in a series to constitute a victory. Because Connect4 uses a 7×6 game board with a four-piece series constituting a win, you can simply calculate `winPlaces` beforehand, which is exactly what is done in `Connect4State`.

The `maxPieces` member specifies the maximum number of pieces that can be placed on the board. It is calculated using the following equation:

```
maxPieces = w*h;
```

This calculation is pretty straightforward. The result is used to detect whether there is a tie; a tie occurs when nobody has won and the number of pieces in the game equals `maxPieces`.

The other constant member, `Empty`, represents an empty space on the board. Each space on the board can contain a player number (0 or 1) or the `Empty` constant, which is set to 2.

Moving right along, the `map` member variable is a three-dimensional array of booleans that holds the lookup table of winning combinations. To better understand how the map is laid out, first think of it as a two-dimensional array with the same dimensions as the board for the game; in other words, think of it as a 7×6 two-dimensional array. Now, add the third dimension by attaching an array of winning positions onto each two-dimensional array entry. Each different winning combination in the game is given a unique position within this array (the winning position array is `winPlaces` in length). Each location in this array is set to `true` or `false` based on whether the winning series intersects the associated board position.

Let's go over a quick example to make sure you understand how the map works. Take a look at the upper-left space on the game board back in Figure 16.1; let's call this position 0,0 on the board. Now, think about which different winning series of pieces would include this position. Give up? Check out Figure 16.5.

As you can see, position 0,0 on the board is a part of three different winning scenarios. Therefore, the winning position array for position 0,0 would have these three entries set to `true`, and all the others would be set to `false`. If the winning moves shown in Figure 16.5 were at positions 11–13 in the winning series array, you would initialize position 0,0 in the map like this:

```
...
map[0][0][9] = false;
map[0][0][10] = false;
map[0][0][11] = true;
map[0][0][12] = true;
```

```
map[0][0][13] = true;
map[0][0][14] = false;
map[0][0][15] = false;
...
```

Figure 16.5.

Winning series possibilities for position 0,0.

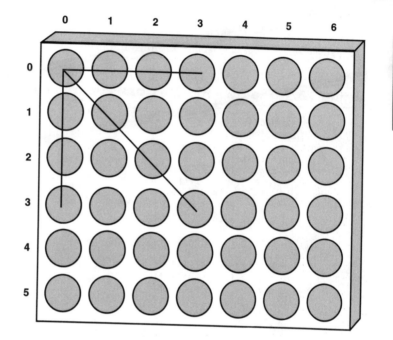

After the entire map is constructed, the AI algorithms can use it to look up winning combinations and determine how close each player is to winning.

The board member variable is simply a 7×6 two-dimensional array of integers that represents the state of the game. Each integer entry can be set to either 0 or 1 (for a player occupying that position on the board) or Empty.

The score member variable contains a two-dimensional array of integers representing the "score" for the players. The main array in score contains a subarray for each player that is winPlaces in length. These subarrays contain information describing how close the player is to completing a winning series. It works like this: Each subarray entry corresponds to a potential winning series and contains a count of how many of the player's pieces occupy the series. If a series is no longer a winning possibility for the player, its entry in the array is set to 0. Otherwise, the entry is set to 2^p, where p is the number of the player's pieces occupying the series. So if one of these entries is set to 16 (2^4), that player has won.

Rounding out the member variables for Connect4State is numPieces, which is just a count of how many pieces have been played in the game. numPieces is really used only in determining whether the game is a tie; in the event of a tie, numPieces is equal to maxPieces.

That covers the member variables for the Connect4State class. You might have realized by now that by understanding the member variables and what they model, you already understand a great deal about how the AI works in the game. Let's move on to the methods in Connect4State, because that's where the fun really begins.

The default constructor for Connect4State takes on the role of initializing the map, board, and score arrays. This constructor is shown in Listing 16.2.

Listing 16.2. The Connect4State class's default constructor.

```java
public Connect4State() {
  // Initialize the map
  int i, j, k, count = 0;
  if (map == null) {
    map = new boolean[7][6][winPlaces];
    for (i = 0; i < 7; i++)
      for (j = 0; j < 6; j++)
        for (k = 0; k < winPlaces; k++)
          map[i][j][k] = false;

    // Set the horizontal win positions
    for (i = 0; i < 6; i++)
      for (j = 0; j < 4; j++) {
        for (k = 0; k < 4; k++)
          map[j + k][i][count] = true;
        count++;
      }

    // Set the vertical win positions
    for (i = 0; i < 7; i++)
      for (j = 0; j < 3; j++) {
        for (k = 0; k < 4; k++)
          map[i][j + k][count] = true;
        count++;
      }

    // Set the forward diagonal win positions
    for (i = 0; i < 3; i++)
      for (j = 0; j < 4; j++) {
        for (k = 0; k < 4; k++)
          map[j + k][i + k][count] = true;
        count++;
      }

    // Set the backward diagonal win positions
    for (i = 0; i < 3; i++)
      for (j = 6; j >= 3; j--) {
        for (k = 0; k < 4; k++)
          map[j - k][i + k][count] = true;
        count++;
      }
  }
}
```

```
  // Initialize the board
  for (i = 0; i < 7; i++)
    for (j = 0; j < 6; j++)
      board[i][j] = Empty;

  // Initialize the scores
  for (i = 0; i < 2; i++)
    for (j = 0; j < winPlaces; j++)
      score[i][j] = 1;

  numPieces = 0;
}
```

The default constructor also sets the number of pieces to zero. There is also a copy constructor for Connect4State, whose source code follows:

```
public Connect4State(Connect4State state) {
  // Copy the board
  for (int i = 0; i < 7; i++)
    for (int j = 0; j < 6; j++)
      board[i][j] = state.board[i][j];

  // Copy the scores
  for (int i = 0; i < 2; i++)
    for (int j = 0; j < winPlaces; j++)
      score[i][j] = state.score[i][j];

  numPieces = state.numPieces;
}
```

If you aren't familiar with copy constructors, they enable you to create new objects that are copies of existing objects. It is necessary to have a copy constructor for Connect4State because the AI algorithms use temporary state objects a great deal, as you'll see in a moment. The copy constructor for Connect4State just copies the contents of each member variable.

The isWinner method in Connect4State checks to see whether either player has won the game:

```
public boolean isWinner(int player) {
  for (int i = 0; i < winPlaces; i++)
    if (score[player][i] == 16)
      return true;
  return false;
}
```

The isWinner method looks for a winner by checking to see whether any member in the score array is equal to 16 (2^4). This indicates victory because it means that four pieces occupy the series.

The isTie method checks for a tie by simply seeing whether numPieces equals maxPieces, which indicates that the board is full. The source code for isTie follows:

```
public boolean isTie() {
  return (numPieces == maxPieces);
}
```

The dropPiece method handles dropping a new piece onto the board:

```
public int dropPiece(int player, int xPos) {
  int yPos = 0;
  while ((board[xPos][yPos] != Empty) && (++yPos < 6))
    ;

  // The column is full
  if (yPos == 6)
    return -1;

  // The move is OK
  board[xPos][yPos] = player;
  numPieces++;
  updateScore(player, xPos, yPos);

  return yPos;
}
```

The dropPiece method takes a player and an X position (column) as its only parameters. It first checks to make sure there is room in the specified column to drop a new piece. Incidentally, you might have noticed from this code that the board is stored upside down in the board member variable. Having the board inverted simplifies the process of adding a new piece a little. If the move is valid, the entry in the board array is set to player, and numPieces is incremented. Then the score is updated to reflect the move with a call to updateScore. You'll learn about updateScore in a moment.

The evaluate method is where the low-level AI in the game takes place. The source code for the evaluate method is shown in Listing 16.3.

Listing 16.3. The Connect4State class's evaluate method.

```
public int evaluate(int player, int level, int depth, int alpha,
  int beta) {
  int goodness, best, maxab = alpha;

  if (level != depth) {
    best = -30000;
    for(int i = 0; i < 7; i++) {
      Connect4State tempState = new Connect4State(this);
      if (tempState.dropPiece(getOtherPlayer(player), i) < 0)
        continue;

      if (tempState.isWinner(getOtherPlayer(player)))
        goodness = 25000 - depth;
```

```
      else
        goodness = tempState.evaluate(getOtherPlayer(player),
          level, depth + 1, -beta, -maxab);
      if (goodness > best) {
        best = goodness;
        if (best > maxab)
          maxab = best;
      }
      if (best > beta)
        break;
    }

    // What's good for the other player is bad for this one
    return -best;
  }

  return (calcScore(player) - calcScore(getOtherPlayer(player)));
}
```

It is the evaluate method's job to come up with the best move for the computer player given the parameters for the depth search algorithm. The algorithm used by evaluate determines the best move based on the calculated "goodness" of each possible move. The alpha and beta parameters specify cutoffs that enable the algorithm to eliminate some moves entirely, thereby speeding things up. It is a little beyond today's focus to go any further into the low-level theory behind the algorithm. If, however, you want to learn more about how it works, look into the Web sites mentioned at the end of yesterday's lesson.

The calcScore method in Connect4State is responsible for calculating the score for a player:

```
private int calcScore(int player) {
  int s = 0;
  for (int i = 0; i < winPlaces; i++)
    s += score[player][i];
  return s;
}
```

In calcScore, the score of a player is calculated by summing each element in the score array. The updateScore method handles updating the score for a player after a move:

```
private void updateScore(int player, int x, int y) {
  for (int i = 0; i < winPlaces; i++)
    if (map[x][y][i]) {
      score[player][i] <<= 1;
      score[getOtherPlayer(player)][i] = 0;
    }
}
```

The updateScore method sets the appropriate entries in the score array to reflect the move; the move is specified in the x and y parameters. The last method in Connect4State is getOtherPlayer, which simply returns the number of the other player:

```
private int getOtherPlayer(int player) {
  return (1 - player);
}
```

That wraps up the game engine. You now have a complete Connect4 game engine with AI support for a computer player. Keep in mind that although you've been thinking in terms of a human versus the computer, the game engine is structured so that you could have any combination of human and computer players. Yes, this means you could set up a game so that two computer players duke it out! Pretty neat, huh?

The `Connect4` Class

The game engine classes are cool, but they aren't all that useful by themselves; they need an applet class with some graphics and a user interface. The `Connect4` class is exactly what they need. The `Connect4` class takes care of all the high-level game issues such as drawing the graphics and managing human moves through mouse event handlers. Even though it doesn't rely on the sprite classes, the `Connect4` applet class is still similar to other applet classes you've developed. Let's look at its member variables first:

```
private Image           offImage, boardImg, handImg;
private Image[]         pieceImg = new Image[2];
private AudioClip       newGameSnd, sadSnd, applauseSnd,
                        badMoveSnd, redSnd, blueSnd;
private Graphics        offGrfx;
private Thread          thread;
private MediaTracker    tracker;
private int             delay = 83; // 12 fps
private Connect4Engine  gameEngine;
private boolean         gameOver = true,
                        myMove;
private int             level = 2, curXPos;
private String          status = new String("Your turn.");
private Font            statusFont = new Font("Helvetica", Font.PLAIN, 20);
private FontMetrics     statusMetrics;
```

The first member variables you probably noticed are the ones for all the graphics and sound in the game. The most important member variable, however, is `gameEngine`, which is a `Connect4Engine` object. There are also two boolean member variables that keep up with whether the game is over (`gameOver`) and whose move it is (`myMove`). The `level` member variable specifies the current level of the game, and the `curXPos` member keeps up with which column the hand selector is currently over. Finally, there are a few member variables for managing the status line text and its associated font and font metrics. Let's move on to the methods.

The `init` method in `Connect4` is pretty standard; it just loads the images and audio clips:

```
public void init() {
  // Load and track the images
  tracker = new MediaTracker(this);
  boardImg = getImage(getCodeBase(), "Res/Board.gif");
  tracker.addImage(boardImg, 0);
  handImg = getImage(getCodeBase(), "Res/Hand.gif");
```

```
      tracker.addImage(handImg, 0);
      pieceImg[0] = getImage(getCodeBase(), "Res/RedPiece.gif");
      tracker.addImage(pieceImg[0], 0);
      pieceImg[1] = getImage(getCodeBase(), "Res/BluPiece.gif");
      tracker.addImage(pieceImg[1], 0);

      // Load the audio clips
      newGameSnd = getAudioClip(getCodeBase(), "Res/NewGame.au");
      sadSnd = getAudioClip(getCodeBase(), "Res/Sad.au");
      applauseSnd = getAudioClip(getCodeBase(), "Res/Applause.au");
      badMoveSnd = getAudioClip(getCodeBase(), "Res/BadMove.au");
      redSnd = getAudioClip(getCodeBase(), "Res/RedMove.au");
      blueSnd = getAudioClip(getCodeBase(), "Res/BlueMove.au");
}
```

Although `init` is certainly important, the `run` method is where things get interesting, because the computer player's move is handled in the main update loop inside it. Listing 16.4 contains the source code for the `run` method.

Listing 16.4. The Connect4 class's run method.

```
public void run() {
  try {
    tracker.waitForID(0);
  }
  catch (InterruptedException e) {
    return;
  }

  // Start a new game
  newGame();

  // Update everything
  long t = System.currentTimeMillis();
  while (Thread.currentThread() == thread) {
    // Make the computer's move
    if (!gameOver && !myMove) {
      Point pos = gameEngine.computerMove(1, level);
      if (pos.y >= 0) {
        if (!gameEngine.isWinner(1))
          if (!gameEngine.isTie()) {
            blueSnd.play();
            status = new String("Your turn.");
            myMove = true;
          }
          else {
            sadSnd.play();
            status = new String("It's a tie!");
            gameOver = true;
          }
        else {
```

continues

Listing 16.4. continued

```
            sadSnd.play();
            status = new String("You lost!");
            gameOver = true;
          }
          repaint();
        }
      }

      try {
        t += delay;
        Thread.sleep(Math.max(0, t - System.currentTimeMillis()));
      }
      catch (InterruptedException e) {
        break;
      }
    }
  }
```

If it is the computer player's turn, the run method attempts a move using the current level by calling computerMove on the gameEngine object. If the move is successful, run checks for a win or tie, and then it plays the appropriate sound and updates the status text.

TIP

The level member variable ultimately determines how smart the computer player is by affecting the depth of the look-ahead search. This is carried out by level being passed as the second parameter of computerMove. If you find the game too easy or too difficult, feel free to tinker with the level member variable, or even supply your own calculation as the second parameter to computerMove.

The update method handles the details of drawing the game graphics. Listing 16.5 shows the source code for the update method.

Listing 16.5. The Connect4 class's update method.

```
public void update(Graphics g) {
  // Create the offscreen graphics context
  if (offGrfx == null) {
    offImage = createImage(size().width, size().height);
    offGrfx = offImage.getGraphics();
    statusMetrics = offGrfx.getFontMetrics(statusFont);
  }
```

16

```
// Draw the board
offGrfx.drawImage(boardImg, 0, 0, this);

// Draw the pieces
int[][] board = gameEngine.getBoard();
for (int i = 0; i < 7; i++)
  for (int j = 0; j < 6; j++)
    switch(board[i][j]) {
    case 0:
      offGrfx.drawImage(pieceImg[0], (i + 1) * 4 + i *
        pieceImg[0].getWidth(this), (6 - j) * 4 + (5 - j) *
        pieceImg[0].getHeight(this) + 67, this);
      break;

    case 1:
      offGrfx.drawImage(pieceImg[1], (i + 1) * 4 + i *
        pieceImg[1].getWidth(this), (6 - j) * 4 + (5 - j) *
        pieceImg[1].getHeight(this) + 67, this);
      break;

    default:
      offGrfx.setColor(Color.white);
      offGrfx.fillOval((i + 1) * 4 + i *
        pieceImg[0].getWidth(this), (6 - j) * 4 + (5 - j) *
        pieceImg[0].getHeight(this) + 67,
        pieceImg[0].getWidth(this),
        pieceImg[0].getHeight(this));
      break;
    }

// Draw the hand selector
if (!gameOver && myMove)
  offGrfx.drawImage(handImg, (curXPos + 1) * 4 + curXPos *
  pieceImg[0].getWidth(this) + (pieceImg[0].getWidth(this) -
  handImg.getWidth(this)) / 2, 63 - handImg.getHeight(this),
  this);

// Draw the game status
offGrfx.setColor(Color.black);
offGrfx.setFont(statusFont);
offGrfx.drawString(status, (size().width -
  statusMetrics.stringWidth(status)) / 2,
  statusMetrics.getHeight());

// Draw the image onto the screen
g.drawImage(offImage, 0, 0, null);
}
```

The update method draws the board, the pieces, the hand selector, and the status text. The only tricky part of update is in drawing the pieces in the correct locations, which takes a few calculations. Other than that, update is pretty straightforward.

The mouseMove method is used to update the hand selector via the curXPos member variable:

```
public boolean mouseMove(Event evt, int x, int y) {
  // Update the current X position (for the hand selector)
  if (!gameOver && myMove) {
    curXPos = x / 28;
    repaint();
  }
  return true;
}
```

In mouseMove, curXPos is set to the currently selected column (0–6), based on the position of the mouse. The mouseDown method is a little more interesting in that it handles making moves for the human player. Listing 16.6 contains the source code for the mouseDown method.

Listing 16.6. The Connect4 class's mouseDown method.

```
public boolean mouseDown(Event evt, int x, int y) {
  if (gameOver) {
    // Start a new game
    newGame();
    return true;
  }
  else if (myMove) {
    // Make sure the move is valid
    Point pos = gameEngine.makeMove(0, x / 28);
    if (pos.y >= 0) {
      if (!gameEngine.isWinner(0))
        if (!gameEngine.isTie()) {
          redSnd.play();
          status = new String("Thinking...");
          myMove = false;
        }
        else {
          sadSnd.play();
          status = new String("It's a tie!");
          gameOver = true;
        }
      else {
        applauseSnd.play();
        status = new String("You won!");
        level++;
        gameOver = true;
      }
      repaint();
    }
    else
      badMoveSnd.play();
  }
  else
    badMoveSnd.play();
  return true;
}
```

The mouseDown method first checks to see whether the game is over, in which case a mouse click starts a new game. If the game is not over, mouseDown attempts to make the human player's move in the specified column. If the move is valid, mouseDown checks for a win or tie, and then it plays the appropriate sound and updates the status text. Notice that if the human player has won, the level of the game is increased.

The last method in Connect4 is newGame, which (surprise!) sets up a new game:

```
public void newGame() {
  // Setup a new game
  newGameSnd.play();
  gameEngine = new Connect4Engine();
  gameOver = false;
  myMove = true;
  status = new String("Your turn.");
  repaint();
}
```

In newGame, the game engine is re-created and all the game status member variables are reinitialized, except for level. This is important, because it results in the level increasing after each win by the human player. The only drawback is that the computer player plays considerably slower (because of the increased depth search) with each increasing level. On the other hand, the computer player gets much smarter after each human player victory, so don't expect to win more than a couple of games.

That concludes the dissection of the Connect4 applet. You now have a complete Java AI strategy game to add to your growing list of Java game accomplishments!

Summary

In today's lesson, you learned how to apply the AI theory from yesterday's lesson toward a real game. You began by developing a preliminary design for a Connect4 game and then progressed into implementing the support classes as well as the main applet class. You learned how to use strategic AI to implement a very capable computer player for the Connect4 game. You also used much of the experience acquired during the past two weeks to add creative graphics and sound to the game.

Today's lesson focused primarily on implementing a computer player for a Connect4 game using AI techniques. But what if you want to play against another real person rather than the computer? Well, you could try to connect two mice to your computer and figure out a way to convince Java to recognize the two. After that approach failed, you would probably come to the conclusion that multiplayer games require an entirely different approach to game design. Over the next few days, you'll learn all about multiplayer network game development, culminating in a network version of Connect4 that enables you to play other people over the Internet. Can you feel the suspense building? I sure can!

Q&A

Q **Could a similar AI approach be used in another board game, such as Checkers?**

A Yes, but the technique of calculating a score for each player would differ, because winning Checkers is based on jumping pieces instead of lining them up in a row.

Q **Is this the best AI approach to take for implementing the Connect4 computer player?**

A Probably not, but it depends on how you define "best." In terms of simplicity, this approach might well be one of the best. I found a few other Connect4 AI strategies on the Web, but I settled on this one because it is relatively easy to implement and understand. No doubt smarter AI strategies exist, but they are almost certainly more difficult to implement. Keep in mind, however, that most other AI strategies in games like Connect4 still use a conceptually similar approach involving look-ahead depth searching. The primary difference usually lies in how the scores are calculated.

Q **Will the Connect4 engine work with a larger board or a different number of pieces to connect in a series?**

A Absolutely. You just need to alter the sizes of the game state arrays as well as all the loops that work with them, along with recalculating the values of the `winPlaces` and `maxPieces` member variables in the `Connect4State` class.

Workshop

The Workshop section provides questions and exercises to help you get a better feel for the material you learned today. Try to answer the questions and at least ponder the exercises before moving on to tomorrow's lesson. You'll find the answers to the questions in Appendix A, "Quiz Answers."

Quiz

1. What is the map used for?
2. Why is the game engine broken into two classes?
3. Why does the hand selector disappear when the computer player is thinking?

Exercises

1. Integrate the sprite classes to animate dropping the pieces.
2. Modify the game engine so that the AI algorithms are executed in a thread.
3. Modify the applet so that two computer players battle it out.
4. In the computer-versus-computer version you just created, try out different values for the level used by each player, and watch the results.

16

Day 17

The Basics of Multiplayer Gaming

In the past couple of days, you've learned what it takes to give the computer the capability to match wits with a human player. Although AI is very important and has countless uses in games, it's hard to discount the human factor in multiplayer games. Today, you learn all about multiplayer games and why they are important in today's gaming landscape. The theory you learn today forms the foundation you need in order to implement a multiplayer networked version of Connect4, NetConnect4, later this week.

The appeal of multiplayer games isn't hard to figure out. Considering how much people enjoy playing games together that don't involve computers, it really was only a matter of time before the appeal of single-player computer games carried over to supporting multiple players. With access to the Internet rapidly extending beyond the circle of techies and computer enthusiasts, the time has come for multiplayer gaming to mature. Java has the potential to lead the way in many regards because of its cross-platform nature and built-in support for networking and tight security.

There are some obstacles, however, when it comes to implementing multiplayer games in Java (or any other language, for that matter). Network games bring with them their own unique set of problems and challenges that must be dealt with at the design level. Today's lesson exposes many of these problems and discusses various techniques for solving them. By the end of today, you'll be ready to move on to the specifics of network programming in Java.

The following topics are covered in today's lesson:

☐ The raw appeal of multiplayer games

☐ Network versus non-network games

☐ Gaming on the Internet

☐ Types of multiplayer games

☐ Network game problems

☐ Network game solutions

☐ Game theory

The Raw Appeal of Multiplayer Games

If you've been fortunate enough to play a multiplayer network game with your friends, you already know how much fun it can be. In many ways, outwitting a real live person is much more fun than competing against a computer player. The reality of going head-to-head with another person can change the whole perspective of a game. I have yet to see a single-player game that evokes the same level of emotion and excitement as is generated from the human factor in multiplayer games.

Arguably one of the most popular multiplayer (and single player, for that matter) games to come along in the past few years is DOOM. DOOM provides a 3D world with previously unheard-of realism and nonstop action. Add to this the ability to share the 3D world with other real people, and it's not hard to see why this game is so compelling.

Even though most of the successful multiplayer games to date, like DOOM, have pitted human players against each other, they don't necessarily have to. The benefits of human interaction in a multiplayer game are just as significant if the human players are working together. I know from experience how fun it can be working together with another person to reach a common goal. One of my favorite games is Super Contra III for the Super Nintendo console game system. This game enables two human players to play together against the computer. In fact, you can get much further in the game with two people cooperating in multiplayer mode than with one player on her own in a single-player game. This approach rewards the players for their cooperation, and in doing so adds another whole dimension to the appeal of the game.

NOTE

I know that the Super Nintendo game system is quickly on its way to becoming outdated. Although I'm not an overly nostalgic person, I find that there are many games on older game systems that are still very fun to play, even in their old age.

Although the discussion thus far has been limited mostly to games involving multiple human players, there is no reason why you can't have a mixture of human and computer players in a multiplayer game. Consider a Poker game, for example. The participants in the game could be any mixture of human and computer players. The ability to have different combinations of players puts an interesting twist on the AI in the game. Moreover, it would be interesting to see how the human players respond to the other players, knowing that some of them are real and some aren't. A few games out there have taken this approach. The computer version of one of my favorite board games, Risk, takes this approach by filling in for missing human players with computer players.

There are endless possibilities for multiplayer games involving both cooperation and competition among human players. Regardless of the scenario, when real people are involved, a certain synthesis of ideas takes place that just isn't possible with computer players. It's then up to game designers like you and me to chart the course and dream up new ways for people to interact with each other through games.

Network versus Non-Network Games

So far, the discussion of multiplayer games has avoided the issue of where the multiple players are physically located. You've probably assumed that I've been referring to multiple players connected over a network, but that doesn't necessarily have to be the case. Because of the relative difficulty in implementing network games, many multiplayer games have relied on two or more players sitting in front of the same computer. In light of recent advances in network standardization and programming libraries, however, this approach of having multiple players using the same machine is losing its appeal rather quickly. It still works pretty well for many console game systems, because they are specifically designed to support two or more players with one set of hardware, but I wouldn't expect to see very many new computer games using this approach.

The point is that you simply must implement a network interface for multiplayer computer games, even if you provide a non-networked multiplayer option. When it comes to Java games, this point is even more important, because Web users will expect to be able to play against other players on the Web.

To better understand the relationship between network versus non-network multiplayer games, check out Figure 17.1 and Figure 17.2.

Figure 17.1.

A two-player game on a non-networked machine.

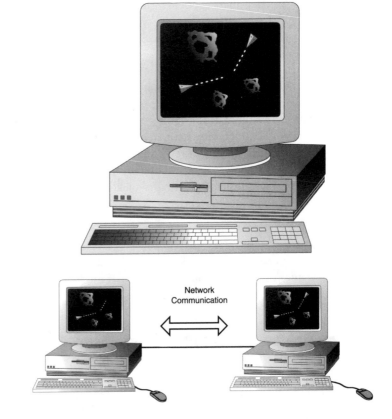

Figure 17.2.

A two-player game on networked machines.

In Figure 17.1, a two-player game is implemented on a single machine; in this situation, the players use different keys on the keyboard. Of course, if you figured out how to get two mice working on one machine, that probably would work too! Although this setup certainly works in the confines of your own home, it doesn't help you much when you want to play with a friend who lives halfway across the world. The bright side is that the design for a game like this wouldn't really be any more difficult than a single-player design; you just process two sets of keyboard inputs rather than one. Nevertheless, all the input still is generated on the same machine and with the same timing. The key point is that although there are two players with two different sets of input, only one instance of the game is running.

Now consider the problems associated with this non-network approach: You're requiring two players to squeeze together next to each other and share the keyboard. Furthermore, this setup wouldn't work for games in which each player needs to see information that should be hidden from the other player, such as your hand in Poker (or any multiplayer card game, for that matter).

The configuration in Figure 17.2 shows a two-player game implemented through some type of network connection between the two machines. There are two computers and therefore two separate instances of the game. Although two instances of the game are running, they effectively operate as one. Notice that there is some form of communication between the two computers across the network connection. This is the communication you must implement to keep the two games operating in conjunction. Fortunately, as you'll learn tomorrow, Java provides a lot of the functionality of establishing and maintaining a network communication channel between players.

Gaming on the Internet

Multiplayer games that can run together on different machines also are known as *network games,* which means that the games are capable of enabling multiple players to connect with each other and play interactively over an external connection between their respective machines. In the case of network Java games, the external network connection is handled through the Internet.

NEW TERM   *Network games* are multiplayer games that can run together on multiple machines.

Even though the ultimate communication medium for network Java games is the Internet, you have to contend with the fact that different game players will access the Internet in different ways. Actually, there are really only two Internet connection scenarios: dedicated and dial-up. A dedicated Internet connection involves a computer being directly connected to the Internet via a direct, high-speed line such as a T1 connection. Actually, slower dedicated lines are available, such as 28,800 baud, but they aren't as popular as their faster counterparts.

A dial-up Internet connection, on the other hand, consists of a computer dialing into an Internet network and establishing a modem connection to the Internet. Technically speaking, a modem connection is certainly physical, but for our purposes, we'll refer to modem connections as *modem networks,* and networks involving physical network hardware connections as *physical networks.*

The primary difference between modem networking and physical networking is the bandwidth of communication. *Bandwidth* refers to how much data can be transferred in a certain amount of time. Most people accessing the Web have already realized that a 28,800 baud modem is a necessity. The absolute minimum modem speed for Web surfing these days is 14,400 baud, but 28,800 baud might as well be the standard, because modems are coming down in price so rapidly.

Bandwidth refers to the amount of data that can be transferred over a network connection in a certain amount of time.

The modem-speed issue is important because the bandwidth can greatly affect the performance of network games. The degree to which the bandwidth affects the game performance, however, is determined by your particular communication strategy. For example, you might be able to figure out a way to send very little data and get by with lower communication speeds. As in all software designs, there are trade-offs, and bandwidth is the big one you must weigh when assessing the communication requirements for your game. This is one aspect of the game design you must be particularly careful about, because the amount of data transferred between games can have a dramatic effect on performance.

As far as managing the details of programming network games in Java, it doesn't matter whether a network is a physical or a modem network. Well, it doesn't matter at least from a protocol and interface perspective. It does matter when you start looking at the performance requirements of a network game. If you haven't guessed already, physical networks are much faster and more reliable than modem networks. Unfortunately, although physical networks provide greater speed and better reliability that helps make multiplayer game design much easier, you can't rely on game players using them. The reality is that few game players have the luxury of a physical Internet connection to play games on. Most physical networks are in the confines of a corporate environment, where game playing generally is frowned upon.

Most game players have available to them only the limited transmission speeds of a modem connection. Therefore, game developers are left programming network games to this lowest common denominator of transmission speed. You simply have to live with the fact that most multiplayer games will be played over modems, so it's your job to design those games accordingly.

Types of Multiplayer Games

Before you get into the design strategies for network games, it's important to understand the fundamental types of network games. The communication design can be affected dramatically by the way the game play progresses, which is determined by the type of game. I've defined two types of network games: turn-based and event-based. Most games should easily fall into one of these two categories.

Turn-Based Games

 Turn-based games are games in which each action in the game is based on a player's turn.

The Connect4 game you developed yesterday is a turn-based game because you are allowed to make a move only when it is your turn. Sure, you are free to think about your move during the other player's turn, but in the context of the game you can take action only during your turn. Most turn-based games are board games or card games, or simple games played on paper such as Tic-Tac-Toe. I can't think of any action games that would be considered turn-based. That would kind of take the action out of it! Nevertheless, turn-based games are very popular and well-suited for networking.

Knowing that turn-based games revolve around whose turn it is, the network communication design is greatly simplified. This is because only one player can interact with the game at a time. Even though multiple players are technically playing the game, only one player is allowed to make a move at a time. The other players must wait their turn before they can do anything. In this way, the game can be designed so that all the players are in a wait state until it becomes their turn. The flow of the game in turn-based games ends up being circular, as in a game of cards. The turn moves around the group of players one by one. Figure 17.3 shows the play flow of a turn-based game involving five players.

Figure 17.3.

Game play flow of a turn-based game with five players.

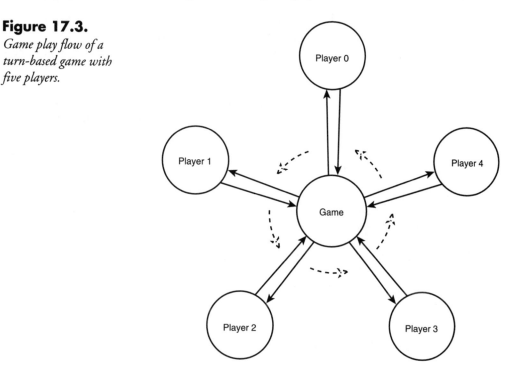

As you can see from the play flow, the game allows each player to take a turn; after each turn, the game processes the turn and allows the next player to take a turn. The play flow occurs this way regardless of the number of players. In a two-player game such as Connect4, the turns just move back and forth between the players.

Event-Based Games

NEW TERM *Event-based* games are games that are dictated by input events that can occur at any time.

Event-based games are much more open-ended than turn-based games. In an event-based game, any player can interact with the game at any time, resulting in an input event. The flow of the game is dictated by the input events rather than turns. As a matter of fact, there is no concept of "turn" in an event-based game. Event-based games include basically all games that don't revolve around turns; examples range from first-person shoot-em-ups such as Duke Nukem 3D to strategy simulators such as CivNet. In the network modes of both these games, any of the players can act independently of any of the other players, generating anywhere from nothing to a massive flood of events.

If you haven't suspected, the communication design for event-based games is much more complex and difficult to implement than that for turn-based games. More importantly, event-based game communication typically requires a much wider bandwidth, because more information is usually being transmitted. It's probably safe to say that each different event-based game you create will have a unique solution. This is because there are so many trade-offs to be made in regard to determining the best way to design the network communication logic. In a game such as Duke Nukem 3D, think about how many things are going on, and even more important, notice how quickly things are happening. Any change in the game from one player's perspective must be communicated to all the other players in some form. Figure 17.4 shows the play flow of an event-based game involving five players.

Notice from the play flow that the game never "allows" the players to do anything, as in turn-based games. The game just sits back and waits for the players to generate input events. Players can generate these events as often or as seldom as they want, fully independent of the other players. This is what enables you to patiently wait behind a corner while another player runs by haphazardly at full speed. Some people never learn!

Figure 17.4.

Game play flow of an event-based game with five players.

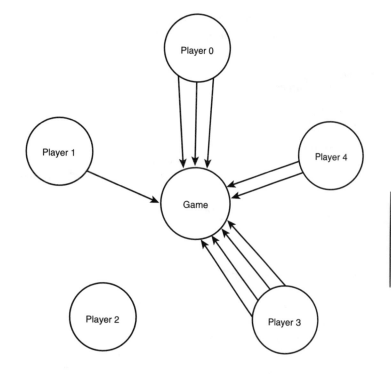

Network Game Problems

Now that you know which type of network games you are dealing with, let's look at some of the common problems you will encounter in a network game design. The overriding concern to be dealt with in designing network games is maintaining synchronization. Synchronization refers to how multiple game instances running on different machines maintain the same game state information. Remember that each player is running a separate instance of the game, but the overall goal is to make each of these different instances function logically as one instance. All the internal data structures modeling the state of the game should match exactly on each player's system.

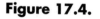 *Synchronization* refers to how multiple instances of a game maintain the same state information.

You can best understand this concept by looking at an example of what can happen when synchronization is lost. Suppose that two players, Heath and Keith, are playing a network adventure game similar to one of the games in the classic Ultima series. As they are walking along together, they run across a monster. Heath is a little more assertive and starts fighting the monster. Keith is low on life points and decides to just sit in the shade and watch. When Heath finishes off the monster, Keith somehow must be notified—and not just as a matter of convenience; any change in the game that potentially can affect other players must be communicated to them.

Another common problem in regard to synchronization involves using random values in games. It is fairly common for games to place some objects randomly when a game starts, such as treasure or even monsters. Sometimes games use random events just to make things vary a little from game to game. In network games this creates big problems unless each game instance uses the same random values as all the other instances. It would totally blow the synchronization for each game to have things going on randomly with respect to each instance. The point here is that many seemingly insignificant things, such as generating random numbers, can cause major headaches in a network game environment.

Network Game Solutions

Now that you understand the problems, let's move on to some solutions. There are many different approaches to designing network game communications, and all of them must somehow address the problem of keeping each player's instance of the game synchronized with all others. You're going to focus on two basic types of network game synchronization strategies: state synchronization and input synchronization.

State Synchronization

NEW TERM   *State synchronization* is a communication method by which each game instance communicates the current state of itself to the other instances.

The state synchronization method is very robust because there is no chance for information loss; everything regarding the current state of the game is sent to the other instances. In a two-player space battle game, for example, the position and speed of all the planets, asteroids, ships, and bullets would be sent as the current state of the game. Figure 17.5 shows a diagram of the information transfer for state synchronization in a two-player network game.

Sounds good so far. But what about a more complex game such as a role-playing adventure game with entire virtual worlds that the players constantly are interacting with? Sending the state of the entire game starts looking a little more difficult because of the vast amounts of information required to model the game state. And don't forget about the bandwidth limitation you learned about earlier, which keeps you from being able to send loads of information between games. Knowing this, it's easy to see that state synchronization is a fairly messy network communication solution. Although state synchronization is functionally a very solid network solution, technically it's just not always feasible.

Figure 17.5.

State synchronization information transfer in a two-player network game.

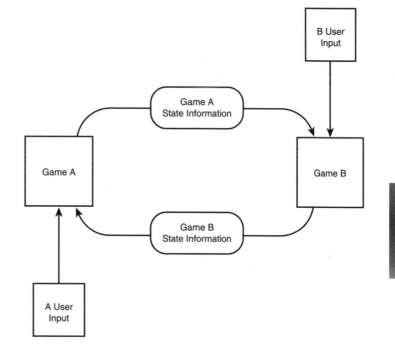

Input Synchronization

NEW TERM *Input synchronization* is a communication method in which each game communicates the input events of its player to the other game instances.

Using input synchronization, each time a player generates input events, such as moving the mouse or pressing keys, the game broadcasts these events to the other games. Using the space battle game example from before, instead of sending the state of all the objects, the game just sends the mouse and keyboard input events generated by the player. Each game then handles each remote (virtual) input from the other games in a similar manner as it handles its own local player's input. Figure 17.6 shows a diagram of the information transfer for input synchronization in a two-player network game.

There has to be a catch, right? Of course there's a catch; there's always a catch! Input synchronization works fine as long as all the changes in the game are dictated solely by the inputs of the players. Practically speaking, this rarely is the case. There are usually random effects in a game such as placement of background objects. These random effects wreak havoc on games relying on input synchronization because they aren't reflected by the player input and therefore are never communicated between games.

Figure 17.6.

Input synchronization in a two-player network game.

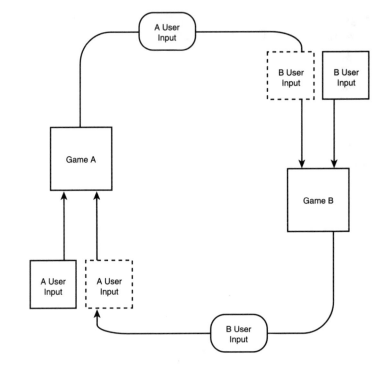

If you happen to have a game in which the entire play flow is dictated by the inputs of the players, input synchronization is for you. Otherwise, you'll have to come up with another solution. Can you think of any games that *are* dictated entirely by the user inputs? Give up? It ends up that most turn-based games are driven completely by the inputs of the users. So you usually can implement network support for turn-based games by using input synchronization.

A Hybrid Solution

Now that I've painted a pretty bleak picture of network game design, I'll let you in on a practical reality in network game design: You usually will have to use some combination of the two methods mentioned. This hybrid solution would include elements of both state and input synchronization. Using the space battle game example again, you could send the user inputs back and forth using input synchronization, and then use state synchronization to send random events such as initial meteor positions. You still don't necessarily need to transmit the entire state of the game, just the aspects of the game state that can't be figured out by each instance on its own. In other words, random events need to be transmitted to each game instance.

If you run across a gaming scenario that doesn't fit well with any of these approaches, you might figure out a communication technique of your own to add to or replace one of these. As I said earlier today, network gaming is a unique area of programming that leaves room for very few general techniques. You usually have to come up with hybrid solutions that draw on what you've learned combined with new ideas you dream up along the way.

Game Theory

Now that you understand the important aspects of handling communications between network game instances, let's shift gears a little and take a look at an area of theoretical research that impacts multiplayer games. An area of increasingly popular academic research, called game theory, can be used to shed light on how people interact with each other in a multiplayer computer game scenario. Applications of this information could breathe fresh insight into the design of multiplayer games. Game theory won't help you with synchronization problems, but it might help you figure out more creative approaches to the game strategy itself.

NEW TERM *Game theory* is a branch of mathematical analysis devoted to the study of decision making in conflict situations.

Such a situation exists when two or more decision makers, or players, with differing objectives act on the same system or share the same resources. Game theory provides a mathematical process for selecting an optimum strategy in the face of an opponent who has a strategy of his own. This mathematical process borders on issues related to both multiplayer computer game design and strategic AI.

In game theory, the following assumptions are usually made:

☐ Each player has available to her two or more well-specified choices or sequences of choices called *plays*.

☐ Every possible combination of plays available to the players leads to a well-defined end-state (win, loss, or draw) that terminates the game.

☐ A specified payoff for each player is associated with each end-state.

☐ Each decision maker has perfect knowledge of the game and of his opposition; that is, he knows in full detail the rules of the game as well as the payoffs for all other players.

☐ All decision makers are rational; that is, each player, given two alternatives, will select the one that yields the greater payoff.

Although general in scope and not originally directed at computer games, game theory touches on many of the same concerns that are raised when strategies for multiplayer computer games are being designed. Two players in a network multiplayer game often go through much of the same thought pattern as people engaged in a verbal conflict. Game theory applies equally well to both scenarios.

Because of its general nature, game theory has seen wide application in areas such as economics, international trade, labor, public policy, natural resources, and development. Individuals making use of game theory in their professions have included philosophers, political scientists, arms-control negotiators, and evolutionary biologists.

You can use game theory in your own multiplayer game designs to help determine how reactions between players impact the game. Game theory is also useful in determining computer player strategies based on the possible range of responses by a human player. It's all a matter of breaking a game down into a sequence of decisions that can be compared to other decisions and what reactions they provoke from other players.

One particular example that shows how game theory raises strategic questions applicable to multiplayer computer games is the Prisoners' Dilemma. The Prisoners' Dilemma is a game that has been, and continues to be, studied by people in various disciplines, ranging from biology to sociology and public policy. Among its interesting characteristics is that it is a "non-zero-sum" game, meaning that the best strategy for a given player is often one that increases the payoff to one's partner as well. It has also been shown that there is no single best strategy; maximizing one's own payoff depends on the strategy adopted by one's partner.

The game works like this: Imagine two criminals arrested under the suspicion of having committed a crime together. The police don't have enough evidence to convict them, so they are isolated from each other and separately offered a deal: The one who offers evidence against the other will be freed. If neither of them accepts the offer, they are effectively cooperating against the police, and both get only a small punishment because of lack of proof. Hence, they both gain. If, however, one of them betrays the other by confessing to the police, he is freed; the one who remained silent receives the full punishment because he did not help the police and because the police now have evidence against him provided by the other prisoner. If both betray each other, they both will be punished, but less severely than if either had refused to talk. The dilemma resides in the fact that each prisoner has a choice between only two options, but neither can make a good decision without knowing what the other one does.

The Prisoners' Dilemma raises some interesting questions regarding strategies involving multiple players competing for a common goal. To try your wits at the Prisoners' Dilemma, check out the online version at http://serendip.brynmawr.edu/~ann/pd.html. Figure 17.7 shows what the Web site looks like with the interactive Prisoners' Dilemma.

Figure 17.7.

The interactive Prisoners' Dilemma Web site.

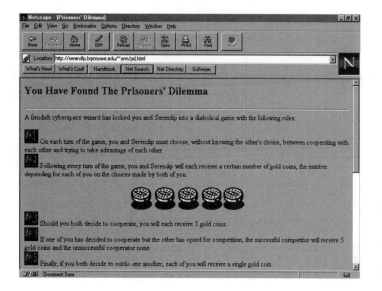

Summary

You should now have some idea about the general theory behind designing games for multiple players. I know that today's lesson didn't really present a rosy image of multiplayer game design, and for good reason; designing games for multiple players over a network is a difficult task that involves a lot of planning and creative design. On the other hand, the capability of supporting multiple human players can make any game orders of magnitude more fun. And with the Internet looming as the ultimate network for playing multiplayer games, it's only a matter of time before network gaming becomes the norm.

Fortunately, the Java language and class libraries provide many features to ease the pain in creating multiplayer games with network support. The task is not necessarily easy, but it's often easier than prior approaches at building Internet games. In tomorrow's lesson, you'll learn exactly what support Java provides for network game development.

Q&A

Q If multiplayer Internet games are so cool, why are there still so few of them?

A One of the main reasons there aren't many network games with full Internet support is that only recently has Internet usage started extending to the general game community. Another reason is that it has been difficult at best to implement Internet communications in games. However, with the advent of Java and various third-party C and C++ libraries, along with a growing acceptance of the Internet among gamers, you should start seeing most new network games sporting Internet support.

Q **Is bandwidth always a concern when you're designing network games?**

A It depends, but more often yes. The only time bandwidth isn't an issue in network games is when a very small amount of information is being transferred between instances. An example of this type of game would be a network Connect4 game, in which the only information transferred would be the column of the move.

Q **Does synchronization get more difficult to maintain when there are more players?**

A Usually not because the amount of synchronization information being sent is the same, regardless of how many players there are.

Workshop

The Workshop section provides questions and exercises to help you get a better feel for the material you learned today. Try to answer the questions and at least think about the exercises before moving on to tomorrow's lesson. You'll find the answers to the questions in Appendix A, "Quiz Answers."

Quiz

1. What are the two basic types of multiplayer games?
2. What is the difference between a modem network connection and a physical network connection?
3. What are the three types of network synchronization solutions?

Exercises

1. Go to a software store and see whether you can find any games that support Internet network play.
2. Of these games, see how many are turn-based and how many are event-based.
3. Check out the Prisoners' Dilemma Web site, and try out your own strategy.

Day 18

Networking with Java

Yesterday you learned what multiplayer games are and why they are so important. Today you take one more step toward creating a networked multiplayer game that can be played over the Internet. I know, you're probably itching to move on and see a full-blown network game. However, you still need to cover some ground in regard to what is required behind the scenes to facilitate network communication in a real game. Trust me, you'll be dealing with the intricacies of network game programming soon enough.

In today's lesson, you learn specifically what Java has to offer in regard to communicating over an Internet network connection. You begin the lesson by taking a look at some basic concepts surrounding the structure of the Internet itself. You then move on to what specific support is provided by the standard Java networking API. Finally, you conclude the lesson by writing a reusable socket class that will prove invaluable tomorrow when you write a complete network game.

The following topics are covered in today's lesson:

☐ Network basics

☐ The client/server paradigm

☐ Sockets

☐ A reusable socket class

Network Basics

Before you look at what type of network support Java provides, it's important that you understand some fundamentals about the structure of the Internet as a network. As you are no doubt already aware, the Internet is itself a global network of many different types of computers connected in various ways. With this wide diversity of both hardware and software all connected together, it's pretty amazing that the Internet is even functional. The functionality of the Internet is no accident and has come at no small cost in terms of planning.

The only way to guarantee compatibility and reliable communication across a wide range of different computer systems is to lay out very strict standards that must be conformed to rigorously. Now, please understand that I'm not the type of person who typically preaches conformity, but conformity in one's personal life is very different from conformity in complex computer networks. When it comes to computers and communication, I make a pretty big exception and embrace conformity for all its worth!

The point is that the only way to allow a wide range of computer systems to coexist and communicate with each other effectively is to hammer out some standards. Fortunately, plenty of standards abound for the Internet, and they share wide support across many different computer systems. Now that I have (I hope) sold you on the importance of communication standards, let's take a look at a few of them.

Addresses

One of the first areas of standardization on the Internet was in establishing a means to uniquely identify each connected computer. It's not surprising that a technique logically equivalent to traditional mailing addresses is the one that was adopted; each computer physically connected to the Internet is assigned an *address* that uniquely identifies it. These addresses, also referred to as *IP addresses,* come in the form of a 32-bit number that looks like this: 243.37.126.82. You're probably more familiar with the symbolic form of IP addresses, which looks like this: sincity.com.

NEW TERM   An *IP address* is a 32-bit number that uniquely identifies each computer physically attached to the Internet.

Addresses provide a unique identifier for each computer connected to the Internet. Each Internet computer has an address for the same reason you have a mailing address and a phone number at your home: to facilitate communication. It might sound simple, and that's because conceptually it is. As long as you can guarantee that each computer is uniquely identifiable, you can easily communicate with any computer without worry. Well, almost. The truth is that addresses are only a small part of the Internet communication equation, but an important part nevertheless. Without addresses, there would be no way to distinguish among different computers.

Protocols

The idea of communicating among different computers on the Internet might not sound like a big deal now that you understand that they use addresses similar to mailing addresses. The problem is that there are many different types of communication that can take place on the Internet, meaning that there must be an equal number of mechanisms for facilitating them. It's at this point that the mailing-address comparison to Internet addressing breaks down. The reason for this is that each type of communication taking place on the Internet requires a unique protocol. Your mail address essentially revolves around one type of communication: the mailman driving up to your mailbox and placing the mail inside.

NEW TERM   A *protocol* is a set of rules and standards defining a certain type of Internet communication.

A protocol specifies the format of data being sent over the Internet, along with how and when it is sent. On the other end of the communication, the protocol also defines how the data is received along with its structure and what it means. You've probably heard mention of the Internet just being a bunch of bits flying back and forth in cyberspace. That's a very true statement, and without protocols those bits wouldn't mean anything.

The concept of a protocol is not groundbreaking or even new; you use protocols all the time in everyday situations, but you just don't call them protocols. Think about how many times you've been involved in this type of dialog:

> "Hi, may I take your order?"
>
> "Yes, I'd like the shrimp special and a soda."
>
> "Thanks, I'll put your order in and bring you your drink."
>
> "Thank you, I sure am hungry."

Although this conversation might not look like anything special, it is a very definite social protocol used to place orders for food at a restaurant. Conversational protocol is important because it gives us familiarity and confidence in knowing what to do in certain situations. Haven't you ever been nervous when entering a new social situation in which you don't quite

18

know how to act? In these cases, you don't really have confidence in the protocol, so you worry about a communication problem that could easily result in embarrassment. For computers and networks, protocol breakdown translates into errors and information transfer failure rather than embarrassment.

Now that you understand the importance of protocols, let's take a look at a couple of the more important ones used on the Internet. Without a doubt, the protocol getting the most attention these days is HTTP, which stands for hypertext transfer protocol. HTTP is the protocol used to transfer HTML documents on the Web. Another important protocol is FTP, which stands for file transfer protocol. FTP is a more general protocol used to transfer binary files over the Internet. These two protocols both have their own unique set of rules and standards defining how information is transferred, and Java provides support for both of them.

NEW TERM   *HTTP*, which stands for Hypertext Transfer Protocol, is the protocol used to transfer HTML documents on the Web.

Ports

Internet protocols make sense only in the context of a service. For example, the HTTP protocol comes into play when you are providing Web content (HTML pages) through an HTTP service. Each computer on the Internet has the capability to provide a variety of services through the various protocols supported. There is a problem, however, in that the type of service must be known before information can be transferred. This is where ports come in. A *port* is a software abstraction that provides a means to differentiate between different services. More specifically, a port is a 16-bit number identifying the different services offered by a network server.

NEW TERM   A *port* is a 16-bit number that identifies each service offered by a network server.

Each computer on the Internet has a bunch of ports that can be assigned different services. To use a particular service and therefore establish a line of communication via a particular protocol, you must connect to the correct port. Ports are numbered, and some of the numbers are specifically associated with a type of service. Ports with specific service assignments are known as standard ports, meaning that you can always count on a particular port corresponding to a certain service. For example, the FTP service is located on port 21, so any other computer wanting to perform an FTP file transfer would connect to port 21 of the host computer. Likewise, the HTTP service is located on port 80, so any time you access a Web site, you are really connecting to port 80 of the host using the HTTP protocol behind the scenes. Figure 18.1 illustrates how ports and protocols work.

Figure 18.1.

A conceptual look at protocols and ports.

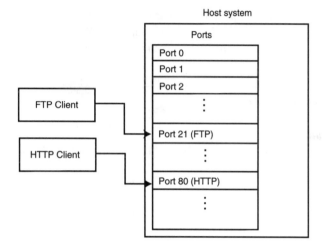

All standard service assignments are given port values below 1024. This means that ports above 1024 are considered available for custom communications, such as those required by a network game implementing its own protocol. Keep in mind, however, that other types of custom communication also take place above port 1024, so you might have to try a few different ports to find an unused one.

The Client/Server Paradigm

So far, I've managed to explain a decent amount of Internet networking fundamentals while dodging a major issue: the client/server paradigm. You've no doubt heard of clients and servers before, but you might not fully understand their importance in regard to the Internet. Well, it's time to remedy that situation, because you won't be able to get much done in Java without understanding how clients and servers work.

The client/server paradigm involves thinking of computing in terms of a client, who is essentially in need of some type of information, and a server, who has lots of information and is just waiting to hand it out. Typically, a client connects to a server and queries for certain information. The server goes off and finds the information and then returns it to the client. It might sound as though I'm oversimplifying things here, but for the most part I'm not; conceptually, client/server computing is as simple as a client asking for information and a server returning it.

In the context of the Internet, clients are typically computers attached to the Internet looking for information, whereas servers are typically larger computers with certain types of information available for the clients to retrieve. The Web itself is made up of a bunch of computers that act as Web servers; they have vast amounts of HTML pages and related data available for people to retrieve and browse. Web clients are those of us who connect to the Web servers and browse through the Web pages. In this way, Netscape Navigator is considered client Web software. Take a look at Figure 18.2 to get a better idea of the client/server arrangement.

Figure 18.2.

A Web server with multiple clients.

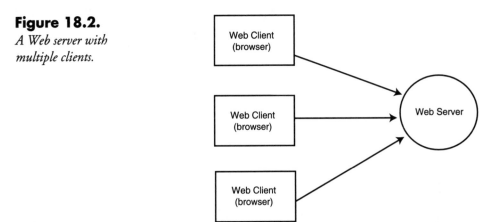

At this point, you might be wondering how the client/server strategy impacts Java game programming. Well, Java games run within the confines of a Web page, which is accessed via client Web browser software such as Netscape Navigator. Each player in a network Java game is running the game within a Web browser, which means that each player is acting as a client. When the players attempt to communicate with each other, you are left with Web clients trying to transfer information among themselves, which can't happen directly. The solution is for the clients (players) to communicate with each other through the server; the server effectively acts as a middleman routing information among the clients. Don't worry if this sounds kind of strange; you'll learn the details later today.

Sockets

One of Java's major strong suits as a programming language is its wide range of network support. Java has this advantage because it was developed with the Internet in mind. The result is that you have lots of options in regard to network programming in Java. Even though there are many network options, Java network game programming uses a particular type of network communication known as sockets.

NEW TERM   A *socket* is a software abstraction for an input or output medium of communication.

18

Java performs all of its low-level network communication through sockets. Logically, sockets are one step lower than ports; you use sockets to communicate through a particular port. So a socket is a communication channel enabling you to transfer data through a certain port. Check out Figure 18.3, which shows communication taking place through multiple sockets on a port.

Figure 18.3.

Socket communication on a port.

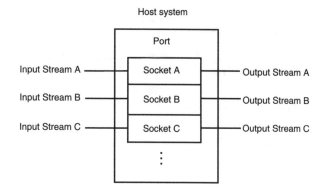

This figure brings up an interesting point about sockets: data can be transferred through multiple sockets for a single port. Java provides socket classes to make programming with sockets much easier. Java sockets are broken down into two types: stream sockets and datagram sockets.

Stream Sockets

NEW TERM A *stream socket*, or connected socket, is a socket over which data can be transmitted continuously.

By continuously, I don't necessarily mean that data is being sent all the time, but that the socket itself is active and ready for communication all the time. Think of a stream socket as a dedicated network connection, in which a communication medium is always available for use. The benefit of using a stream socket is that information can be sent with less worry about when it will arrive at its destination. Because the communication link is always "live," data is generally transmitted immediately after you send it. This method of communication is the method you will use tomorrow to write a sample network game, NetConnect4.

> **NOTE**
> A practical example of data being sent through a streaming mechanism is RealAudio, a technology that provides a way to listen to audio on the Web as it is being transmitted in real time.

Java supports streamed socket programming primarily through two classes: Socket and ServerSocket. The Socket class provides the necessary overhead to facilitate a streamed socket client, and the ServerSocket class provides the core functionality for a server. Here is a list of some of the more important methods implemented in the Socket class:

```
Socket(String host, int port)
Socket(InetAddress address, int port)
synchronized void close()
InputStream getInputStream()
OutputStream getOutputStream()
```

The first two methods listed are actually constructors for the Socket class. The host computer you are connecting the socket to is specified in the first parameter of each constructor; the difference between the two constructors is whether you specify the host using a string name or an InetAddress object. The second parameter is an integer specifying the port you want to connect to. The close method is used to close a socket. The getInputStream and getOutputStream methods are used to retrieve the input and output streams associated with the socket.

The ServerSocket class handles the other end of socket communication in a client/server scenario. Here are a few of the more useful methods defined in the ServerSocket class:

```
ServerSocket(int port)
ServerSocket(int port, int count)
Socket accept()
void close()
```

The first two methods are the constructors for ServerSocket, which both take a port number as the first parameter. The count parameter in the second constructor specifies a timeout period for the server to automatically "listen" for a client connection. This is the distinguishing factor between the two constructors; the first version doesn't listen for a client connection, whereas the second version does. If you use the first constructor, you must specifically tell the server to wait for a client connection. You do this by calling the accept method, which blocks program flow until a connection is made. The close method simply closes the server socket.

You might be thinking that the socket classes seem awfully simple. In fact, they are simple, which is a good thing. Most of the actual code facilitating communication via sockets is handled through the input and output streams connected to a socket. In this way, the communication itself is handled independently of the network socket connection. This might not seem like a big deal at first, but it is crucial in the design of the socket classes; after you've created a socket, you connect an input or output stream to it and then forget about the socket.

The Socket and ServerSocket classes are the classes you'll use a little later today to build a simple networking applet. You'll get to see how easy it is to communicate using Java and sockets.

18

Datagram Sockets

The other type of socket supported by Java is the datagram socket. Unlike stream sockets, in which the communication is akin to a live network, a datagram socket is more akin to a dial-up network, in which the communication link isn't continuously active.

NEW TERM   A *datagram socket* is a socket over which data is bundled into packets and sent without requiring a "live" connection to the destination computer.

Because of the nature of the communication medium involved, datagram sockets aren't guaranteed to transmit information at a particular time, or even in any particular order. The reason datagram sockets perform this way is that they don't require an actual connection to another computer; the address of the target computer is just bundled with the information being sent. This bundle is then sent out over the Internet, leaving the sender to hope for the best.

On the receiving end, the bundles of information can be received in any order and at any time. For this reason, datagrams also include a sequence number that specifies which piece of the puzzle each bundle corresponds to. The receiver waits to receive the entire sequence, in which case it puts them back together to form a complete information transfer. As you might be thinking, datagram sockets are less than ideal for network game programming, simply because of the implied time delays and sequencing complexities.

A Reusable Socket Class

You've now learned enough about network theory and the Java networking support to write some code. Before you can think in terms of writing network game code, however, you need to develop some code that helps facilitate the core communications necessary for a game. In doing so, you'll have reliable, reusable code that can easily be applied to provide functionality specific to a particular game communication protocol.

As you learned earlier, the primary purpose of sockets is to provide a channel of communication through a particular port. You also learned that sockets have associated input and output streams that actually handle the details of transferring information via the socket. Even though the standard Java socket classes provide much of this support, some code still must be handled on your end; this is the code you're going to focus on at this point.

The first layer of code necessary to facilitate network communications comes in the form of a socket helper class that handles the details of initializing a socket and managing the associated data streams. The SocketAction class was developed by Greg Turner to help ease the pain in establishing a communication channel using Java sockets. The SocketAction class

18

is derived from Thread so that it has its own thread of execution. Let's start by looking at the member variables of SocketAction, which follow:

```
private DataInputStream inStream = null;
protected PrintStream    outStream = null;
private Socket           socket = null;
```

The first two members, inStream and outStream, are the input and output streams used to receive and send data through the socket. The third member variable, socket, is the socket object itself.

The constructor for SocketAction takes a Socket object as its only parameter:

```
public SocketAction(Socket sock) {
  super("SocketAction");
  try {
    inStream = new DataInputStream(new
      BufferedInputStream(sock.getInputStream(), 1024));
    outStream = new PrintStream(new
      BufferedOutputStream(sock.getOutputStream(), 1024), true);
    socket = sock;
  }
  catch (IOException e) {
    System.out.println("Couldn't initialize SocketAction: " + e);
    System.exit(1);
  }
}
```

The constructor creates the buffered data streams and initializes the socket member variable with the Socket object passed in. If there was a problem in initializing the streams, the constructor detects it by using the catch clause. Note that if there is an error in creating the streams, something is seriously wrong, which explains why the entire program exits.

The send and receive methods are possibly the most useful methods in SocketAction, even though they contain very little code:

```
public void send(String s) {
  outStream.println(s);
}

public String receive() throws IOException {
  return inStream.readLine();
}
```

The send method simply sends a string out over the socket connection by using the output data stream. Similarly, the receive method receives a string by using the input data stream.

The closeConnections method simply closes the socket:

```
public void closeConnections() {
  try {
    socket.close();
    socket = null;
  }
```

```
  catch (IOException e) {
    System.out.println("Couldn't close socket: " + e);
  }
}
```

The `isConnected` method verifies that the input and output streams, as well as the `socket` object, are valid:

```
public boolean isConnected() {
  return ((inStream != null) && (outStream != null) && (socket != null));
}
```

Finally, the `finalize` method closes the socket as an added safety precaution:

```
protected void finalize () {
  if (socket != null) {
    try {
      socket.close();
    }
    catch (IOException e) {
      System.out.println("Couldn't close socket: " + e);
    }
    socket = null;
  }
}
```

And that's all there is to the `SocketAction` class. That wasn't too bad, was it? As you saw, the `SocketAction` class is pretty elementary. Nevertheless, its simple function of providing a clean management class for sockets and their associated streams will make life much easier tomorrow when you build a complete network game.

Summary

Today you broke away from the confines of programming for a single user and moved into the world of network programming. You learned that Java makes network programming surprisingly easy by providing standard classes that hide most of the nastiness typically associated with network programming. You began the lesson with some network fundamentals, progressing onward to learn all about sockets and how to use them. You then finished the lesson by developing a reusable socket class that provides much of the overhead involved in network communications.

Even though little of today's lesson had anything to do with game programming specifically, you learned enough about Java network programming to move on to tomorrow's lesson, which does deal with game programming. In fact, tomorrow's lesson is entirely devoted to converting the Connect4 game from Day 16's lesson into a multiplayer network game playable over the Internet.

18

Q&A

Q **Why is the client/server paradigm so important in Java network programming?**

A The client/server model was integrated into Java because it has proven time and again to be superior to other networking approaches. By dividing the act of serving data from the act of viewing and working with data, the client/server approach provides network developers with the freedom to implement a wide range of solutions to common network problems.

Q **Does the client/server strategy really make sense for games?**

A Based on the traditional role of a server strictly providing information to a "dumb" client, the answer is no. When it comes to games, however, the concept of what the clients and server are responsible for changes somewhat. For example, a game server is responsible for receiving client player events and dispatching them to the other players. In turn, the clients are responsible for generating and sending the events to the server, as well as updating themselves based on other player events received from the server. When you view the client/server model from this admittedly altered perspective, it makes complete sense for games.

Q **Why aren't datagram sockets suitable for network game communications?**

A The primary reason is speed, because you have no way of knowing when information transferred through a datagram socket will reach its destination. Admittedly, you don't really know for sure when stream socket data will get to its destination either, but you can rest assured it will be faster than with the datagram socket. Also, datagram socket transfers have the additional complexity of requiring you to reorganize the incoming data, which is an unnecessary and time-consuming annoyance for games.

Workshop

The Workshop section provides questions and exercises to help you get a firmer grasp on the material you learned today. Try to answer the questions and at least think about the exercises before moving on to tomorrow's lesson. You'll find the answers to the questions in Appendix A, "Quiz Answers."

Quiz

1. What is a port?
2. What is the significance of using sockets for network communications?
3. What is the difference between stream sockets and datagram sockets?
4. What's the big deal about writing a reusable socket class?

Exercises

1. If you have a dedicated Internet connection, find out what your numeric IP address is.

2. Try out some networked Java applets and see if you can figure out how they are using Java sockets. Note: You can find many networked Java applets at the Gamelan Web site (http://www.gamelan.com).

3. Spend some time relaxing, because tomorrow's lesson dives straight into developing a complete network game.

18

Day 19

NetConnect4: Human versus Human

In yesterday's lesson, you learned how Java supports network communications through a client/server model. You even built a simple socket class to help make network communications a little easier. In today's lesson, you carry the client/server approach a step forward and build a complete network game supporting multiple players. Actually, instead of writing a whole new game, you modify a game you already wrote to support network play. By the end of today's lesson, you'll have the skills necessary to begin developing your own network games.

Today you take the Connect4 game you wrote on Day 16 and adapt it to network play between two players. In doing so, you put the socket class developed yesterday to good use; you use the socket class as a basis for implementing a complete network game protocol facilitating game communication between multiple clients and a server. Sounds like fun, right? You bet!

The following topics are covered in today's lesson:

☐ Designing NetConnect4

☐ Sample applet: NetConnect4

Designing NetConnect4

If you recall, the Connect4 game you wrote in Day 16's lesson was a single-player game utilizing artificial intelligence to simulate an intelligent computer player. The goal now is to take that game and adapt it for two human players playing the game over the Web. This task might sound a little daunting, but keep in mind that the game itself is already written; you're just adding the network support code.

As you learned yesterday, the core of Java network game programming revolves around a client/server communication strategy. Knowing this, you've probably guessed that a Java network game design will involve some type of client/server arrangement. In fact, the design of the NetConnect4 game can be divided cleanly into the client side and the server side. These two components are logically separate, communicating entirely through a game protocol defined between them. Let's take a look at what each of these pieces is responsible for.

The Server

In any Java game, the server side of the game acts almost like a referee, managing the different players and helping them communicate effectively. More specifically, a game server takes on the role of handling the network connection for each player, along with querying for and responding to events for the players. The role of a generic game server can be broken down into the following actions:

1. Initialize the server socket.
2. Wait for a client to connect.
3. Accept the client connection.
4. Create a daemon thread to support the client.
5. Go back to step 2.

The most crucial aspect of this series of events is step 4, when the server creates a daemon thread to support the client. You're probably wondering what I mean by "support." Well, in a generic sense, I don't know what I mean. The reason is that the daemon thread is where the applet-specific code goes. So a generic server only knows that it needs to create a daemon thread; it doesn't know or care about what that thread actually does. You'll learn more about daemon threads a little later today when you actually get into the code for NetConnect4.

NEW TERM A *daemon* is a process that runs in the background of a system performing some type of support function.

You now have an idea about the role a generic game server plays in the context of a network game. The question, then, is what role does such a server play in the context of a specific game, namely NetConnect4? The role of the NetConnect4 server ends up being not much different from that of the generic server, but it is important that you understand exactly what it needs to do differently.

Because Connect4 is a two-player game, the first job of the server is to pair up players (clients) as they connect to the game. A more limited approach would be to permit only the first two players who connect to play the game. But you're smarter than that and hopefully demand a more powerful game server. Your game server enables multiple games to be played at once simply by pairing additional client players together for each game. In this way, a typical NetConnect4 server session might have six or eight players playing at once. Of course, the players know only about the other player in their immediate game.

To keep things a little simpler, don't worry about players choosing who they play against; in other words, just pair players on a first-come first-served basis.

After the server has detected two players and paired them up for a game, it becomes the responsibility of the server's daemon thread to dictate the flow of the game between the players. The daemon accomplishes this by informing each player of the state of the game, while also modifying the state according to each player's turn. The responsibilities of the NetConnect4 server and daemon can be summarized as shown here:

- [ ] Accept client player connections.
- [ ] Pair up players to form separate games.
- [ ] Manage the flow of the game.
- [ ] Communicate each player's move to the other player.
- [ ] Notify the players of the state of the game.

The Client

The other side of a Java network game is the client. The client portion of a network game corresponds to the applet being run by each player. Because game players interact with the client, the client program is usually much fancier than the server in regard to how information is displayed. As a matter of fact, game servers typically don't even have user interfaces; they crank away entirely behind-the-scenes doing all the dirty work while the client applets dazzle the users.

The basic responsibility of a game client is to connect to the server and communicate the user's actions, along with receiving game state information from the server and updating itself accordingly. Of course, along with this comes the responsibility of displaying the game graphics and managing the entire game interface for the user. You can probably already see that game clients tend to require the most work, at least from a strictly design perspective.

The good news is that you've already written most of the client for NetConnect4. The Connect4 game you wrote on Day 16 is essentially a non-networking game client in that it handles all the work of managing a game with a user; it displays the graphics, interfaces with the user, and keeps up with the state of the game. The focus of building a NetConnect4 client then becomes modifying the original Connect4 code to transform it into a full-blown client that can communicate with the NetConnect4 server. The following is a summary of what functionality the NetConnect4 client needs to provide:

☐ Connect to the server.

☐ Notify the player of the connection/game state.

☐ Communicate the player's move to the server.

☐ Receive the other player's move from the server.

☐ Update the game with the state received from the server.

Putting Them Together

You might be wondering how this whole client/server game scenario works in regard to a Web server, because it's apparent that the game server must be running at all times. For a network game to work, you must have the game server always running in the background, meaning that it must somehow be launched by the Web server or by some type of system startup feature. This makes it available to connect clients who come along wanting to play.

When a Web client shows up to play a game, the game server accepts the client's connection and then takes on the role of hooking the client up with another client to play a game. The game server is entirely responsible for detecting when clients arrive as well as when they leave, creating and canceling game sessions along the way. Because the game server is being run in the background all the time, it must be extremely robust.

WARNING

Because the game server is responsible for detecting and pairing clients, it is imperative that the server be running at all times. Without the server, you have no knowledge of or communication between clients.

Sample Applet: NetConnect4

The NetConnect4 sample applet demonstrates all the details of using Internet network communication to develop a multiplayer Java game. Even though the focus of today's lesson is on the actual programming involved in making NetConnect4 a reality, you'll probably find the code a little easier to follow if you run the finished product first. Knowing that, let's put NetConnect4 through its paces and see how to use it. By the way, the complete source code, executable, images, and sounds for the NetConnect4 game are located on the accompanying CD-ROM.

Running NetConnect4

This discussion on running the NetConnect4 sample game assumes that you either have access to a Web server or can simulate a network connection on your local machine. When I refer to running the server side of the game, you need to run it in the way that you typically execute a program based on your Web server configuration.

NOTE

I tested the game myself by simulating a network connection on my local Windows 95 machine. I did this by changing the TCP/IP configuration on my machine so that it used a specific IP address; I just made up an address. If you make this change to your network configuration, you won't be able to access a real network using TCP/IP until you set it back, so don't forget to restore things when you're finished testing the game.

As you already know, the NetConnect4 game is composed of two parts: a client and a server. The NetConnect4 server is the core of the game and must be running in order for the clients to work. So to get the game running, you must first run the server by using the Java interpreter (java). You do this from a command line, like this:

```
java NetConnect4Server
```

The other half of NetConnect4 is the client, which is an applet that runs from within a browser such as Netscape Navigator. Incidentally, the NetConnect4 client applet is called Connect4, to keep the name consistent with the original single-player game. After you have the server up and running, fire up a Java-compatible browser, and load an HTML document including the NetConnect4 client applet. On the CD-ROM, this HTML document is called Example1.html, in keeping with the standard JDK demo applets. After running the Connect4 client applet, you should see something similar to what's shown in Figure 19.1.

At this point, you have the server up and running with a single client attached to it. Because two players are required to start a game, the client is in a wait state until another player comes along. Now, load a second instance of the Web browser with the same Example1.html document; this is your second player. When the server detects this player, it pairs the two players and starts the game. Figure 19.2 shows this scenario.

19

Figure 19.1.

The NetConnect4 game with a single client player.

Figure 19.2.

The NetConnect4 game with two client players in a new game.

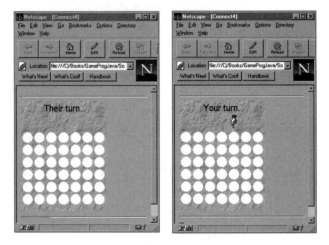

By switching between the Web browsers, you can simulate a network game between the two players. Go ahead and outwit yourself so that you can see what happens when one of the players wins. This situation is shown in Figure 19.3.

For another game to start between the same two players, each player just needs to click once in the applet window. You can see now how two players interact together in a game of NetConnect4. Now, if you really want to test the game, try loading two more instances of the Web browser and starting another game between two new players. In this scenario, you have a total of four players involved in two separate games, all running off the same server. The game server supports an unlimited number of players and games, although at some point it might be wise to impose a limit so that performance doesn't start dragging. A couple of hundred players banging away at your game server might tend to slow things down!

Figure 19.3.
The NetConnect4 game with two client players in a finished game.

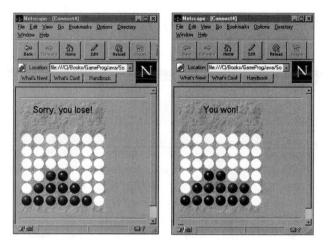

You now understand how the game plays, along with the roles of the client and server, so you're ready to actually dig into the source code and really see how things work. You've come to the right place.

Developing NetConnect4

The client/server nature of NetConnect4 doesn't just apply at the conceptual level, it also plays a role in how the code is laid out for the game. Because the client and server components function as separate programs, it makes sense to develop the code for them as two different efforts. With that in mind, let's tackle each part separately.

The Server

The NetConnect4 server is composed of four classes:

- ☐ Connect4Server
- ☐ Connect4Daemon
- ☐ Connect4Player
- ☐ Game

The Connect4Server class serves as a stub program to get the server started. Check out the source code for it:

```
class Connect4Server {
  public static void main(String args[]) {
    System.out.println("NetConnect4 server up and running...");
    new Connect4Daemon().start();
  }
}
```

As you can see, the Connect4Server class contains only one method, main, which prints a message and creates a Connect4Daemon object. The Connect4Daemon class is where the server is actually created and initialized. The Connect4Daemon class is responsible for creating the server socket and handling client connections. Take a look at the member variables defined in the Connect4Daemon class:

```
public static final int PORTNUM = 1234;
private ServerSocket     port;
private Connect4Player  playerWaiting = null;
private Game            thisGame = null;
```

Other than the constant port number, Connect4Daemon defines three member variables consisting of a ServerSocket object, a Connect4Player object, and a Game object. The Connect4Player and Game classes are covered a little later in the lesson. The ServerSocket member object, port, is created using an arbitrary port number above 1024. If you recall from yesterday's lesson, all ports below 1024 are reserved for standard system services, so you must use one above 1024. More specifically, I chose 1234 as the port number, which is represented by the PORTNUM constant.

WARNING

Using a port number greater than 1024 doesn't guarantee that the port will be available. It does guarantee, however, that the port isn't already assigned to a common service. Nevertheless, any other extended services, such as game servers, could potentially conflict with your port number. If your port number conflicts with another server, just try a different one.

The run method in Connect4Daemon is where the details of connecting clients are handled:

```
public void run() {
  Socket clientSocket;
  while (true) {
    if (port == null) {
      System.out.println("Sorry, the port disappeared.");
      System.exit(1);
    }
    try {
      clientSocket = port.accept();
      new Connect4Player(this, clientSocket).start();
    }
    catch (IOException e) {
      System.out.println("Couldn't connect player: " + e);
      System.exit(1);
    }
  }
}
```

The run method first retrieves the socket for a connecting client via a call to the ServerSocket class's accept method. If you recall from yesterday's lesson, the accept method waits until a client connects and then returns a socket for the client. After a client connects, a Connect4Player object is created using the client socket.

NOTE

Even though the Connect4Daemon class functions very much like a daemon thread, you don't specify it as a Java daemon thread because you don't want it to be destroyed by the runtime system. You might be wondering why the Java runtime system would go around killing innocent threads. Because daemon threads always run as support for other non-daemon threads or programs, the Java runtime system kills them if there are no non-daemon threads executing.

The waitForGame method is where players are paired up with each other. Listing 19.1 contains the source code for the waitForGame method.

Listing 19.1. The Connect4Daemon class's waitForGame method.

```
public synchronized Game waitForGame(Connect4Player p) {
  Game retval = null;
  if (playerWaiting == null) {
    playerWaiting = p;
    thisGame = null;       // just in case!
    p.send("PLSWAIT");
    while (playerWaiting != null) {
      try {
        wait();
      }
      catch (InterruptedException e) {
        System.out.println("Error: " + e);
      }
    }
    return thisGame;
  }
  else {
    thisGame = new Game(playerWaiting, p);
    retval = thisGame;
    playerWaiting = null;
    notify();
    return retval;
  }
}
```

19

The `waitForGame` method is called from within the `Connect4Player` class, which you'll learn about in a moment. `waitForGame` is passed a `Connect4Player` object as its only parameter. If no player is waiting to play, this player is flagged as a waiting player, and a loop is entered that waits until another player connects. A null `Game` object is then returned to indicate that only one player is present. When another player connects and `waitForGame` is called, things happen a little differently. Because a player is now waiting, a `Game` object is created using the two players. This `Game` object is then returned to indicate that the game is ready to begin.

The `finalize` method in `Connect4Daemon` is simply an added measure to help clean up the server socket when the daemon dies:

```
protected void finalize() {
  if (port != null) {
    try {
      port.close();
    }
    catch (IOException e) {
      System.out.println("Error closing port: " + e);
    }
    port = null;
  }
}
```

To clean up the server socket, `finalize` simply calls the `close` method on the port.

The `Connect4Daemon` class made a few references to the `Connect4Player` class, which logically represents a player in the game. Listing 19.2 contains the source code for the `Connect4Player` class.

Listing 19.2. The `Connect4Player` class.

```
class Connect4Player extends SocketAction {
  private Connect4Daemon daemon = null;

  public Connect4Player(Connect4Daemon server, Socket sock) {
    super(sock);
    daemon = server;
  }

  public void run() {
    daemon.waitForGame(this).playGame(this);
  }

  public void closeConnections() {
    super.closeConnections();
    if (outStream != null) {
      send("GAMEOVER");
    }
  }
}
```

19

The Connect4Player class represents a player from the server's perspective. Connect4Player is derived from SocketAction, which is the generic socket class you developed yesterday. I told you it would come in handy. The only member variable defined in Connect4Player is daemon, which holds the Connect4Daemon object associated with the player.

The constructor for Connect4Player takes Connect4Daemon and Socket objects as its two parameters. The Connect4Daemon object is used to initialize the daemon member variable, and the Socket object is passed on to the parent constructor in SocketAction.

The run method for Connect4Player calls back to the daemon's waitForGame method to get a Game object for the player. The playGame method is then called on the Game object to get the game underway. The closeConnections method closes the client connection and is typically used to end the game.

The last class the NetConnect4 server comprises is the Game class, which handles the details associated with managing the game logic and the communication between players. The Game class takes on the bulk of the work involved in maintaining the state of the game, as well as communicating that state between the players. The Game class contains a group of member constants that define the different states in the game:

```
public static final int ERROR = -1;
public static final int IWON = -2;
public static final int IQUIT = -3;
public static final int ITIED = -4;
public static final int YOURTURN = -5;
public static final int SENTSTRING = -6;
```

Along with the constants, the Game class has member variables representing each player, along with an event queue for each player and a string used to send messages to the other player:

```
private Connect4Player  player1 = null;
private Connect4Player  player2 = null;
private Vector          p1Queue = null;
private Vector          p2Queue = null;
private String          sentString;
```

NEW TERM An *event queue* is a list of events that take place within a particular context.

In the case of NetConnect4, an event consists of player moves and related game states. So the event queue is used to keep up with the latest player moves and game states.

The workhorse method in the Game class is playGame, which essentially manages the game flow and logic for each player. Listing 19.3 contains the source code for the playGame method.

19

Listing 19.3. The Game class's playGame method.

```
public void playGame(Connect4Player me) {
  String instr;
  boolean playgame = true;
  boolean theirturn = false;

  try {
    if (me == player2) {
      theirturn = true;
    }
    else if (me != player1) {
      System.out.println("Illegal call to playGame!");
      return;
    }

    while (playgame) {
      if (!theirturn) {
        me.send("YOURTURN");
        instr = me.receive();
        instr = instr.toUpperCase();
        instr = instr.trim();
        if (instr.startsWith("IQUIT")) {
          sendStatus(me, IQUIT);
          playgame = false;
        }
        else if (instr.startsWith("IWON")) {
          sentString = me.receive();
          sentString = sentString.toUpperCase();
          sentString = sentString.trim();
          sendStatus(me, IWON);
          sendStatus(me, SENTSTRING);
          playgame = false;
        }
        else if (instr.startsWith("ITIED")) {
          sentString = me.receive();
          sentString = sentString.toUpperCase();
          sentString = sentString.trim();
          sendStatus(me, ITIED);
          sendStatus(me, SENTSTRING);
        }
        else {
          sentString = instr;
          sendStatus(me, SENTSTRING);
        }
      }
      else {
        theirturn = false;
      }

      if (playgame) {
        me.send("THEIRTURN");
        int stat = getStatus(me);
        if (stat == IWON) {
          me.send("THEYWON");
          if (getStatus(me) != SENTSTRING) {
```

19

```
          System.out.println("Received Bad Status");
          me.closeConnections();
        }
        me.send(sentString);
        playgame = false;
      }
      else if (stat == ITIED) {
        me.send("THEYTIED");
        if (getStatus(me) != SENTSTRING) {
          System.out.println("Received Bad Status");
          me.closeConnections();
        }
        me.send(sentString);
        playgame = false;
      }
      else if (stat == IQUIT) {
        me.send("THEYQUIT");
        playgame = false;
      }
      else if (stat == SENTSTRING) {
        me.send(sentString);
      }
      else if (stat == ERROR) {
        me.send("ERROR");
        me.closeConnections();
        playgame = false;
      }
      else {
        System.out.println("Received Bad Status");
        sendStatus(me,ERROR);
        me.closeConnections();
        playgame = false;
      }
    }
  }
  me.closeConnections();
  return;
}
catch (IOException e) {
  System.out.println("I/O Error: " + e);
  System.exit(1);
}
}
}
```

19

The logic used in playGame is fairly simple in that it models the way a game of Connect4 takes place; basically, each player waits while the other takes her turn. The only potentially confusing aspect of playGame is the mechanism it uses to communicate between the players. Each player has an event queue, which contains game information sent by the other player. The players communicate with each other in an indirect fashion by using the event queue. The state of the game is encoded into event messages using the state constants, along with strings. The playGame method interprets this information for each player.

The getStatus method gets the status of the game for the player passed in the me parameter. Listing 19.4 contains the source code for the getStatus method.

Listing 19.4. The Game class's getStatus method.

```
private synchronized int getStatus(Connect4Player me) {
  Vector ourVector = ((me == player1) ? p1Queue : p2Queue);
  while (ourVector.isEmpty()) {
    try {
      wait();
    }
    catch (InterruptedException e) {
      System.out.println("Error: " + e);
    }
  }
  try {
    Integer retval = (Integer)(ourVector.firstElement());
    try {
      ourVector.removeElementAt(0);
    }
    catch (ArrayIndexOutOfBoundsException e) {
      System.out.println("Array index out of bounds: " + e);
      System.exit(1);
    }
    return retval.intValue();
  }
  catch (NoSuchElementException e) {
    System.out.println("Couldn't get first element: " + e);
    System.exit(1);
    return 0; // never reached, just there to appease compiler
  }
}
```

The getStatus method waits until the player's event queue contains status information, and then it grabs the information and returns it.

The sendStatus method is the complement of getStatus; it's used to update a player's event queue with status information:

```
private synchronized void sendStatus(Connect4Player me, int message) {
  Vector theirVector = ((me == player1) ?  p2Queue : p1Queue);
  theirVector.addElement(new Integer(message));
  notify();
}
```

The integer status message passed in as the second parameter to sendStatus is added to the player's event queue. The notify method is then called, which causes the wait call in getStatus to return. This shows the synchronized nature of these two methods: getStatus waits until sendStatus provides the information it needs.

That sums up the code for the server. At this point, you have half a game. Too bad you can't do much with it yet; you still need a client. Knowing that, let's take a look at the code involved in making the client side work.

The Client

The client side of NetConnect4 consists of four classes, three of which you've seen before:

- [ ] `Connect4State`
- [ ] `Connect4Engine`
- [ ] `Connect4`
- [ ] `Connect4ClientConnection`

The first two classes, `Connect4State` and `Connect4Engine`, come directly from the original Connect4 game. They provide the core logic for establishing the rules of the game and determining whether the game has been won, lost, or tied. These two classes require no modification for NetConnect4, so refer to Day 16 if you need to refresh your memory on how they work.

The `Connect4` applet class should also be familiar from the original game. A few modifications have been made to this version of `Connect4` to accommodate the fact that the game is running over a network. The primary changes to the `Connect4` class are in the `run` method, which handles establishing a server connection and coordinating the state of the game with the graphics and user interface. Listing 19.5 contains the source code for the `run` method.

Listing 19.5. The `Connect4` class's `run` method.

```
public void run() {
  // Track the images
  int gameState = 0;
  newGame();
  try {
    tracker.waitForID(0);
  }
  catch (InterruptedException e) {
    return;
  }

  try {
    // Create the connection
    connection = new Connect4ClientConnection(this);
    while (connection.isConnected()) {
      int istatus = connection.getTheirMove();
      if (istatus == Connect4ClientConnection.GAMEOVER) {
        myMove = false;
        gameState = 0;
        return;
```

continues

Listing 19.5. continued

```
        }
        // Wait for the other player
        else if (istatus == Connect4ClientConnection.PLSWAIT) {
          if (gameState == 0) {
            gameState = Connect4ClientConnection.PLSWAIT;
            status = new String("Wait for player");
            repaint();
          } else {
            System.out.println("Gameflow error!");
            return;
          }
        }
        else if (istatus == Connect4ClientConnection.THEIRTURN) {
          status = new String("Their turn.");
          myMove = false;
          gameState = Connect4ClientConnection.THEIRTURN;
          repaint();
        }
        else if (istatus == Connect4ClientConnection.YOURTURN) {
          gameState = Connect4ClientConnection.YOURTURN;
          status = new String("Your turn.");
          repaint();
          myMove = true;
        }
        else if (istatus == Connect4ClientConnection.THEYWON) {
          gameState = Connect4ClientConnection.THEYWON;
        }
        else if (istatus == Connect4ClientConnection.THEYQUIT) {
          gameState = Connect4ClientConnection.THEYQUIT;
          status = new String("Opponent Quit!");
          myMove = false;
          repaint();
          return;
        }
        else if (istatus == Connect4ClientConnection.THEYTIED) {
          gameState = Connect4ClientConnection.THEYTIED;
        }
        else if (istatus == Connect4ClientConnection.ERROR) {
          System.out.println("error!");
          gameState = Connect4ClientConnection.ERROR;
          status = new String("Error! Game Over");
          myMove = false;
          repaint();
          return;
        }
        else {
          if (gameState == Connect4ClientConnection.THEIRTURN) {
            // Note that we make the move, but wait for the *server*
            // to say YOURTURN before we change the status. Otherwise,
            // we have a race condition - if the player moves before
            // the server says YOURTURN, we go back into that mode,
            // allowing the player to make two turns in a row!
            Point pos = gameEngine.makeMove(1, istatus);
            blueSnd.play();
            repaint();
```

```
      }
      else if (gameState == Connect4ClientConnection.THEYWON) {
        status = new String("Sorry, you lose!");
        myMove = false;
        gameOver = true;
        repaint();
        sadSnd.play();
        return;
      }
      else if (gameState == Connect4ClientConnection.THEYTIED) {
        status = new String("Tie game!");
        myMove = false;
        gameOver = true;
        repaint();
        sadSnd.play();
        return;
      }
      else {
        System.out.println("Gameflow error!");
        return;
      }
    }
  }
}
catch (IOException e) {
  System.out.println("IOException: "+e);
}
}
```

The logic used in the run method flows directly from the logic you just learned about in the Game class. This logic revolves around handling whose turn it is, along with communicating whether a game has been won, lost, or tied.

The mouseDown method also has been modified a little to accommodate sending game information to the server. Listing 19.6 shows the source code for the mouseDown method.

Listing 19.6. The Connect4 class's mouseDown method.

```
public boolean mouseDown(Event evt, int x, int y) {
  if (gameOver) {
    thread = null;
    thread = new Thread(this);
    thread.start();
  }
  else if (myMove) {
    // Make sure the move is valid
    Point pos = gameEngine.makeMove(0, x / 28);
    if (pos.y >= 0) {
      if (!gameEngine.isWinner(0))
        if (!gameEngine.isTie()) {
```

continues

Listing 19.6. continued

```
                redSnd.play();
                status = new String("Their turn.");
                connection.sendMove(pos.x);
                myMove = false;
              }
              else {
                sadSnd.play();
                status = new String("It's a tie!");
                gameOver = true;
                connection.sendITIED();
                connection.sendMove(pos.x);
              }
              else {
                applauseSnd.play();
                status = new String("You won!");
                gameOver = true;
                connection.sendIWON();
                connection.sendMove(pos.x);
              }
          repaint();
        }
    }
    else
      badMoveSnd.play();
    return true;
}
```

The mouseDown method is actually where each player's physical move is sent to the server. Notice that this information is sent using the client member variable, which is a Connect4ClientConnection object. This brings up a neat aspect of the design of the Connect4 client: The client communication details in the Connect4 class are hidden in the Connect4ClientConnection class.

The Connect4ClientConnection class is in charge of managing the client socket and ensuring that information is sent back and forth to the server correctly. Connect4ClientConnection is derived from SocketAction, which is another good example of code reuse. The constructor for Connect4ClientConnection takes an Applet object as its only parameter:

```
Connect4ClientConnection(Applet a) throws IOException {
  super(new Socket(a.getCodeBase().getHost(), PORTNUM));
}
```

The Connect4ClientConnection constructor creates a socket connection based on the applet parameter and a port number. Note that this port number must match the port number used by the server.

WARNING

> If the port numbers for the client and server don't match, none of the
> socket communication will be able to take place. In other words, the
> game won't run if the port numbers don't match.

The getTheirMove method in Connect4ClientConnection is used to get the other player's
move so that the client game can be updated. Listing 19.7 contains the source code for the
getTheirMove method.

Listing 19.7. The Connect4ClientConnection class's getTheirMove method.

```
public int getTheirMove() {
  // Make sure we're still connected
  if (!isConnected())
    throw new NullPointerException("Attempted to read closed socket!");

  try {
    String s = receive();
    System.out.println("Received: " + s);
    if (s == null)
      return GAMEOVER;
    s = s.trim();
    try {
      return (new Integer(s)).intValue();
    }
    catch (NumberFormatException e) {
      // It was probably a status report error
      return getStatus(s);
    }
  }
  catch (IOException e) {
    System.out.println("I/O Error: " + e);
    System.exit(1);
    return 0;
  }
}
```

The getTheirMove method basically just receives a string from the server and resolves it down
to an integer, which is then returned. The integer it receives is a game state constant as defined
in Connect4ClientConnection. The following are the game state constants defined in
Connect4ClientConnection:

```
static final int ERROR = -1;
static final int PLSWAIT = -2;
static final int YOURTURN = -3;
static final int THEIRTURN = -4;
```

```
static final int THEYWON = -5;
static final int THEYQUIT = -6;
static final int THEYTIED = -7;
static final int GAMEOVER = -8;
```

Although these game state constants are similar in function to the ones defined on the server side in the Game class, keep in mind that they are client-specific and make sense only in the context of a client. The constants are all negative, which is based on the fact that the integer state constant is also used to convey the location of a player's move; all moves are in the range 0 through 6, which corresponds to the column into which a piece is being dropped.

The getStatus method resolves a string status message into an integer game state constant. Listing 19.8 contains the source code for getStatus.

Listing 19.8. The Connect4ClientConnection class's getStatus method.

```
private int getStatus(String s) {
  s = s.trim();
  if (s.startsWith("PLSWAIT"))
    return PLSWAIT;
  if (s.startsWith("THEIRTURN"))
    return THEIRTURN;
  if (s.startsWith("YOURTURN"))
    return YOURTURN;
  if (s.startsWith("THEYWON"))
    return THEYWON;
  if (s.startsWith("THEYQUIT"))
    return THEYQUIT;
  if (s.startsWith("THEYTIED"))
    return THEYTIED;
  if (s.startsWith("GAMEOVER"))
    return GAMEOVER;

  // Something has gone horribly wrong!
  System.out.println("received invalid status from server: " + s);
  return ERROR;
}
```

The getStatus method is used by getTheirMove to convert incoming text messages to their integer equivalent.

The sendMove method is pretty straightforward; it simply sends the player's move to the server:

```
public void sendMove(int col) {
  String s = (new Integer(col)).toString();
  send(s);
}
```

Likewise, the send`IQUIT`, send`IWON`, and send`ITIED` methods are used to send the corresponding messages `IQUIT`, `IWON`, and `ITIED` to the server:

```
public void sendIQUIT() {
  send("IQUIT");
}

public void sendIWON() {
  send("IWON");
}

public void sendITIED() {
  send("ITIED");
}
```

That wraps up the client side of NetConnect4. If you're still a little dizzy from all the code, feel free to go through it again and study the details until you feel comfortable with everything. Trust me, it's perfectly normal to get confused during your first dealings with network game programming—I sure did!

Summary

Today you wrote your fourth complete Java game. Well, you actually modified one of the games you had already written. However, turning a single-player game into a two-player game that can be played over the Web might as well constitute a whole new game. In learning how the game was implemented, you saw how the client/server architecture and Java socket services are used in a practical scenario. You also reused the generic socket class you developed yesterday, thereby reinforcing the values of applying OOP techniques to Java game programming.

With four complete Java games under your belt, you're probably ready to chart some new territory in regard to Java game development. That's a good thing, because tomorrow's lesson focuses on a subject that has long been crucial to successful game programming: optimization. Tomorrow's lesson guides you through some tricks and techniques for speeding up your Java game code.

Q&A

Q I still don't follow the whole client/server strategy as it applies to NetConnect4. Can you briefly explain it again?

A Of course. The game server sits around in a never-ending loop waiting for client players to show up. When a player connects to the server, the server spawns a daemon thread to manage the communications necessary to support a single game.

This daemon serves as a communication channel between the two clients (players) involved in the game, which is necessary because there is no facility to enable clients to communicate directly with each other.

Q Would this same client/server strategy work for a game with more than two players?

A Absolutely. The code would get a little messier because the daemon would have to manage a group of clients rather than just two, but conceptually there is no problem with adding more client players to the mix.

Q How do I incorporate NetConnect4 into a Web site?

A Beyond simply including the client applet in an HTML document that is served up by your Web server, you must also make sure that the NetConnect4 server (`NetConnect4Server`) is running on the Web server machine. Without the game server, the clients are worthless.

Workshop

The Workshop section provides questions and exercises to help you get a better feel for the material you learned today. Try to answer the questions and at least ponder the exercises before moving on to tomorrow's lesson. You'll find the answers to the questions in Appendix A, "Quiz Answers."

Quiz

1. What is a daemon thread?
2. What is the significance of the `Game` class?
3. What is the purpose of the `Connect4ClientConnection` class?

Exercises

1. Enhance the NetConnect4 game to display the name of each player as he is making his move. Hint: To get the name of a player, use the `getHostName` method after getting an `InetAddress` object for a socket using `getInetAddress`.

2. Modify the NetConnect4 game to enable players to choose who they want to play with. Admittedly, this is a pretty big modification, but I think you can handle it. Hint: This task involves modifying the client/server design so that clients connect and are added to a list of potential players. A player can then choose an opponent from the list, in which case they are paired together normally.

19

Day 20

Optimizing Java Code for Games

Execution speed has always had a unique importance to game developers. More so than any other area of software, games typically must squeeze every ounce of performance out of the host system. This is distressing news for those of us writing games in Java, simply because Java is so removed from the specifics of the host system that it's extremely difficult to cut corners while coding. However, even though you can't get down and dirty with the hardware, you can still optimize Java code in various ways to improve performance in your games.

Today's lesson deals with Java code optimization and how it can be used to speed up Java games. You'll learn various optimization techniques that will help you become a more efficient Java programmer. To really understand how these optimizations help, you have to go under the hood of Java, so roll up your sleeves and prepare to get a little dirty.

As you go through today's lesson, keep in mind that it's one of the last lessons in the book for a very good reason: Any thoughts of optimizing your code should occur near the end of the development cycle. In other words, focus on getting your game up and running, and then focus your attention on looking for ways to optimize.

The following topics are covered in today's lesson:

- ☐ What is code optimization?
- ☐ Understanding the JDK compiler
- ☐ Costs of common operations
- ☐ Isolating problem code
- ☐ Optimization techniques

What Is Code Optimization?

Code optimization is the process of modifying working code to a more optimal state based on a particular goal. The fact that optimization takes place on working code is an important point; always perform optimizations on code *after* you get the code working. The type of optimization performed is dependent on the desired goal; code optimization can be divided into three distinct types, which are based on the needs of the developer:

- ☐ Maintainability
- ☐ Size
- ☐ Speed

Maintainability

Maintainability optimization is performed to help make code more manageable in the future. This type of optimization is usually geared toward the structure and organization of code, rather than modifications of the algorithms used in the code. In general, maintainability optimization involves a programmer studying the code at large and making changes to help other programmers understand and modify the code in the future.

If you haven't guessed, maintainability optimization doesn't rank very high on the list of important optimizations used by game developers. It's still important to organize your code and enforce some structure, but just don't let maintainability optimization become an overriding concern.

Size

Another popular optimization is size optimization, which involves making changes to code that result in a smaller executable class file. The cornerstone of size optimization is code reuse, which comes in the form of inheritance for Java classes. Fortunately, good OOP design strategies naturally favor size optimization, so you will rarely need to go out of your way to perform this type of optimization. For example, it's just good design practice to put code that is reused a few times in a method. In this way, most size optimizations naturally take place during the initial code development.

Although not entirely crucial, size optimization can't be completely ignored in regard to Java game programming. This is because the size of your compiled Java classes will directly impact the amount of time it takes your game to load and initially execute. If, however, you leverage as much of the standard Java API code as possible and reuse code by deriving from other classes, you're probably doing enough for the cause of reducing class size.

Speed

And now, introducing the real subject of today's lesson: speed optimization. Speed optimization is without a doubt the most important aspect of game development after the game is up and running correctly. Speed optimization includes all the techniques and tricks used to speed up the execution of code. Considering the performance problems inherent in Java, speed optimization takes on an even more important role in Java than in other languages such as C and C++. Because the Java compiler has the last word on how code is generated, most speed optimizations will be performed with the compiler in mind.

The rest of today's lesson focuses on issues of speed optimization and how to get the best performance out of your Java code. At times, you will sacrifice the other areas of optimization for the sake of speed. In most cases, this sacrifice is entirely acceptable, even expected, because the organization of the code and size of the executable classes won't matter much if your game is too slow to play.

Optimizing with the JDK Compiler

All optimizations begin and end with the Java compiler. If you don't understand the compiler, you're largely guessing at which optimizations will have a positive effect on your code. So let's take a look at the JDK compiler and see what role it plays in turning out speedy Java bytecodes.

NEW TERM   A *bytecode* is a Java term referring to the intermediate processor-independent code generated by the Java compiler. Bytecode executables (classes) are interpreted by the Java runtime system.

20

> Third-party Java compilers are turning up and will continue to turn up
> that outclass the JDK compiler in regard to speed optimization.
> Nevertheless, the JDK compiler is the standard Java compiler and
> currently the most reliable.

The JDK compiler (javac) includes a switch for generating optimized Java bytecode executables: -0. In release 1.0 of the JDK, this switch results in only two optimizations taking place: inline methods and exclusion of line numbers. The first of these optimizations is the only one that affects the speed of the executable bytecode; final, static, and private methods are inlined by the compiler, resulting in less method call overhead.

NEW TERM   *Method inlining* is the process of replacing each call to a method with the actual method code. Inlining can often increase the size of the resulting class file, but it can help improve performance.

The second optimization performed by the JDK compiler results in the exclusion of line number information from the executable class file. This is a size optimization and does nothing in terms of helping speed up the code.

As you can see, the JDK compiler does little for you in regard to optimization. This basically means that you need to plan on doing a lot of optimization by hand. A future release of the JDK should (I hope) improve this situation, but you can't afford to stand around waiting for miracles—you've got games to write!

Costs of Common Operations

Now that you understand what the JDK compiler does (or doesn't do) for you in regard to optimization, it's time to focus on the Java runtime system. By examining the runtime system, you can get an idea of how fast certain types of code run and make smarter decisions about the way you write Java code. What do I mean by examining the runtime system? Well, I mean running different types of code and timing each type to see how the speeds match up. This operation gives you a very realistic look at how code differs in terms of execution speed and consequently gives you a place to start making appropriate code optimizations.

The speed of an operation is often referred to as the *cost* of the operation. Code optimization can almost be likened to accounting, in which you try to keep from blowing a performance budget with your code costs. As if optimization weren't tedious enough as it is, I had to make a reference to accounting! Anyway, Jonathan Hardwick performed a very neat analysis on the cost of common Java operations on various systems, the results of which I've included in Tables 20.1 through 20.3. These tables contain approximate times in microseconds for common Java operations. Incidentally, the systems used to perform the cost analysis were a Sun Sparcstation 5 running Solaris, an AMD 486 DX4-120 running Windows 95, and an AMD 486 DX4-120 running Linux 1.2.13.

 In terms of speed optimization, *cost* refers to the speed required to perform an operation.

Table 20.1. The costs of Java variable accesses.

Description	Operation	Solaris	486 Win95	486 Linux
Method variable assignment	`i = 1;`	0.4	0.3	0.5
Instance variable assignment	`this.i = 1;`	2.4	0.7	0.9
Array element assignment	`a[0] = 1;`	1.1	1.0	1.3

Table 20.2. The costs of increment with Java data types.

Description	Operation	Solaris	486 Win95	486 Linux
Byte variable increment	`byte b++;`	1.2	1.2	1.3
Short variable increment	`short s++;`	1.4	1.2	1.3
Int variable increment	`int i++;`	0.3	0.1	0.3
Long variable increment	`long l++;`	1.1	1.1	1.3
Float variable increment	`float f++;`	0.9	1.1	1.2
Double variable increment	`double d++;`	1.0	1.3	1.5

20

Table 20.3. The costs of miscellaneous Java operations.

Description	Operation	Solaris	486 Win95	486 Linux
Object creation	`new Object();`	10.7	13.8	12.8
Method invocation	`null_func();`	3.1	2.1	2.4

continues

Table 20.3. continued

Description	Operation	Solaris	486 Win95	486 Linux
Synchronized method	`sync_func();`	16.3	20.1	15.9
Math function	`Math.abs(x);`	5.6	4.8	5.6
Equivalent math code	`(x < 0) ? -x : x;`	0.6	0.4	0.6

These tables point out lots of interesting information regarding the performance of Java code. From Table 20.1, it's readily apparent that method variables are more efficient to use than instance variables. Furthermore, you can see that array element assignment is slower than method variable assignment due to the fact that Java performs bounds checking operations whenever an array element is accessed. Keep in mind that this table isn't meant as an argument to get rid of all your class member data. Rather, think of it as providing insight into making those decisions in which the design could go either way.

Table 20.2 shows timing data relating to the use of the standard Java data types. As you might have expected, the two 32-bit data types, `int` and `float`, showed the best performance because the tests were performed on 32-bit systems. It is interesting to note that the performance difference between using an `int` over a `byte`, `short`, or `long` is much more significant than for using a `float` over a `double`.

Even though the floating-point types show comparable performance to the integer types, don't be misled about using integer math over floating-point math. This timing table reflects only an increment operation, which is much different than more complex operations performed in the context of a game. Integer math is much more efficient than floating-point math. So use the table as a measure of the relative speeds among integer types, and then try to use integer math throughout your code.

Table 20.3 focuses on a few miscellaneous operations that are worth thinking about. First, it shows the high cost of creating an object. This should serve as an incentive to eliminate the creation of temporary objects within a loop where the creation occurs over and over. Rather, you can place the temporary object above the loop and reinitialize its members as needed inside the loop.

Table 20.3 also shows the dramatic performance costs of using a normal method versus a synchronized method. Even though synchronization is very important in multithreaded programming, this should be some encouragement to minimize the usage of synchronized methods in games.

Finally, Table 20.3 shows you how using the standard Java math methods can sometimes be a burden. Even something as simple as taking the absolute value of a number imposes much greater performance costs when you call the `Math.abs` method, as opposed to inlining the equivalent code yourself.

Isolating Problem Code

The biggest mistake you can make in regard to optimizing your game code is trying to optimize *all* the code. Being smart about what code you attack is crucial in not spending years trying to improve the performance of your game. More important, it's a well-established fact that a relatively small portion of code is usually responsible for the bulk of the performance drain. It's your job to isolate this code and then focus your optimization efforts accordingly.

WARNING

Don't attempt to optimize code as you write it. Many programmers have the tendency to think they can do it all the first time through, which includes developing perfectly optimized error-free code. If you truly think you are capable of filling this tall order, then be my guest. Meanwhile, the rest of us mere mortals have to contend with our fair share of mistakes, even without worrying how optimized a piece of code is. Throw in the complexities of trying to optimize code that doesn't even work yet, and you're setting yourself up for disaster. In all fairness, it's usually okay to make minor optimizations that don't significantly impact the structure of your code; just don't get carried away.

Fortunately, isolating problem code isn't all that difficult if you use the proper tools. The most useful tool in finding bottlenecks in your code is a profiler. A profiler's job is to report on the amount of time spent in each section of code as a program is executing. The Java runtime interpreter has an undocumented built-in profiler that is easy to use and works pretty well. To use the runtime interpreter profiler, simply specify the `-prof` option when using the interpreter, like this:

```
java -prof Classname
```

`Classname` is the name of the class you want to profile. Of course, this technique doesn't work too well for applets, because they must be run within the context of the applet viewer tool or a browser. Fortunately, you can use the profiler with applets by altering the arguments to the interpreter a little, like this:

```
java -prof sun.applet.AppletViewer Filename
```

In this case, `Filename` is the name of the HTML file containing a link to your applet. When you finish running the applet, the interpreter will write a file named `java.prof` to the current directory. This file contains profile information for the applet you just ran.

20

To get an idea of what kind of information the Java profiler generates, check out Listing 20.1, which contains a few lines of profile information generated for the Traveling Gecko sample game. I've cleaned up the listing a little by hand just to make it easier to read.

Listing 20.1. A partial profile listing for the Traveling Gecko sample game.

```
count callee                             caller                         time
25261 java/util/Vector.size()            SpriteVector.testCollision(      19
22780 java/util/Vector.elementAt(I)      SpriteVector.testCollision(      38
20258 java/awt/Rectangle.intersects()    Sprite.testCollision(LSprite;)   56
20258 Sprite.getCollision()              Sprite.testCollision(LSprite;)    4
20258 Sprite.testCollision(LSprite;)     SpriteVector.testCollision(     102
10360 Sprite.getPosition()               SpriteVector.update()V            2
 4075 java/lang/Object.<init>()          java/awt/Rectangle.<init>(IIII)   0
 3800 sun/awt/image/Image.getImageRep(II) sun/awt/win32/Win32Image.getImage 60
```

As you can see, the profile information is broken down into four columns. The first column specifies how many times a particular method was called, and the second column states the name of the method. The third column specifies the calling method, the one that invoked the method in question. Finally, the fourth column specifies the relative amount of time spent in the method during each call. The larger this number is, the more costly the method.

You can easily use this information as a guide to determine the code on which to focus your optimization efforts. The methods appearing at the top of the list should receive much greater attention, because they are being called far more times than methods farther down in the list. Making small performance gains in a method that is being called 20,000 times will have a much greater impact than speeding up a method that is called only a couple of hundred times. The cool thing is that you can try different optimizations and then run the profiler again to see whether the relative times have changed. This is a very practical, if somewhat time-consuming, way to make great strides in speeding up your games.

Optimization Techniques

Now that you've isolated the code that is making your game crawl, it's time to look into exactly what optimizations you can perform to speed things up. The rest of today's lesson is aimed at different techniques you can apply to code that you know could stand some improvement. You won't always be able to optimize every piece of problem code; the goal is to make big dents in the areas that can be optimized.

NOTE

Incidentally, make sure that you have already tried your game with compiler optimizations turned on (the -0 option). I know it's not much, but it's free!

Rethink Algorithms

Many C/C++ programmers have traditionally resorted to assembly language when the issue of performance is raised. As a Java programmer, you don't have this option. This is actually a good thing, because it forces you to take a closer look at your design approach instead of relying on heavier processor dependence to solve your problems. What the assembly heads don't realize is that much more significant gains can be made by entirely rethinking an algorithm than by porting it to assembly. And trust me, the amount of time spent hand-coding tedious assembly could easily result in a leaner, more efficient algorithm.

This same ideology applies to Java programming. Before you run off writing native methods and expanding loops to get every little ounce of performance, which you'll learn about in a moment, take a step back and see whether the algorithm itself has any weaknesses. To put this all into perspective, imagine if programmers had always resorted to optimizing the traditional bubble sort algorithm and had never thought twice about the algorithm itself. The quick sort algorithm, which is orders of magnitude faster than bubble sort without any optimization, would never have come about.

Use Native Methods

I kind of hate to recommend them, but the truth is that native methods (methods written in C or C++ that can be called from Java code) are typically much faster than Java methods. The reason I'm reluctant to promote their use is that they blow the platform independence benefit of using Java, therefore limiting your game to a particular platform. If platform independence isn't high on your list, however, by all means look into rewriting problem methods in C.

Use Inline Methods

Inline methods, whose bodies appear in place of each method call, are a fairly effective means of improving performance. Because the Java compiler already inlines final, static, and private methods when you have the optimization switch turned on, your best bet is to try to make as many methods as possible final, static, or private. If this isn't possible and you still want the benefits of inlined code, you can always inline methods by hand: just paste the body of the method at each place where it is called. This is one of those cases in which you are sacrificing both maintainability and size for speed. The things we do for speed!

Replace Slow Java API Classes and Methods

There might be times when you are using a standard Java API class for a few of its features, but the extra baggage imposed by the class is slowing you down. In situations like this, you might be better off writing your own class that performs the exact functionality you need and no more. This streamlined approach can pay off big, even though it comes at the cost of rewriting code.

Another similar situation is when you are using a Java API class and you isolate a particular method in it that is dragging down performance. In this situation, instead of rewriting the entire class, just derive from it and override the troublesome method. This is a good middle-of-the-road solution because you leverage code reuse against performance in a reasonable manner.

Use Look-Up Tables

An established trick up the sleeve of every experienced game programmer is the look-up table. Look-up tables are tables of constant integer values that are used in place of time-consuming calculations. For example, a very popular type of look-up table is one containing values for trigonometric functions, such as sine. The use of trigonometric functions is a necessity when you are working with rotational objects in games. If you haven't noticed, trigonometric functions are all floating-point in nature, which is a bad thing. The solution is to write an integer version of the desired function using a look-up table of values. This relatively simple change is practically a necessity considering the performance hit you take by using floating-point math.

Eliminate Unnecessary Evaluations

Moving along into more detailed optimizations, you can often find unnecessary evaluations in your code that are serving only to eat up extra processor time. The following is an example of some code that unnecessarily performs an evaluation that acts effectively as a constant:

```
for (int i = 0; i < size(); i++)
  a = (b + c) / i;
```

The addition of b + c, although itself a pretty efficient piece of code, is better off being calculated before the loop, like this:

```
int tmp = b + c;
for (int i = 0; i < size(); i++)
  a = tmp / i;
```

This simple change could have fairly dramatic effects, depending on how many times the loop is iterated. Speaking of the loop, there's another optimization you might have missed. Notice that size() is a method call, which might bring to mind the costs involved in calling a method that you learned about earlier today. You might not realize it, but size() is being called every time through the loop as part of the conditional loop expression. The same technique used to eliminate the unnecessary addition operation can be used to fix this problem. Check out the resulting code:

```
int s = size;
int tmp = b + c;
for (int i = 0; i < s; i++)
  a = tmp / i;
```

Eliminate Common Subexpressions

Sometimes you might be reusing a costly subexpression without even realizing it. In the heat of programming, it's easy to reuse common subexpressions instead of storing them in a temporary variable, like this:

```
b = Math.abs(a) * c;
d = e / (Math.abs(a) + b);
```

The multiple calls to Math.abs() are costly compared to calling it once and using a temporary variable, like this:

```
int tmp = Math.abs(a);
b = tmp * c;
d = e / (tmp + b);
```

Expand Loops

One optimization that is popular among C/C++ game programmers is loop expansion, or loop unrolling, which is the process of expanding a loop to get rid of the overhead involved in maintaining the loop. You might be wondering exactly what overhead I'm talking about. Well, even a simple counting loop has the overhead of performing a comparison and an increment each time through. This might not seem like much, but with game programming you could well end up in the position of clawing for anything you can get!

NEW TERM *Loop expansion*, or *loop unrolling*, is the process of expanding a loop to get rid of the inherent overhead involved in maintaining the loop.

Loop expansion basically involves replacing a loop with the brute-force equivalent. To better understand it, check out the following piece of code:

```
for (int i = 0; i < 1000; i++)
  a[i] = 25;
```

20

That probably looks like some pretty efficient code, and in fact it is. But if you want to go the extra distance and perform a loop expansion on it, here's one approach:

```
int i = 0;
for (int j = 0; j < 100; j++) {
  a[i++] = 25;
  a[i++] = 25;
  a[i++] = 25;
  a[i++] = 25;
  a[i++] = 25;
  a[i++] = 25;
  a[i++] = 25;
  a[i++] = 25;
  a[i++] = 25;
}
```

In this code, you've reduced the loop overhead by an order of magnitude, but you've introduced some new overhead by having to increment the new index variable inside the loop. Overall, this code does outperform the original code, but don't expect any miracles. Loop expansion can be effective at times, but I don't recommend placing it too high on your list of optimization tricks.

Summary

Today you learned about a somewhat murky area of Java game development: code optimization. You began the lesson by learning about the fundamental types of optimization, including the type that game programmers are mostly concerned with: speed optimization. You then learned about the optimizations (or lack thereof) provided by the JDK compiler. From there, you got a little dose of realism by looking into the timing costs of common Java operations. Finally, you finished off the lesson with an in-depth look at some practical code optimizations you can apply to your own games.

Incidentally, after going through today's lesson, you might be wondering how well the sample code throughout the book is optimized. I'm sorry to report that it is optimized very little, mainly for the sake of keeping it easier to follow. It ends up that optimized code is often much harder to understand, so I opted to err on the side of clarity. Now that you're disillusioned with my coding practices, prepare to turn your attention toward tomorrow's lesson, which is putting together a Java game programming toolkit.

Q&A

Q Do all games require lots of code optimization to run at acceptable speeds?

A No. First, many games simply aren't speed-intensive, which immediately eliminates the need for any optimization. Second, even those games that could benefit from

20

optimization will often run at reasonable speeds without it. The sample games you've studied in this book are very good examples of this fact.

Q I keep hearing about just-in-time compilers. How will they impact the whole optimization issue?

A Just-in-time compilers (Java compilers that turn bytecodes into platform-dependent code at runtime) are music to the ears of Java game programmers, because they will undoubtedly increase the speed of all Java code by an order of magnitude. Even so, Java game programmers will likely use the new speeds afforded by just-in-time compilers to add more complexity to their games. When this happens, you will still be left optimizing your code. Our greed seems to keep us from winning!

Q I really enjoy hacking through cryptic bytecodes; is there anything else I can do to speed up my Java code?

A But of course, the Java class file disassembler is the tool for you. The disassembler (javap) comes standard with the JDK, and it enables you to see the bytecodes generated for a class. Just use the -c option, and you'll get complete bytecode listings for each method. You can then use these listings to study the intricate results of your source code optimizations.

Workshop

The Workshop section provides questions and exercises to help you with the material you learned today. Try to answer the questions and at least go over the exercises before moving on to tomorrow's lesson. You'll find the answers to the questions in Appendix A, "Quiz Answers."

Quiz

1. What are the three major areas of code optimization?
2. What type of speed optimization does the JDK compiler perform?
3. What is the significance of using a profiler?
4. When should you use a look-up table?

Exercises

1. Run the Java profiler on the Traveling Gecko sample game and see whether you can isolate any methods for performing optimizations.
2. Try your hand at making a few optimizations to Traveling Gecko; then run the profiler again to see whether your changes helped. Hint: There is an unnecessary evaluation in SpriteVector::testCollision just waiting for you to fix it.

Day 21

Assembling a Game Development Toolkit

In case you didn't realize it, today is your final lesson! Because it is your last lesson, it only makes sense to cover a topic that will help you as you move on to your own game programming projects. Today's focus is on assembling a Java game development toolkit. Like any craftsman, a Java game programmer needs an easily accessible set of tools that can be used in various situations. Today you learn about some of the major tools out there now, and on the horizon, that will aid you as you begin developing your own Java games.

The Java programming tools market is extremely young and very dynamic. The seemingly limited number of development tools available today could easily double in a matter of months. Although sometimes frustrating, this dynamic is also very exciting, and it ultimately results in stronger technologies for Java developers. The goal of this lesson is to highlight some of the more promising Java development tools and give you a place to begin researching which tools will work best for you.

You learn today that two primary types of tools are necessary for game development: content tools and development tools. You've already seen some content tools throughout the book, so today's lesson focuses more on development tools.

The following topics are covered in today's lesson:

- [ ] The importance of tools
- [ ] Content tools
- [ ] Java Developer's Kit
- [ ] Integrated development environments
- [ ] Programming tools and technologies

The Importance of Tools

Back in the early days of Windows programming, I was extremely frustrated by the lack of available development tools. At the time, you had to develop and compile Windows programs from a DOS command line, and then launch Windows to test them. Although I suspected that Windows was here to stay, I refused to take Windows seriously until some decent development tools were available. I simply saw Windows programming as more trouble than it was worth at the time. Fortunately, Windows development tools eventually started to appear, which greatly eased the pain of Windows programming. These days, Windows development tools are extremely advanced and provide a glimpse into the types of Java development tools that will emerge.

In similar ways, Java is going through the same difficulties shared by Windows back in the early days of Windows. Although developing Java applets using the Java Developer's Kit is significantly easier than developing Windows applications using the original Windows Software Development Kit, a lot of improvement could be done when it comes to Java development tools. Fortunately, third-party Java development tools are available today and many more are in the works.

Technically speaking, all that is required to develop Java programs is a text editor, a compiler, and a runtime environment. The Java Developer's Kit (JDK) supplies all of these components. However, saying that these three components are sufficient for Java development is like saying a hammer and a handsaw are sufficient for building a house. Sure, they get the job done, but at what cost to you in terms of time and frustration? In all fairness, the JDK isn't all that bad, but contrast it with the integrated visual programming environments for other languages such as C++ and BASIC and you'll want more.

You might think that programming is programming, and no flashy visual tools are ever going to change that. In a way, you're right. In regard to games especially, your main development efforts will always be spent hacking away at Java code. However, a certain degree of organizational busy work can be reduced or streamlined by integrated development environments. For example, having your source files organized into a project structure is often very useful for managing all your classes and keeping them in perspective. Furthermore, it's hard to argue over the power of using an integrated graphical debugger, which is often indispensable in tracking down hard to find bugs.

The point is that even though I'm not ruling out command-line tools such as the JDK, I encourage you to look into some integrated Java development environments and see whether they might save you some time and trouble. You'll learn about some of these environments throughout the rest of today's lesson. However, before doing that, let's take a look at another type of development tool: content tools.

Content Tools

Content tools consist of the tools necessary to create the content for games. Content includes graphics, sound, music, and any other types of media you plan to integrate into your games. Unlike development tools, content tools are used to create and edit game resources rather than source code. There are two main types of content tools: graphics utilities and sound utilities.

> Eventually, music utilities could establish themselves as yet another content tool, but currently you have to handle music like normal sampled sounds in Java. In other words, Java music currently must be created using a sound utility.

You already learned about some useful content tools in earlier lessons dealing with graphics and sound. More specifically, you saw some popular graphics utilities on Day 4, "The Basics of Graphics." You learned about some useful sound utilities on Day 11, "The Basics of Sound." Refer to these lessons if you operate primarily on short-term memory, like me!

Java Developer's Kit

The Java Developer's Kit (JDK) provides the core tools and documentation necessary for developing Java applets, including games. The JDK is the first thing you should take into consideration when putting together your own Java development toolkit. Although third-party add-ons and development environments promise to make Java development smoother and easier, the JDK provides the essentials. Many third-party development environments

21

require the JDK to operate. Also, the JDK is Sun's official development kit for Java, which means you can always count on it providing the most extensive and up-to-date Java support.

The JDK includes a Java runtime interpreter, a compiler, a debugger, lots of applet demos, and the complete Java API source code, along with a few other useful tools. All the sample code you've seen throughout the book was developed using only the JDK, so don't underestimate its power and usefulness. Version 1.02 of the JDK is included on the accompanying CD-ROM.

Integrated Development Environments

The development tools provided with the JDK are all command-line tools. Most modern development environments include graphical editors, graphical debuggers, and visual class browsers. These environments are known as integrated development environments (IDEs), because all the disparate development tools are integrated together. Java is too modern a language not to have a modern development interface to match, and Java programmers know this. Fortunately, the software tool developers know this, too. Most of the major players in the development-tool business have announced Java IDEs. A lot of them have already released their products in at least a beta form.

These third-party development environments span different operating systems and range from C/C++ environment add-ons to entirely new products themselves developed in Java. Any of these environments will aid in Java game development and probably save you time in the long run.

Sun's Java Workshop

Java Workshop, from the creators of Java itself, has the potential to be a very interesting Java development tool. Using a very Web-centric design, Java Workshop is itself implemented using a great deal of HTML for maximum configurability. Sun's Java Workshop is currently available for Solaris and Windows 95/NT systems. The following is a list of the main features provided by Java Workshop:

- [ ] Project manager
- [ ] Build manager
- [ ] Portfolio manager
- [ ] Applet viewer
- [ ] Source editor
- [ ] Source browser

☐ Integrated debugger

☐ Online help including Java API

Sun offers a try-and-buy program for Java Workshop in which you can download it and try it out before making the purchase. For more information, check out Sun's Java Workshop Web site, which is located at `http://www.sun.com/sunsoft/Developer-products/java/Workshop` (see Figure 21.1).

Figure 21.1.
Sun's Java Workshop Web site.

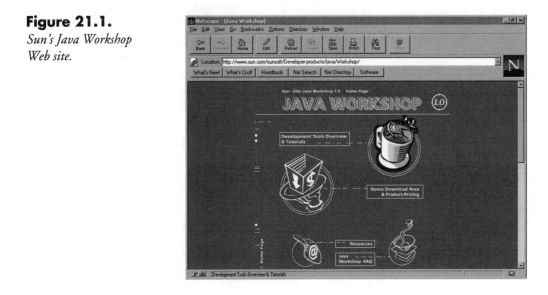

Symantec Café

Symantec is the first major PC tool developer to have a working Java development environment on the market. Symantec Café is a Java development environment based on the Symantec C++ development environment for Windows 95/NT. Café is not, however, limited to the Windows 95/NT platform; Symantec recently released a version for Macintosh. Figures 21.2 and 21.3 show what the Café development environment looks like for Windows and Macintosh.

21

Figure 21.2.

The Symantec Café development environment for Windows 95/NT.

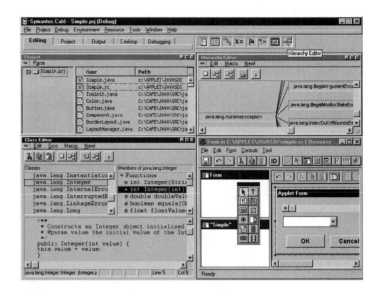

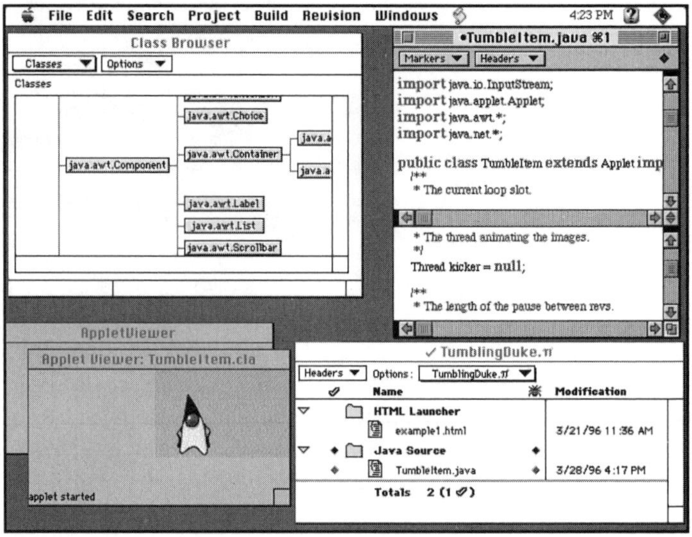

Figure 21.3.

The Symantec Café development environment for Macintosh.

The following list gives the main features provided by Symantec Café:

☐ Project management

☐ Class editor

☐ Hierarchy editor

☐ Visual drag-and-drop design tool

☐ Integrated debugger

☐ Source editor

☐ Faster bytecode compiler

☐ Faster Java runtime virtual machine

☐ Agents for automated applet/application creation

☐ Online help including Java API

Symantec has also released a Just-In-Time (JIT) compiler that integrates into either Café or the standard JDK. Symantec's JIT compiler promises to significantly speed up the execution of Java applets, which is a major issue for game development. You can find out more about Café and the JIT compiler at the Symantec Café Web site, which is located at `http://cafe.symantec.com` (see Figure 21.4).

NOTE

If you happen to already have Symantec C++, you can use Symantec's Java add-on, Espresso, which is specifically designed to add Java functionality to Symantec C++.

Figure 21.4.
The Symantec Café Web site.

Borland C++ 5.0 and Borland's Java Debugger

Borland, one of the largest development tool makers for the PC, has focused significant efforts toward bringing Java tools to market. Because of the apparent urgency surrounding its internal development efforts, Borland appears to have divided its Java tool offerings across two product lines: Borland C++ 5.0 and Borland Latté.

Borland has decided to make its first commercial Java offering a part of its Borland C++ 5.0 product. Borland C++ has long been a popular C++ compiler for PCs, and it now includes a complete integration of Java tools.

The Borland C++ 5.0 Java development environment includes the following features:

- ☐ Project management
- ☐ Integrated visual debugger
- ☐ Source editor with color syntax highlighting
- ☐ Object scripting
- ☐ Just-in-time compiler
- ☐ Online help including Java API

Borland's second wave of Java tools, code named Latté, are themselves being completely developed in Java. Borland's long-term goal appears to be focused on the Latté technology, but Borland C++ 5.0 is a sensible alternative until Latté matures. The first offering of the Latté technology is the Borland Debugger for Java, which is currently in a beta release.

For more information on Borland C++ 5.0 and the Latté technology, check out Borland's Java Web site at `http://www.borland.com/Product/java/java.html` (see Figure 21.5).

Figure 21.5.

Borland's Java Web site.

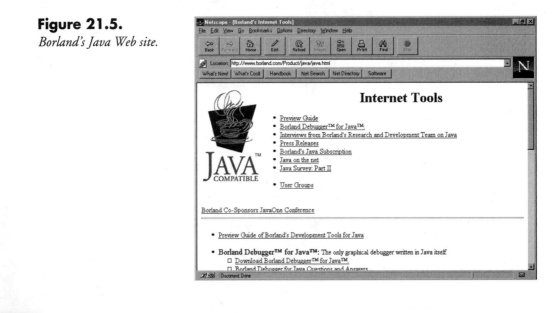

Microsoft Jakarta

Just when everyone thought Microsoft was in too deep with Visual Basic, they turn around and announce plans for their own Java development environment, code named Jakarta. Jakarta is planned as an integration into the already popular Developer Studio product for Windows 95/NT, which encompasses Visual C++, Fortran Powerstation, Visual Test, and the Microsoft Developer Network. It's therefore safe to assume that many of the Jakarta tools will resemble the existing C++ tools included with Visual C++.

NOTE Having worked extensively with Visual C++ developing Windows 95/NT games in C++, I can attest to its usefulness as a key component in my Windows game development toolkit. Let's hope Jakarta is just as good, or even better.

Natural Intelligence's Roaster

One of the early entrants into the Macintosh Java development tool market is Natural Intelligence's Roaster. Roaster boasts a wide array of features:

- ☐ Project management
- ☐ Integrated debugger
- ☐ Integrated browser and class tree
- ☐ Programming editor
- ☐ Faster bytecode compiler
- ☐ Class disassembler
- ☐ Online help including Java API
- ☐ Extensive HTML support

For more information about Roaster, check out Natural Intelligence's Roaster Web site at `http://www.natural.com/pages/products/roaster` (see Figure 21.6).

Metrowerks CodeWarrior Gold

Another neat integrated development environment for Macintosh is CodeWarrior Gold, by Metrowerks. CodeWarrior Gold 9 boasts a complete development solution, including support for Java, C/C++, and Object Pascal. As far as Java goes, CodeWarrior Gold sports the following major features:

- ☐ Project management
- ☐ Integrated debugger
- ☐ Class browser
- ☐ Programming editor
- ☐ Bytecode disassembler
- ☐ Online help including Java API

Figure 21.6.

Natural Intelligence's Roaster Web site.

For more information regarding CodeWarrior Gold, check out Metrowerk's CodeWarrior Web site at `http://www.metrowerks.com/products/cw/gold.html` (see Figure 21.7).

Silicon Graphics Cosmo Code

One of the most powerful Java development environments to come out thus far is Cosmo Code by Silicon Graphics, which is a component of the larger Cosmo Web development system. Cosmo itself is aimed at providing more extensive multimedia and 3D graphics support for the Web. Cosmo Code is the primary development component of Cosmo and is currently available for Irix systems. Cosmo Code contains the following major features:

- ☐ Project management
- ☐ Graphical debugger
- ☐ Visual source browser
- ☐ Programming editor
- ☐ Cosmo Multimedia Libraries

Figure 21.7.

Metrowerk's CodeWarrior Gold Web site.

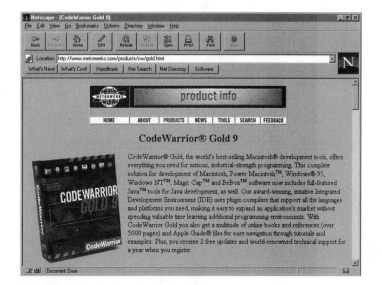

To find out the latest information about Cosmo Code or to download a copy to try out, go to the Cosmo Web site at `http://www.sgi.com/Products/cosmo/code` (see Figure 21.8).

Figure 21.8.

Silicon Graphics Cosmo Code Web site.

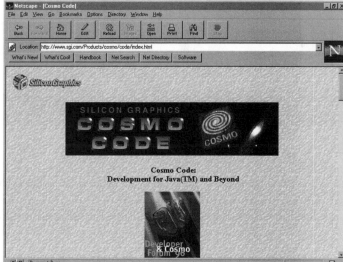

Java WebIDE

The last integrated development environment is probably the most interesting, simply because it is integrated into the Web itself. The Java WebIDE Web site, by Chami

Wickremasinghe, is itself a development environment, operating solely on Web pages and embedded Javascript. Although not up to par with many of the features found in the environments previously mentioned, Java WebIDE is nevertheless useful in its own right. The following are a few of the features in Java WebIDE:

- ☐ Source editing and compiling
- ☐ Syntax highlighting
- ☐ Java API searching

To try out Java WebIDE, head over to its Web site at `http://www.chamisplace.com/prog/javaide` (see Figure 21.9).

Figure 21.9.

The Java WebIDE Web site.

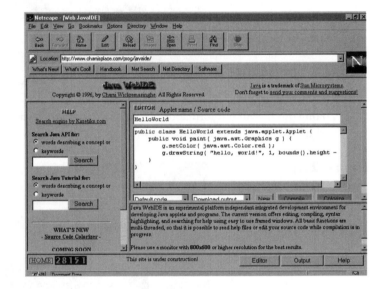

Programming Tools and Technologies

After you've settled on an IDE (if you decide to use one at all), you will probably want to keep an eye open for programming tools and emerging technologies to find other ways to enhance your development toolkit. The current offerings of Java-related programming tools are still fairly slim, but expect new ones to appear rapidly.

Keep in mind that new technologies will no doubt emerge that are built on top of, or that integrate with, Java. You might find that you can leverage the usage of some of these technologies to enhance and streamline your game development efforts. In the world of Java game programming, as in most areas of software development, the programmer who can leverage technological advances and reuse the most code usually wins. Let's take a look at a few programming tools and technologies.

Liquid Motion

Liquid Motion, by Dimension X, is a tool that enables you to graphically generate 2D Java animations. You animate objects by graphically drawing a path of motion, allowing Liquid Motion to handle the details of actually animating the object. Liquid Motion sports the following major features:

- ☐ Sequence sprites and audio clips
- ☐ Control motion path of objects
- ☐ Select from various motions and animation speeds
- ☐ Create events for user interaction
- ☐ Motion Engine API

To find out more about Liquid Motion, check out the Liquid Motion Web site at `http://web.dimensionx.com/products/lm` (see Figure 21.10).

Figure 21.10.
The Liquid Motion Web site.

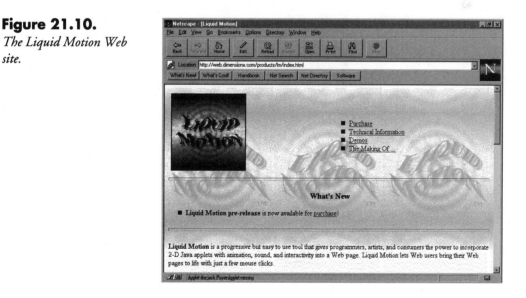

CodeColorizer

CodeColorizer, also by Chami Wickremasinghe, is a Web-based tool used to colorize Java source code. This process, also known as syntax highlighting, can be useful in deciphering code. You could use CodeColorizer to colorize your own code or, even better, use it on someone else's code to aid you in figuring out how it works. To try out CodeColorizer, go to the CodeColorizer Web site at `http://www.chamisplace.com/prog/cc` (see Figure 21.11).

21

> Most of the third-party Java integrated development environments
> provide a code colorization feature. However, you still might find the
> CodeColorizer useful if you are solely using the JDK.

Figure 21.11.

*The CodeColorizer Web
site.*

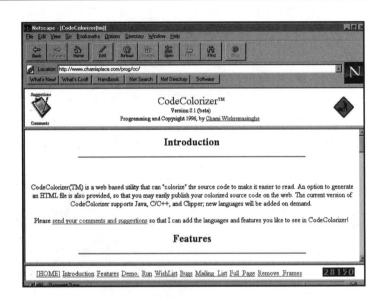

ActiveX

If you haven't heard of ActiveX yet, don't worry, you will. I know, I'm starting to sound like
an AT&T commercial, but ActiveX really is a technology that has the potential to shake up
the Web. ActiveX, by Microsoft, is a technology that defines controls (objects) that can be
inserted into Web pages to add functionality. Sounds a lot like Java, right? ActiveX controls
are in fact a lot like Java applets, the major difference being that ActiveX controls can be
integrated into applications developed using various other environments such as Visual C++,
Visual Basic, and Borland's Delphi.

ActiveX is not meant to replace Java; rather, expect ActiveX controls to coexist comfortably
with Java and possibly even merge with Java applets in some respects. It's not yet clear what
effect ActiveX will have on Java game programming, but it is an exciting enough technology
that you should keep an eye on it. To find out more about ActiveX, visit Microsoft's ActiveX
Web site at `http://www.microsoft.com/intdev/inttech/controls.htm` (see Figure 21.12).

Figure 21.12.
Microsoft's ActiveX Web site.

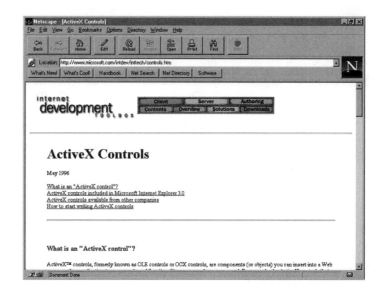

Summary

Today's lesson presented you with a suitable ending to your three-week journey through Java game development: assembling a Java game programming toolkit. You started off learning about the different kinds of tools suited to the various aspects of game development. You then moved on to learning about each type of tool in detail, focusing on specific software products along the way. Although this lesson might have appeared almost like an advertisement, it was really only meant to show you what is out there in the way of Java game development tools. It's now up to you to pick and choose which ones best suit your needs.

This lesson marks the last day of your foray into Java game programming. If you're still hungry for more, you can read a few appendixes! Better yet, take some time and work out some game designs of your own. Then see whether you have what it takes to turn them into Java games that the whole Web community can enjoy. The ultimate goal of these three weeks has been to teach you the skills necessary for you to get going writing your own Java games. So what are you waiting for?

Q&A

Q **Can I use just the Java Developer's Kit to write Java games?**

A Absolutely. As a matter of fact, that's all I used to write the sample code throughout this book.

21

Q **If I only need the JDK to write games, why bother with using an integrated development environment, like those mentioned in today's lesson?**

A You would want to use an IDE because it handles a lot of the busy work required when using the JDK alone, along with making everything graphical and more intuitive. The difference between using the JDK and using an IDE is roughly the same difference between using a command-line shell and using a GUI interface. If you're a PC user, it's like using Windows as opposed to DOS...get the picture?

Q **Are there any programming packages to aid in Java game development?**

A Not yet. I've seen some Java animation packages that certainly could be used for games, but no professional Java game programming packages have emerged yet. However, you already have all you need to get started! The sprite classes you've used throughout the book serve as a very good basis for building a Java game programming package of your own.

Workshop

The Workshop section provides questions and exercises to help you get a better feel for the material you learned today. Try to answer the questions and go over the exercises before moving on to the appendixes. You'll find the answers to the questions in Appendix A, "Quiz Answers."

Quiz

1. What are the two main types of content tools?
2. Which development tool is the best?
3. What is the focus of tomorrow's lesson?

Exercises

1. Itemize the tools you think would make good additions to your game development toolkit, factoring in the cost of each tool.
2. Go to some of the Web sites mentioned throughout today's lesson and try out some of the tools, keeping in mind your specific development resources and needs.
3. Go out and celebrate the fact that you are now a Java game programmer!

Week

3

In Review

Give yourself a big pat on the back, because you deserve it! You've weathered the storm and finished this three-week whirlwind tour of Java game programming. In this last week, you learned about some pretty advanced game programming concepts, including artificial intelligence, networking, and Java code optimization. Let's recap what you learned this week before you move on to turning your own game ideas into Java realities.

Day 15

In Day 15's lesson, you learned the fundamentals of artificial intelligence, including the major types of AI used in games. You moved on to learning about the AI techniques used in some popular commercial games, which provided you with some insight into where AI is headed in the gaming industry. You finished up the lesson by seeing some resources on the Web for doing further research on AI.

Day 16

On Day 16, you developed a complete game, Connect4, that used artificial intelligence to provide the "brains" for a computer player. You began by defining the rules of the game and studying basic AI strategies. You then developed a Connect4 game engine complete with AI, along with an applet that utilized the engine.

Day 17

Day 17's lesson focused on the basics of multiplayer gaming, including the two primary types of multiplayer games. You then learned about the most common problems associated with developing multiplayer games, along with corresponding solutions. The lesson concluded with a discussion of game theory, which is an interesting area of academic research that can be applied to multiplayer game design.

Day 18

Day 18's lesson presented Java's support for networking, along with some strategies for developing networked applets in Java. You learned about the client/server approach to network programming and how it can be used to facilitate interaction between multiple users on the Internet. You finished by developing a powerful network class, SocketAction, which provides the overhead for performing streamed socket communication.

Day 19

On Day 19, you developed a complete network Java game, NetConnect4, that allows two players to play Connect4 over the Internet. You began by studying the network requirements of the game, and then moved on to developing the client/server classes necessary for network communication. You then integrated this code into the original Connect4 game to build the complete NetConnect4 game.

Day 20

On Day 20, you learned about techniques for optimizing Java code in games. Although Java is a fairly high-level language, you learned a variety of ways to squeeze more performance out of your game code. You first took a look at the different approaches to dealing with optimizations, including the use of a profiler. You then finished up by learning a wide range of techniques for altering Java code to be more efficient.

Day 21

Your final lesson focused on the tools of the Java trade. You learned about the latest Java development environments and how they can be used to improve the game development process. Although writing cool Java games ultimately boils down to writing efficient, well-organized Java code, putting together a powerful toolkit will no doubt save you time and energy in the long run.

APPENDIX A

Quiz Answers

This appendix contains answers to the quiz questions presented at the end of each lesson. Please refer to these answers to check your own answers to the questions. I would tell you to feel free to grade yourself, but this is supposed to be fun!

Day 1

1. This is just too easy—it's Visual Basic! Just kidding, the correct answer is Java.
2. The opportunity to allow people from all over to share in an interactive gaming experience.

Day 2

1. The keyboard and mouse.
2. It only supports the ULAW sound format and doesn't provide any means to manipulate sound data.
3. A piece of multimedia data used by a game, such as an image or a sound.
4. To tell the story of a game graphically, scene by scene, by using rough sketches of each scene.

Day 3

1. Software bundles of data and the methods that act on that data.
2. The process of packaging an object's data together with its methods.
3. Because it allows parts of a program to change without subsequently affecting other parts, resulting in far better control over code maintenance.
4. Performance.

Day 4

1. CompuServe created the GIF image format in 1987 as a means to establish platform-independence in graphical images.
2. The technique of storing an image so that it can be drawn incrementally as it is being loaded. Interlacing is used frequently in Web page images.
3. The process of reducing the colors in an image to a lesser number of colors, while still maintaining a similar look.
4. A graphical object with multiple animation frames, which are also known as phases of the object.

A

5. Decide how much you can afford to pay for the artwork, find out if the artist has experience with computer graphics, and develop a good idea of what specific artwork you want the artist to create.

Day 5

1. Red, green, blue, and alpha.
2. An abstract representation of a drawing surface.
3. The `FontMetrics` class.
4. To provide a means of monitoring the load progress of images and (eventually) other media objects.

Day 6

1. The illusion of movement is created by displaying images in rapid succession with small changes in content between each.
2. Frame-based animation and cast-based (sprite) animation.
3. Transparency is a technique used to draw only the relevant part of a rectangular image. This is extremely useful in sprite animation, where many objects have irregular shapes yet are modeled as rectangular images.
4. Flicker is the annoying phenomenon created when the screen is erased between each frame of an animation sequence. This is caused by the rapid combination of erasing and then drawing the next frame, and it can be fixed only by eliminating the requirement of erasing the screen.
5. Double buffering is a technique that helps eliminate flicker when displaying an animation. It involves drawing the next frame of animation to an offscreen buffer and then drawing the buffer to the screen. This eliminates flicker because the screen never has to be erased; the offscreen buffer is erased with each new frame.

Day 7

1. By the integers 0 to 7, where 0 represents 0 degrees (facing up) and each other integer represents angles increasing by 45 degrees each time. For example, 3 represents 135 degrees and 4 represents 180 degrees.
2. The velocity multipliers are used to alter the velocity based on the direction. For example, if the direction is 2, the angle is 90 degrees and the sprite is facing right. Therefore, the X velocity needs to be positive and the Y velocity needs to be zero.

3. In the update method of the Tarantula class, the decision of whether to create new spiderlings is determined in a completely random fashion.

4. The same way that they determine whether to create spiderlings: randomly via the update method.

5. Two reasons. First, because you want to limit to 10 the number of sprites that could be added to the list. Second, because you want to eliminate collision detection and let the tarantulas walk all over each other.

Day 8

1. Absolute and relative.

2. Sorry, this was a little bit of a trick question. The answer is whichever one works best! The point is that there are no hard rules when determining the best user input approach in games.

3. In Java, it's not! This is a little inside joke for DOS (yikes!) game programmers. Fortunately, Java frees you from the burdens of low-level, processor-specific coding such as interrupt routines, and it lets you deal with input at a more meaningful level.

Day 9

1. An event is simply something that happens that you might want to know about.

2. Call the shiftDown method on the Event object that is passed into the mouseMove event handler method.

3. By overriding the mouseExit event handler method.

4. The keyboard controls for the saucer are implemented by overriding the keyDown event handler method and setting the velocity of the saucer according to which arrow key was pressed. The mouse controls for the saucer are implemented by overriding the mouseDown and mouseDrag methods and setting the position of the saucer based on the mouse position.

Day 10

1. Frogger! That was just too easy.

2. With some lousy, meaningless points!

A

3. The keyDown event handler method is used to detect when the arrow keys are pressed. If an arrow key is pressed, the gecko's velocity is set accordingly. To only allow one movement per key press, the gecko's velocity is reset to zero in the update method for Gecko.

4. Pretty well. Geckos are extremely fast—much faster than your Java-handicapped gecko.

5. By overriding the action method and checking to see whether the event target is of type Button. If so, the arg parameter is cast to a String and compared to the string "New Game". If there is a match, the button was indeed pressed, so the newGame method is called.

Day 11

1. A sound wave is a series of traveling pressure changes in the air.

2. A/D converters handle the task of converting analog audio signals to digital audio signals that can be represented in a computer.

3. 8000 Hz.

4. The amount of time between when you play a sound in an applet and when the user actually hears it.

Day 12

1. Unfortunately, the answer is no. You'll have to wait for a future release of Java to remedy this situation. However, all is not lost, because on Day 11 you learned that many popular sound editing tools enable you to convert sounds across a wide variety of formats.

2. The getCodeBase method returns the base URL for the location of the current applet, whereas the getDocumentBase method returns the base URL for location of the HTML document containing the applet. Because resources such as sounds are typically stored relative to the applet, it is both safer and smarter to use getCodeBase when you need a URL for loading a resource.

3. When you need to play a looped sound or when you plan on playing a sound more than once.

4. By calling the stop method on the AudioClip object used to loop the sound.

Day 13

1. Sky Harbor Airport in Phoenix, Arizona.

2. Because you need to be able to ignore the net sprite when looking to see whether the player clicked a scorpion. It also enables you to override the default response to collision detections.

3. Because they're nocturnal creatures.

4. Because it is necessary to stop the looped music when the update thread is stopped. Otherwise, it would be possible for the music to keep playing even though the rest of the applet was stopped.

5. Because it must be accessible by other classes. More specifically, the lost member variable is incremented in the update method of the Scorpion class.

Day 14

1. Single-stepping provides you with a means to see exactly how your code is being executed, one line at a time.

2. A runtime error in your code.

3. When a derived class adds a variable with the same name as a variable in one of its parent classes.

4. A list of the methods called en route to the currently executing code.

Day 15

1. Chasing, evading, and patterned.

2. Different behaviors are assigned probabilities for an object and then selected based on these probabilities; each behavior represents a particular type of action for an object, such as fighting or fleeing.

3. Calculating a score based on the current state of the game.

4. Because hardware has only recently reached a point where it can begin dealing with the heavy amount of processing required of most AI systems.

Day 16

1. The map is used to provide an efficient and logical way of representing all the different winning scenarios in the game. Without the map, you would have a

significantly more difficult time calculating scores and determining whether a player has won.

2. Because it logically makes sense to divide it into two separate components. More important, however, is the fact that `Connect4State` must be able to be copied and used temporarily in a recursive manner. This usage wouldn't be possible if everything was combined in a single class.

3. Because the computer player's thinking algorithm is not implemented in a thread. This results in the algorithm tying up the system while it is running. Because the system is tied up, the screen isn't updated and, therefore, the hand selector isn't drawn.

Day 17

1. Turn-based and event-based.

2. From a strictly game design perspective, there is no difference. The difference arises when you assess the bandwidth limitations of each. Modem connections have much smaller bandwidths than physical connections.

3. State synchronization, input synchronization, and hybrid.

Day 18

1. A software abstraction that represents a communication channel for a particular service such as FTP or HTTP.

2. Sockets are significant to network programming because they allow you to focus on input and output operations, independent of the intricacies and specifics involved with the network itself.

3. Stream sockets act like active connections, with data being transferred immediately in real time; datagram sockets just broadcast data over the Internet and hope that it eventually makes it to the intended destination at some point in the future.

4. The generic socket class is important because it isolates the common code involved in establishing general communications between clients and a server. This code can be easily reused in more specific client/server classes designed to support a particular game.

Day 19

1. A daemon thread is a thread that runs in the background and performs some type of support function, such as managing client communications in the NetConnect4 game.

2. The Game class handles the details of managing the game logic and the communication between players from the server side.

3. The Connect4ClientConnection class handles establishing a client socket connection, along with managing the communication between players from the client's perspective.

Day 20

1. Maintainability, size, and speed.

2. Method inlining.

3. A profiler helps you isolate which code is being called the most and how much time is being spent there, which tells you where to direct your optimization efforts.

4. When your code is reliant on costly calculations that can be replaced with a table of integer constants.

Day 21

1. Graphics utilities and sound utilities.

2. The one that works for you! That's no joke, because a development tool is only useful to the degree that it saves you time and energy. Research the tools for yourself and decide which, if any, of them might suit your needs.

3. Rest and relaxation! Come on, you've finished the book; go have a little fun and unwind!

APPENDIX

B

Keeping Up-to-Date on Java Game Programming

Perhaps the most important aspect of continued success in Java game programming is keeping up with the latest trends and technologies. Fortunately, there are plenty of resources—both online and other—for keeping your game programming skills up-to-date. This appendix points you to some of the more useful resources, which you should attempt to make use of as often as possible.

Sun's JavaSoft Web Site

Sun's official Java site on the Web is maintained by JavaSoft and contains all of the latest Java information and tools produced by JavaSoft, the Sun subsidiary responsible for Java. You'll definitely want to keep an eye on this site because it is the central location for obtaining official Java updates. It also has a pretty extensive set of online documentation, including a really nice Java tutorial. The Sun JavaSoft Web site is located at `http://www.javasoft.com` (see Figure B.1).

Figure B.1.

Sun's JavaSoft Web site.

Gamelan Web Site

Gamelan is currently the end-all Java resource directory! Besides the official Java Web site at Sun, Gamelan is by far the most useful and comprehensive source of Java information anywhere. It conveniently divides Java up into different categories, with each leading to a wealth of information, source code, and sample applets. Check out Gamelan yourself and you'll see what I mean. It's located at `http://www.gamelan.com` (see Figure B.2).

Figure B.2.

The Gamelan Web site.

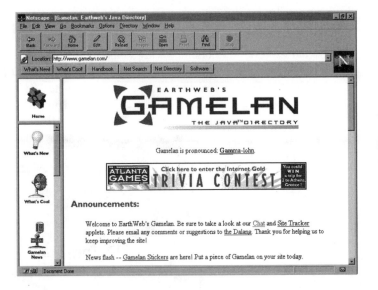

JavaWorld Online Journal

The JavaWorld online journal is an excellent publication by IDG Communications that always has some interesting Java programming articles. You can even subscribe to JavaWorld and receive Java information via e-mail. The JavaWorld Web site is located at http://www.javaworld.com (see Figure B.3).

Figure B.3.

The JavaWorld online journal Web site.

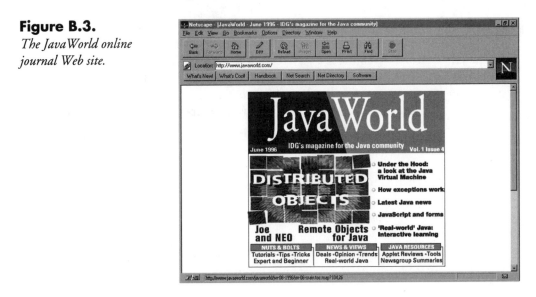

Digital Espresso Online Summary

Digital Espresso is an online weekly summary of the traffic appearing in the various Java mailing lists and news groups. Digital Espresso is an excellent Java resource because it pulls information from a variety of sources into a single Web site. It is located at `http://www.io.org/~mentor/DigitalEspresso.html` (see Figure B.4).

Figure B.4.

The Digital Espresso Web site.

Java Developer Web Site

The Java Developer Web site is a very good Web site for sharing information and finding answers to Java programming questions. It has a section called "How Do I…" that lists common (and not so common) Java programming questions and their corresponding answers, including example source code. The Java Developer Web site is located at `http://www.digitalfocus.com/faq` (see Figure B.5).

Figure B.5.

The Java Developer Web site.

Applet Arcade Web Site

When you want to get some game ideas or just check out what other Java game programmers are up to, head over to the Applet Arcade. The Applet Arcade is a Web site containing links to a wide variety of Java games. The Applet Arcade is located at `http://members.aol.com/shadows125/arcade.htm` (see Figure B.6).

Figure B.6.

The Applet Arcade Web site.

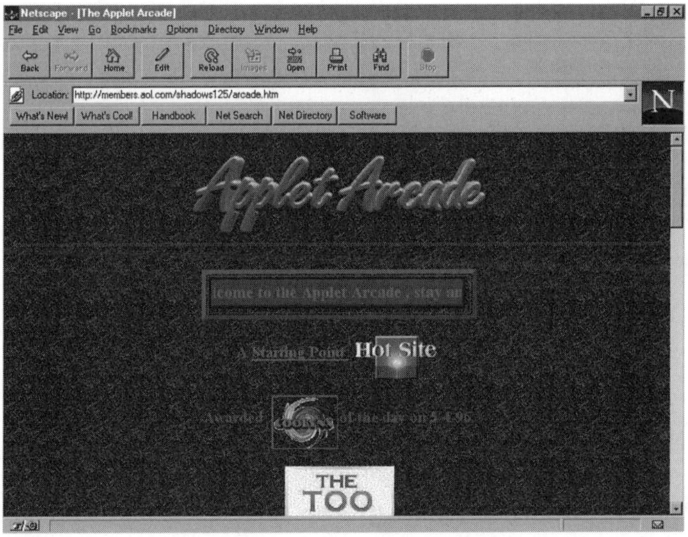

Game Developer Magazine

An excellent source for general game programming tips and tricks is *Game Developer* magazine. *Game Developer* isn't likely to include a great deal of Java information, but it is indispensable in keeping up with the latest game programming techniques. You can pick up a copy of the magazine at your local bookstore, or check out their Web site at `http://www.gdmag.com` (see Figure B.7).

Figure B.7.

The Game Developer *magazine Web site.*

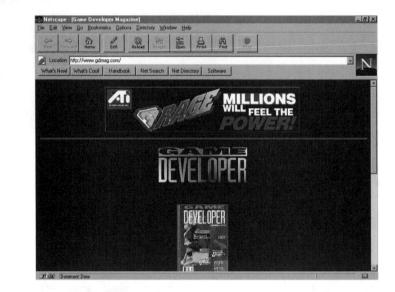

Games Domain Web Site

Another cool source of general game information is the Games Domain Web site. The Games Domain contains a variety of game information, including reviews and a complete section devoted to game programming. It is located at `http://www.gamesdomain.co.uk` (see Figure B.8).

Figure B.8.

*The Games Domain
Web site.*

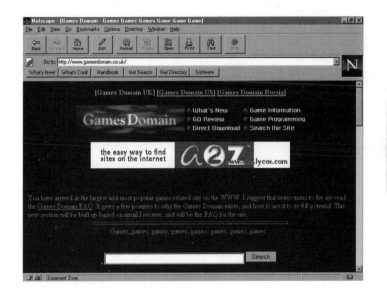

Differences Between Java and C/C++

It is no secret that the Java language is highly derived from the C and C++ languages. Because C++ is currently one of the more popular game programming languages, it is important to understand the aspects of C++ that Java inherits. Of possibly even more importance are the aspects of C++ that Java doesn't support. Because Java is an entirely new language, it was possible for the language architects at Sun to pick and choose which features from C++ to implement in Java and how to implement them.

The focus of this appendix is to point out the differences between Java and C++. If you are a C++ programmer, you can appreciate the differences between Java and C++. Even if you don't have any C++ experience, you can gain some insight into the Java language by understanding the C++ discrepancies that it clears up in its implementation. If you have a C/C++ game you are thinking of porting to Java, this appendix will help you sort out the major areas to target in your porting efforts.

NOTE

> Because C++ backwardly supports C, many of the differences pointed out in this appendix refer to C++, but inherently apply to C as well.

The Preprocessor

All C/C++ compilers implement a stage of compilation known as the preprocessor. Part of the responsibility of the C++ preprocessor is to perform an intelligent search and replace on identifiers that have been declared using the #define or #typedef directives. Although most advocators of C++ discourage this usage of the preprocessor, which was inherited from C, it is still widely used by most C++ programmers. Most of the processor definitions in C++ are stored in header files, which complement the actual source code files.

The problem with the preprocessor approach is that it provides an easy way for programmers to inadvertently add unnecessary complexity to a program. Many programmers using the #define and #typedef directives end up inventing their own sublanguage within the confines of a particular project. This results in other programmers having to go through the header files and sort out all of the #define and #typedef information to understand a program, which makes code maintenance and reuse almost impossible. An additional problem with the preprocessor approach is that it is very weak when it comes to type checking and validation.

Java does not have a preprocessor. It provides similar functionality (#define, #typedef, and so on) to that provided by the C++ preprocessor, but with far more control. Constant data members are used in place of the #define directive, and class definitions are used in lieu of the #typedef directive. The end result is that Java source code is much more consistent and easier to read than C++ source code. Additionally, Java programs don't use header files; the

Java compiler builds class definitions directly from the source code files, which contain both class definitions and method implementations.

Pointers

Most developers agree that the misuse of pointers causes the majority of bugs in C/C++ programming. Put simply, when you have pointers, you have the ability to trash memory. C++ programmers regularly use complex pointer arithmetic to create and maintain dynamic data structures. In return, C++ programmers spend a lot of time hunting down complex bugs caused by their complex pointer arithmetic.

The Java language does not support pointers. Java provides similar functionality by making heavy use of references. Java passes all arrays and objects by reference. This approach prevents common errors due to pointer mismanagement. It also makes programming easier in a lot of ways because the correct usage of pointers is easily misunderstood by all but the most seasoned programmers.

You might be thinking that the lack of pointers in Java will keep you from being able to implement many data structures such as dynamic arrays. The reality is that any pointer task can be carried out just as easily, and more reliably, with objects and arrays of objects. You then benefit from the security provided by the Java runtime system; it performs boundary checking on all array indexing operations.

Structures and Unions

C++ has three types of complex data types: classes, structures, and unions. Java only implements one of these data types: classes. Java forces programmers to use classes when the functionality of structures and unions is desired. Although this sounds like more work for the programmer, it actually ends up being more consistent, because classes can imitate structures and unions with ease. The Java designers really wanted to keep the language simple, so it only made sense to eliminate aspects of the language that overlapped.

Functions

In C, code is organized into functions, which are defaulted as global subroutines accessible to a program. C++ added classes and, in doing so, provided class methods, which are functions that are connected to classes. C++ class methods are very similar to Java class methods. However, because C++ still supports C, nothing is discouraging C++ programmers from using functions. This results in a mixture of function and method use that makes for confusing programs.

Java has no functions. Being a more pure object-oriented language than C++, Java forces programmers to bundle all routines into class methods. No limitation is imposed by forcing programmers to use methods instead of functions. As a matter of fact, implementing routines as methods encourages programmers to better organize code. Keep in mind that, strictly speaking, nothing is wrong with the procedural approach of using functions; it just doesn't mix well with the object-oriented paradigm that defines the core of Java.

Multiple Inheritance

Multiple inheritance is a feature of C++ that enables you to derive a class from multiple parent classes. Although multiple inheritance is indeed powerful, it is complicated to use correctly and causes lots of problems otherwise. It is also very complicated to implement from the compiler perspective.

Java takes the high road and provides no direct support for multiple inheritance. You can implement functionality similar to multiple inheritance by using interfaces in Java. Java interfaces provide object method descriptions, but contain no implementations.

Strings

C and C++ have no built-in support for text strings. The standard technique adopted among C and C++ programmers is that of using null-terminated arrays of characters to represent strings.

In Java, strings are implemented as first class objects (`String` and `StringBuffer`), meaning that they are at the core of the Java language. Java's implementation of strings as objects provides several advantages:

- ☐ The manner in which you create strings and access the elements of strings is consistent across all strings on all systems.
- ☐ Because the Java string classes are defined as part of the Java language, and not part of some extraneous extension, Java strings function predictably every time.
- ☐ The Java string classes perform extensive runtime checking, which helps eliminate troublesome runtime errors.

The `goto` Statement

The dreaded `goto` statement is pretty much a relic these days even in C and C++, but it is technically a legal part of the languages. The `goto` statement has historically been cited as the cause for messy, impossible to understand, and sometimes even impossible to predict code known as "spaghetti code." The primary usage of the goto statement has merely been as a convenience to substitute not thinking through an alternative, more structured branching technique.

For all of these reasons and more, Java does not provide a goto statement. The Java language specifies goto as a keyword, but its usage is not supported. I suppose the Java designers wanted to eliminate the possibility of even using goto as an identifier! Not including goto in the Java language simplifies the language and helps eliminate the option of writing messy code.

Operator Overloading

Operator overloading, which is considered a prominent feature in C++, is not supported in Java. Although roughly the same functionality can be implemented by classes in Java, the convenience of operator overloading is still missing. However, in defense of Java, operator overloading can sometimes become very tricky. Undoubtedly the Java developers decided not to support operator overloading in order to keep the Java language as simple as possible.

Automatic Coercions

Automatic coercion refers to the implicit casting of data types that sometimes occurs in C and C++. For example, in C++ you are allowed to assign a float value to an int variable, which can result in a loss of information. Java does not support C++ style automatic coercions. In Java, if a coercion will result in a loss of data, you must always explicitly cast the data element to the new type.

Variable Arguments

C and C++ allow you to declare functions that take a variable number of arguments, such as printf. Although this is a convenient feature, it is impossible for the compiler to thoroughly type check the arguments, which means problems can arise at runtime without you knowing it. Again, Java takes the high road and doesn't support variable arguments at all.

Command-Line Arguments

The command-line arguments passed from the system into a Java program differ in a couple of ways from the command-line arguments passed into a C++ program. First, the number of parameters passed differs between the two languages. In C and C++, the system passes two arguments to a program: argc and argv. argc specifies the number of arguments stored in argv. argv is a pointer to an array of characters containing the actual arguments. In Java, the system passes a single value to a program: args. args is an array of Strings that contains the command-line arguments.

In C and C++, the command-line arguments passed into a program include the name used to invoke the program. This name always appears as the first argument, and it is rarely ever used. In Java, you already know the name of the program because it is the same name as the class, so there is no need to pass this information as a command-line argument. Therefore, the Java runtime system only passes the arguments following the name that invoked the program.

Summary

You learned in this appendix about the differences between Java and C++. Although no knowledge of C++ is required for Java game programming, it can certainly be beneficial to understand where Java inherits many of its features.

INDEX

MindSpring™

is proud to sponsor

TEACH YOURSELF INTERNET GAME PROGRAMMING with JAVA in 21 DAYS

by Hosting their Web site at http://www.thetribe.com/

MindSpring Web Services provides a reliable, cost effective solution for individuals and organizations wishing to have a "virtual" Web presence (http://www.yourdomain.com/).

Here is a sample of the services we provide:
RealAudio™
Shockwave™
Java™
Secure transactions
24 hour FTP access
Daily Statistics
Custom cgi scripts

For additional information:
1-800-719-4332
http://web.mindspring.com/
sales@mindspring.com

© 1996 MindSpring Enterprises, Inc. All other brand or product names are trademarks or registered trademarks of their respective holders.

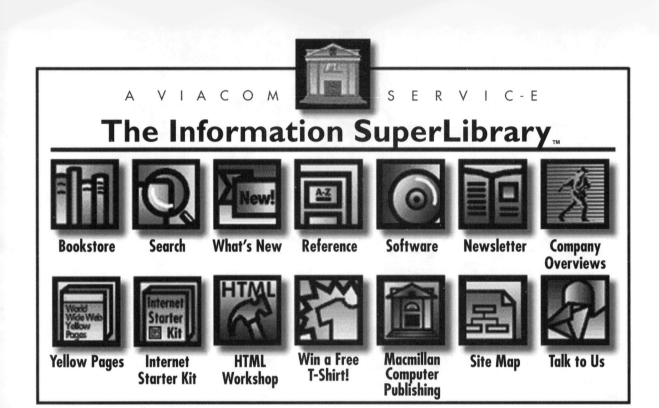

Teach Yourself Java in 21 Days

Laura Lemay, et al.   *Internet/Programming*

Introducing the first, best, and most detailed guide to developing applications with the hot new Java language from Sun Microsystems.

CD-ROM includes the Java Developer's Kit

Provides detailed coverage of the hottest new technology on the World Wide Web

Shows readers how to develop applications using the Java language

Includes coverage of browsing Java applications with Netscape and other popular Web browsers

Covers Java

$39.99 USA, $56.95 CDN, 1-57521-030-4, 500 pp.

Casual - Accomplished - Expert

Web Site Construction Kit for Windows 95

Christopher Brown & Scott Zimmerman   *Internet/Programming*

The *Web Site Construction Kit for Windows 95* provides readers with everything they need to set up, develop, and maintain a Web site with Windows 95. It teaches the ins and outs of planning, installing, configuring, and administering a Windows 95–based Web site for an organization, and it includes detailed instructions on how to use the software on the CD-ROM to develop the Web site's content: HTML pages, CGI scripts, image maps, and so on.

Provides a blueprint and all the tools needed to set up a complete Web site

Teaches how to install, configure, and administer a Windows 95 server

CD-ROM contains all the source code from the book and useful utilities

Covers Windows 95

$49.99 USA, $70.95 CDN, 1-57521-072-X, 560 pp.

Casual - Accomplished

Java Unleashed

Michael Morrison, et al.   *Internet/Programming*

Java Unleashed is the ultimate guide to the year's hottest new Internet technologies: the Java language and the HotJava browser from Sun Microsystems. *Java Unleashed* is a complete programmer's reference and a guide to the hundreds of exciting ways Java is being used to add interactivity to the World Wide Web.

Includes a helpful and informative CD-ROM

Describes how to use Java to add interactivity to Web presentations

Shows readers how Java and HotJava are being used across the Internet

Covers Java 1.1

$49.99 USA, $70.95 CDN, 1-57521-049-5, 1,008 pp.

Casual - Accomplished - Expert

Teach Yourself JavaScript in a Week

Arman Danesh   *Internet/Programming*

Teach Yourself JavaScript in a Week is the easiest way to learn how to create interactive Web pages with LiveScript, Netscape's Java-like scripting language. It is intended for nontechnical people and will be equally of value to users on the Macintosh, Windows, and UNIX platforms.

Teaches how to design and create attention-grabbing Web pages with JavaScript

Shows how to add interactivity to Web pages

Covers JavaScript

$39.99 USA, $56.95 CDN , 1-57521-073-8, 576 pp.

Accomplished - Expert

Java Developer's Guide

Jamie Jaworski & Carie Jardean   *Internet/Programming*

Java is one of the major growth areas for developers on the World Wide Web. It brings with it the capability to download and run small applications called applets from a Web server. *Java Developer's Guide* teaches developers everything they need to know to effectively develop Java applications.

CD-ROM includes source code from the book and valuable utilities

Covers Java interface, VRML extensions, security, and more

Explores new technology and future trends of Java development

Covers Java 1.1

$49.99 USA, $70.95 CDN, 1-57521-069-x, 768 pp.

Accomplished - Expert

Teach Yourself Web Publishing with HTML 3.2 in 14 Days, Professional Reference Edition

Laura Lemay   *Internet/Web Publishing*

This is the updated edition of Lemay's previous bestseller, *Teach Yourself Web Publishing with HTML in 14 Days, Premier Edition*. In it, readers will find all the advanced topics and updates—including adding audio, video, and animation—to Web page creation.

CD-ROM included

Explores the use of CGI scripts, tables, HTML 3.2, the Netscape and Internet Explorer extensions, Java applets and JavaScript, and VRML

Covers HTML 3.2

$59.99 USA, $84.95 CDN, 1-57521-096-7, 1,104 pp.

New - Casual - Accomplished

Web Page Wizardry: Wiring Your Site for Sound and Action

Dick Oliver *Internet/Web Publishing*

Readers learn how to create stunning Web pages by adding full-motion video, animations, sounds, music, and 3D worlds with dazzling examples from the author.

CD-ROM includes powerful utilities and source code from the book

$39.99 USA, $56.95 CDN, 1-57521-092-4, 500 pp.

Accomplished - Expert

Tricks of the Java Programming Gurus

Glenn Vanderburg, et al. *Internet/Programming*

This book is a guide for experienced Java programmers who want to take their Java skills beyond simple animations and applets. It shows readers how to streamline their Java code, how to achieve unique results with undocumented tricks, and how to add advanced-level functions to existing Java programs.

CD-ROM includes all the source code from the book

Skilled Java professionals show how to improve garbage collection before and after compilation for improved performance

Provides a fast-paced guide to advanced Java programming

Covers Java 1.1

$39.99 USA, $56.95 CDN, 1-57521-102-5, 750 pp.

Accomplished - Expert

Add to Your Sams.net Library Today
with the Best Books for Internet Technologies

ISBN	Quantity	Description of Item	Unit Cost	Total Cost
1-57521-030-4		Teach Yourself Java in 21 Days (Book/CD-ROM)	$39.99	
1-57521-072-X		Web Site Construction Kit for Windows 95 (Book/CD-ROM)	$49.99	
1-57521-049-5		Java Unleashed (Book/CD-ROM)	$49.99	
1-57521-073-8		Teach Yourself JavaScript in a Week	$39.99	
1-57521-069-X		Java Developer's Guide (Book/CD-ROM)	$49.99	
1-57521-096-7		Teach Yourself Web Publishing with HTML 3.2 in 14 Days, Professional Reference Edition (Book/CD-ROM)	$59.99	
1-57521-092-4		Web Page Wizardry: Wiring Your Site for Sound and Action (Book/CD-ROM)	$39.99	
1-57521-102-5		Tricks of the Java Programming Gurus (Book/CD-ROM)	$39.99	
		Shipping and Handling: See information below.		
		TOTAL		

Shipping and Handling: $4.00 for the first book, and $1.75 for each additional book. If you need to have it NOW, we can ship product to you in 24 hours for an additional charge of approximately $18.00, and you will receive your item overnight or in two days. Overseas shipping and handling adds $2.00. Prices subject to change. Call between 9:00 a.m. and 5:00 p.m. EST for availability and pricing information on latest editions.

201 W. 103rd Street, Indianapolis, Indiana 46290

1-800-428-5331 — Orders   1-800-835-3202 — FAX   1-800-858-7674 — Customer Service

Book ISBN 1-57521-148-3

What's on the Disc

The companion CD-ROM contains the Java™ Developer's Kit from Sun Microsystems, plus the source code and Java samples from the book.

Windows 3.1 or NT Installation Instructions

1. Insert the CD-ROM disc into your CD-ROM drive.
2. From File Manager or Program Manager, choose Run from the File menu.
3. Type **<drive>CDSETUP** and press Enter, where **<drive>** corresponds to the drive letter of your CD-ROM. For example, if your CD-ROM is drive D:, type **D:CDSETUP** and press Enter.
4. Follow the on-screen instructions in the installation program. Files will be installed to a directory named \JAVAGAME, unless you choose a different directory during installation.

CDSETUP creates a Windows program manager group called *TY Internet Game Programming*. This group contains icons for exploring the CD-ROM.

Windows 95 Installation Instructions

1. If Windows 95 is installed on your computer and you have the AutoPlay feature enabled, the Guide to the CD-ROM program starts automatically whenever you insert the disc into your CD-ROM drive.

Macintosh Installation Instructions

1. Insert the CD-ROM disc into your CD-ROM drive.
2. When an icon for the CD appears on your desktop, open the disc by double-clicking on its icon.

3. Double-click on the icon named Guide to the CD-ROM, and follow the directions that appear.

Technical Support from Macmillan

We can't help you with Windows or Macintosh problems or software from third parties, but we can assist you if a problem arises with the CD-ROM itself.

E-mail support: Send e-mail to support@mcp.com.

CompuServe: GO SAMS to reach the Macmillan Computer Publishing forum. Leave us a message, addressed to SYSOP. If you want the message to be private, address it to *SYSOP.

Telephone: (317) 581-3833

Fax: (317) 581-4773

Mail: Macmillan Computer Publishing
Attention: Support Department
201 West 103rd Street
Indianapolis, IN 46290-1093

Here's how to reach us on the Internet:

World Wide Web (*The Macmillan Information SuperLibrary*)
http://www.mcp.com/samsnet